NEW YORK THEATRE ANNUAL

Volume 2

NEW YORK THEATRE ANNUAL
1977-78

edited by Catharine Hughes

Gale Research Company • Book Tower • Detroit, Michigan 48226

NEW YORK THEATRE ANNUAL

Lynn Fox, *Production Editor*
Roger D. Hubbard, *Photography Coordinator*
Linda Hubbard, *Assistant Editor*
Arthur Chartow, *Cover Design*

Copyright©1978
GALE RESEARCH COMPANY

Library of Congress Catalog Card Number 78-50757
ISBN 0-8103-0417-1

Contents

Preface

Volume 2 of the *New York Theatre Annual,* which covers the 1977-78 season (June 1, 1977-May 31, 1978), has been considerably expanded from the first edition.

Several plays, in particular award-winners or those that attracted major attention, such as *"Da," Ain't Misbehavin', The Act* and *Runaways,* receive double-page coverage, including additional photos and extended review excerpts.

A second addition to this volume is a full listing of all major theatre awards for the 1977-78 season. There are also now two indexes: one for plays, the second for individuals and organizations.

As in volume 1, the *Annual* is divided into four principal sections: Broadway; Broadway/Continuing Plays; Off and off-Off Broadway; and Off and off-Off Broadway/Continuing Plays. The new plays are arranged according to date of opening. The continuing plays are presented in alphabetical order.

Unless otherwise indicated, the casts are those that appeared on the opening night. The review excerpts reflect a balanced overview of the commentary that appeared in major daily and periodical publications.

Catharine Hughes

Broadway

1977-78 Season
through May 31, 1978

Beatlemania

Mitch Weissman, Leslie Fradkin, Justin McNeill
and Joe Pecorino as the Beatles

Songs written by John Lennon, Paul McCartney and George Harrison; editorial content by Robert Rabinowitz, Bob Gill, Lynda Obst; visuals director, Charles E. Hoefler; multimedia images by Robert Rabinowitz, Bob Gill, Shep Kerman, Kathleen Rabinowitz; original concept by Steven Leber, David Krebs and Jules Fisher; setting by Robert D. Mitchell; lighting by Jules Fisher; sound by Abe Jacob; musical supervision by Sandy Yaguda; special consultant, Murray Thek; hair designed by Phyllis Della; production stage manager, Robert V. Straus; production supervised by Jules Fisher. Winter Garden Theatre, Broadway and 49th Street.

Beatlemania blends many of the Beatles' best-known songs into a collage including slides, films and lighting effects, following the quartet from its February 1964 American debut to its breakup.

Reflecting the changes that occurred in the styles of the Beatles, it includes such numbers as "Making It" and "Tripping."

Beatlemania, which did not have a press opening, began performances on May 26, 1977.

Opened May 26, 1977

With: Joe Pecorino, rhythm guitar; Mitch Weissman, bass guitar; Leslie Fradkin, lead guitar; Justin McNeill, drums

REVIEWS

"It's an ingratiating enough affair, if you don't take it too seriously. . . . The four young men in the cast do a pretty fine job in imitating the Beatles's looks, vocal timbres, personal mannerisms, arrangements and overall impact. . . . The mechanics of the show are flashy in a nice sense." — John Rockwell, *The New York Times (6-17-77, p. C 3)*

"It is often blatant in its outline of the world surrounding the Beatles' era . . . but it is often subtle, showing the changes which occurred in the group without slamming the audience over the head. . . . It's not a brilliant show, but it's very good and certainly well worth seeing." — *Variety (2-15-78, p. 68)*

"A harmless and amusing musical celebration. . . . The four unknowns do a fine job of mimicking their gestures and recreating the Beatles' distinctive music." — Carl Arrington, *New York Post*

The Importance of Being Earnest

Kathleen Widdoes, John Glover, Patricia Conolly,
James Valentine, Elizabeth Wilson, G. Wood and Mary Louise Wilson

THE CAST

Algernon Moncrieff . . . . John Glover
Lane, Manservant . . . . Munson Hicks
John Worthing . . . . .James Valentine
Lady Bracknell . . . . Elizabeth Wilson
Gwendolen Fairfax . . . . . .Patricia Conolly
Cecily Cardew. . . . . .Kathleen Widdoes
Miss Prism . . . . Mary Louise Wilson
Rev. Canon Chasuble, D. D.. . . . . .G. Wood
Merriman. . . . . .Thomas Ruisinger

By Oscar Wilde. Presented by Circle in the Square; directed by Stephen Porter; setting by Zack Brown; costumes by Ann Roth; lighting by John McLain; wigs and hair styles by Paul Huntley; production stage manager, Randall Brooks. Circle in the Square Theatre, 50th Street West of Broadway.

Wilde's 1895 comedy is almost universally considered his best play, and by many regarded as one of the outstanding farces of the nineteenth century. Its plot revolves around two couples (John Worthing and Gwendolen Fairfax and Algernon Moncrieff and Cecily Cardew) as they wend their ways toward inevitable marriages.

But plot is not its essence, though it abounds in often outlandish events, among them a baby found in a handbag, a man (Worthing) who invents a dissolute brother and another who then proceeds to impersonate him.

The play's success, however, is a result of what has been called its "stylistic brilliance," best exemplified in its epigrams and aphorisms, its literacy and sometimes stunning wit.

Opened June 16, 1977, for a limited engagement
Closed August 28, 1977

REVIEWS

"Agreeable and sometimes better than that. . . . But a great deal does not get beyond a reading of pleasantly familiar lines upon an exuberantly designed set. . . . The director, Stephen Porter, is frequently unable quite to meet the difficulties." — Richard Eder, *The New York Times (6-17-77, p. C5)*

"It was gratifying to find the production so good it makes Oscar Wilde's glittering comedy seem more delightful than ever. . . . The resourceful Porter has come up with a novel approach to the play, not a self-consciously revolutionary one opposite to the author's but a quietly daring one still. . . . One would ordinarily expect him to stage an exemplary *Importance of Being Earnest,* and he could, with his eyes shut. With his eyes open he has created an exceptional one." — Martin Gottfried, *New York Post (6-17-77, p. 31)*

"Even in a spotty production, Oscar Wilde's satirical farce about Victorian society remains witty and refreshing after 82 years. . . . In general, this is a flawed edition of a comic masterpiece." — *Variety (6-22-77, p. 102)*

"They play it not brilliantly, but gracefully and well. . . . Stephen Porter has directed a nice production: nice in the sense of cozily pleasant, and nice in the sense of delicately precise." — Julius Novick, *The Village Voice (7-4-77, p. 85)*

"Apart from a wonderfully sly-tongued cast, which this production has, the play demands a director who can crack the combination of its elegant wit and satirical wisdom with the silky fingers of a safe robber. Stephen Porter is just that sort of director, and the stamp of his assurance is his total trust in the playwright." — T. E. Kalem, *Time (6-27-77, p. 61)*

Man of La Mancha

THE CAST

Don Quixote (Cervantes) . . . . Richard Kiley
Sancho . . . . Tony Martinez
The Horse . . . . Ben Vargas
The Mule . . . . Hector Mercado
The Innkeeper' . . . . Bob Wright
Maria, the Innkeeper's Wife . . . . Marceline Decker
Pedro, Head Muleteer . . . . Chev Rodgers
Anselmo, a Muleteer . . . . Ted Forlow
Juan, a Muleteer . . . . Mark Holliday
Tenorio, a Muleteer . . . . Ben Vargas
Paco, a Muleteer . . . . Anthony DeVecchi
Jose, a Muleteer . . . . Hector Mercado
Aldonza. . . . . Emily Yancy
Fermina, a Slavey . . . . Joan Susswein
Guitarist . . . . Robin Polseno
Jorge, a Muleteer. . . . . Edmond Varrato
Fernando, a Muleteer . . . . David Wasson
Antonia. . . . . Harriett Conrad
The Housekeeper. . . . . Margret Coleman
The Padre . . . . Taylor Reed
Dr. Carrasco. Ian Sullivan
The Barber. . . . . Ted Forlow
Moorish Dancer. . . . . Joan Susswein
The Captain . . . . Renato Cibelli
Guards . . . . Michael St. Paul
David Wasson

Richard Kiley

By Dale Wasserman; music by Mitch Leigh; lyrics by Joe Darion. Presented by Eugene V. Wolsk; production and musical staging by Albert Marre; setting and lighting by Howard Bay; costumes by Howard Bay and Patton Campbell; music arrangements by Music Makers, Inc.; assistant to the director, Greg Hirsch; musical director, Robert Brandzel; production stage manager, Patrick Corrigan. Palace Theatre, Broadway at 47th Street.

First produced in 1965, with the same star, after which it ran for 2,328 performances, *Man of La Mancha* is one of the most popular musicals of our time.

The story (based on Cervantes's *Don Quixote*) tells of the mad Don (Cervantes himself) and his visionary quest after his delusions. Accompanied by the loyal Sancho, he must initially defend himself against accusations that he is a bad poet and an honest man. He recites the serio-comic tale of the Knight of the Woeful Countenance and goes off to pursue his dreams, eventually to die.

Man of La Mancha's success, however, derives more from its songs than from its book, and principal among them are "Dulcinea," "I Really Like Him," "Little Bird, Little Bird," "The Impossible Dream" and "Aldonza."

Opened September 15, 1977, for a limited engagement
Closed December 31, 1977

REVIEWS

"The production is big and generally first-rate. It would be hard to improve upon Mr. Kiley's performance, or those of several other members of the cast. The trouble is in the parts they have to play; the trouble is that *Man of La Mancha* is a work that fights itself and loses." — Richard Eder, *The New York Times (9-16-77, p. C 3)*

"Though the musical still isn't anything to get excited about, its success is understandable. . . . This revival's greatest asset is Richard Kiley, giving the performance of his career. . . . He is a commanding figure on stage without ever seeming possessive about it and he is superb." — Martin Gottfried, *New York Post (9-16-77, p. 43)*

"I am content to hail the work and commend to my readers this exceptionally stirring production of it. . . . If [Richard Kiley] was marvellous to begin with, he is still more marvellous now." — Brendan Gill, *The New Yorker (9-26-77, p. 100)*

"To death and taxes, we may now add a third, similarly unpleasant, certainty: revivals of *Man of La Mancha*. . . . This show is an equal insult to Cervantes, the American musical theater, and humanity." — John Simon, *New York (10-3-77, p. 78)*

"Richard Kiley is back in the title role, giving a thoroughly satisfying performance, both vocally and dramatically, perhaps with added assurance and authority. The part of the strumpet peasant girl, Aldonza, is well played by Emily Yancy. . . . Tony Martinez is well cast as the hero's selfless servant, Sancho. . . . Wasserman's book . . . still seems somewhat ponderous and slow-starting." — *Variety (9-21-77, p. 98)*

Tartuffe

Tammy Grimes, John Wood and Stefan Gierasch

THE CAST

Flipote, Mme. Pernelle's maid . . . . .Ruth Livingston
Dorine, Mariane's lady's-maid . . . . .Patricia Elliott
Mme. Pernelle, Orgon's mother . . . . .Mildred Dunnock
Elmire, Orgon's wife . . . . Tammy Grimes
Mariane, Orgon's daughter,
    Elmire's stepdaughter. . . . . .Swoosie Kurtz
Damis, Orgon's son, Elmire's stepson. . . . . Ray Wise
Cléante, Orgon's brother-in-law . . . . Peter Coffield
Orgon, Elmire's husband. . . . . Stefan Gierasch
Valère, in love with Mariane . . . . Victor Garber
Tartuffe, a hypocrite . . . . John Wood
M. Loyal . . . . .Roy Brocksmith
A police officer. . . . . Jim Broaddus
Deputies . . . . Timothy Landfield, Steven Gilborn

REVIEWS

"[A] spectacular but lopsided production. . . . Mr. Wood indisputably takes over. His presence, his outsize artistic energy and resources, his quivering sense of each comic moment. . . make it difficult to notice anything else. . . . The danger in such performances is not mainly that they can overshadow the other actors. . . . But to a considerable degree, by making it impossible to look away from him, he undermines other aspects of the play. . . .

"Was there any way of harnessing Mr. Wood to the rest of the cast? Probably, but it would not be easy. It would require direction more powerful than the imaginative but indulgent guidance provided by Stephen Porter." — Richard Eder, *The New York Times* (9-26-77, p. 40)

"I can guardedly recommend this *Tartuffe,* even if Stephen Porter's staging has flaws ranging beyond what I consider a basically vulgar conception. . . . When you throw together a brilliantly headstrong actor and a not incompetent but less than forceful director, there is bound to be imbalance. With Wood at one end of the seesaw and Porter at the other, the evening becomes a plane so steeply inclined that the play pretty nearly slides off it." — John Simon, *New York* (10-10-77, p. 56)

"The present production is infectiously high-spirited, but it scants the biting melancholy wisdom that animates Molière's satiric moral vision. . . . In the title role, John Wood radiates evil. . . . Yet we are too conscious that he is a self-aware villain, scoring stunning acting points without carrying complete emotional conviction." — T. E. Kalem, *Time* (10-10-77, p. 108)

"The production is satisfactory, if not very illuminating. . . . I have serious reservations about Stephen Porter's direction. . . . He has certainly encouraged far more horseplay and mere bustling about than I can find any reason for." — Brendan Gill, *The New Yorker* (10-3-77, p. 109)

"The exhilaration of such unusual and in many ways substantiable re-interpretation is one of the most satisfying rewards a classical theater can provide. This is seeing a great play and a new play at the same time. . . . This production is that rare treat, an adventure in high theater." — Martin Gottfried, *New York Post* (9-26-77, p. 23)

By Molière. English verse translation by Richard Wilbur. Presented by Circle in the Square; directed by Stephen Porter; scenery and costumes by Zack Brown; lighting by John McLain; wigs and hair styles by Paul Huntley; production stage manager, Randall Brooks. Circle in the Square Theatre, 51st Street, West of Broadway.

Molière's *Tartuffe* was first produced for Louis XIV in 1664, when it offended many and was banned. In 1669, in its third version, it was authorized.

A Parisian bourgeois named Orgon compels his family to accept the presence of the hypocritically pious Tartuffe. He wishes him to marry his daughter Mariane. Tartuffe, however, is hardly what he seems, but rather a parasite with particularly sensual inclinations. He takes a fancy to Orgon's wife Elmire, and when Orgon discovers it, he wants to drive him out of his house. Unfortunately, he already has made over the whole of his estate to him and placed in his hands some compromising political documents. For his part, Tartuffe would have Orgon turned out of his own house. The King, fortunately for Orgon, discovers that Tartuffe was a criminal and, in the end, it is he who is arrested.

Opened September 25, 1977, for a limited engagement
Closed November 20, 1977

Miss Margarida's Way

Estelle Parsons

THE CAST

Miss Margarida . . . . .Estelle Parsons
One of her students . . . . Colin Garrey
The rest of her students . . . . . . The Audience

By Roberto Athayde. A New York Shakespeare Festival Production, presented by Joseph Papp; associate producer, Bernard Gersten; directed by Mr. Athayde; setting and costumes by Santo Loquasto; lighting by Martin Tudor; stage manager, Penny Gebhard. Originally presented at the Public Theatre, 425 Lafayette Street. Ambassador Theatre, 215 West 49th Street.

Miss Margarida's Way is the way of all tyrants, all authoritarians, whether political, social or personal. Whether she turned up in a classroom, a country club or a cabinet room, the figure on stage is the quintessence of power, influence and would-be omniscience run amok.

Miss Margarida is at least nominally a schoolteacher and the audience, which is expected to participate, makes up her eighth-grade class. Almost from the start, she reminds them that the "deserving ones" are "those who obey" without question, those who remain silent. The last thing she wants her "students" to do is make decisions. Docility and the acceptance of her "way" are the principal criteria for acceptance and success.

Fleeting early cajolery and attempts to ingratiate soon give way to demagoguery; brief efforts to lecture to paranoia: "All you kids wanna do is grab my tits, right?" Yet, at the end and even at moments throughout, she is a surprisingly sympathetic figure, if only because she becomes a symbol of everyone's vulnerability.

Opened (on Broadway) September 27, 1977
Closed January 1, 1978

REVIEWS

"Mordant, funny, sometimes subtle and ultimately moving. Dramatically it is a mixed success, however, despite its ingenious format and the spectacular performance of Estelle Parsons. . . . The undependable relationship of the audience to Miss Margarida is one of the dramatic difficulties with the play. More serious is the fact that once Miss Margarida is established on stage with her whips and hysteria, her changeableness and foolishness, all that happens for a while is repetition." — Richard Eder, *The New York Times (9-28-77, p. C 16)*

"It died because the dynamic between the performer and the audience means so much to this play and without it, the flaws — the repetitiousness, the lack of story — are underlined from dreariness to weariness. . . . Miss Parsons' performance is tremendous . . . but ultimately she cannot make a character of Miss Margarida because as written this is only a 'character' — an eccentric." — Martin Gottfried, *New York Post (9-28-77, p. 56)*

"[Estelle Parsons] blows the roof off Broadway's Ambassador Theatre in a drama that merits little more than a stray snore." — T. E. Kalem, *Time (10-10-77, p. 108)*

"This play is really an absurdist farce much more than any sort of structured piece of symbolism. The author is far too undisciplined and, I am afraid, fuzzy-minded to give us anything so controlled as a tidily working satirical metaphor. . . . What helps . . . is the performance of Estelle Parsons." — John Simon, *New York (10-17-77, p. 124)*

"Where Athayde fails as a dramatist is in the obviousness of the character study, the repetitiousness of the pathetic woman's harangue . . . and ultimately the boredom that overcomes the audience. . . . Under the author's direction, Estelle Parsons gives an admirably energetic performance, with shrewd variations of mood and tone." — *Variety (10-5-77, p. 94)*

The Grand Kabuki

The National Theatre of Japan. Presented by Kazuko Hillyer, in two plays: *Kurozuka* and *Yoshitsune Senbon Zakura*; stage director Takeshiba Norio; stage manager, Toshi Ogawa. Beacon Theatre, 2124 Broadway.

Headed by the actor Ennosuke Ichikawa III, a virtuoso performer who comes from an acting dynasty dating back to the mid-nineteenth century, this is one of the leading Kabuki troupes in Japan.

Large on spectacle and primarily an actors' theatre, the Grand Kabuki offers two plays on its program. The first is derived from an eighteenth-century Kabuki classic, *Yoshitsune Senbon Zakura,* and here is presented only in excerpt form.

Opened August 31,1977, for a limited engagement
Closed September 18, 1977

With: Ichikawa En-nosuke III, Ichikawa Mon-nosuke VII, Ichikawa Danshiro IV, Nakamura Yonekichi IV, Ichikawa Dan-en, Ichikawa Juy-en, Nakamura Tokicho, Katacka Hidejyu, Ichikawa Takajiro, Kusanagi Akira, Kihara Hirokazu, Oishi Hirotsugu.
Singers and Musicians: *Nagauta* — Imafuji Choshi, Kineya Rokuzo, Kineya Shunjyuro, Matsunaga Tetsujiro, Kineya Katsuroku, Kineya Katsutoshiharu, Kineya Rokunobu, Kineya Sukesaburo, Kineya Toshihiro; *Narimono* — Tosha Roshu, Fukuhara Tsurujiro, Tanaka Kanshiro, Tanaka Chojyuro, Mochizuke Takisaku, Nakai Kazuo; *Koto* — Miyahara Yokio, Sugino Masataka; *Shakuhachi* — Sakai Suizan; *Gidayu* — Takemoto Fujitayu, Tsurusawa Genjiro, Toyosawa Shigematsu

REVIEWS

"There is no doubt that this is very grand theatre indeed. . . . Ennosuke III . . . is, in the best of this tradition, a virtuoso performer and one with a singular introspective flavor." — Anna Kisselgoff, *The New York Times (9-1-77, p. B 11)*

"What Kabuki offers us is the exitement of absorbing theater through the senses rather than through the mind, and the rare joy of sitting on the edge of a theater seat, breathlessly awaiting the next move." — Sylviane Gold, *New York Post (9-1-77, p. 20)*

"One might say that Kabuki is chiefly for theatrical epicures, but I am more inclined to assert that the person who finds no pleasure in Kabuki has no real taste for *theatre*." — Harold Clurman, *The Nation (9-24-77, p. 286)*

"These performances have a credibility that seems to come from combining Kabuki with the more naturalistic approach of the Western theatre. . . . And once you get the unusualness of the story squared away and accept that the characters, in moments of high emotion, will lapse into poems sung by the reciter. There is nothing to prevent your finding analogies in the best of our own acting." — Michael Feingold, *The Village Voice (9-12-77, p. 67)*

Estrada

The 1977 Music and Dance Festival from the Soviet Union. Nikolai Laktionov, artistic director, Nadezhda Kazantzeva, administrative director. Tamara Golovanova, choreographer; Savely Onishchenko, production manager. Presented by United Euram. Majestic Theatre, 245 West 44th Street.

Estrada offers a selection of songs, dances, acrobatics and mime acts from various regions of the Soviet Union, some of them legitimately folkloric, others more of the nightclub variety.

Among the highlights are the Orera group from Georgia, which is dressed in black velvet and switches from almost scat-like singing into a crooning love song with its "Serdtse" and "Svetlyachok," then swings into "East Side, West Side" and "Give My Regards to Broadway" (in English). Another group, the folk-rock Pesnyary, comes on armed with a variety of instruments, including one called a zhaleika, to deliver a Byelorussian folk song. Two dancers, sporting large mustaches, parody Russian folk-dance.

Opened September 20, 1977
Closed

With: Nani Bregvadze, Grigori Davidenko and Vladimir Kononovich, Natalia and Oleg Kiriushkin, Larisa Kudeyarova, Yefim Levinson and Galina Korzina, Orera, Pesnyary, Vladimir Serov, Souvenir Ensemble, Alla, Vyacheslav and Vyacheslav Rasshivkin, Jr.

REVIEWS

"There is some charm and occasionally some mild excitement in the songs, dances, acrobatics and mime acts. . . . Taken as a whole, though, it is depressingly like the displays at airport souvenir stands. A few of the articles have an authentic feeling to them. . . . But a great deal is a kind of nightclub package tour through the more obvious forms of Soviet entertainment." — Richard Eder, *The New York Times (9-21-77, p. C 15)*

"It invites a tourist's condescension since if it were American it would fold in Toledo." — Martin Gottfried, *New York Post (9-21-77, p. 18)*

"Some of it [is] sweet and stirring, some loaded with cliches and contradiction but too dated for modern consumption." — *Variety (9-28-77, p. 71)*

"A shoddy collection of third-rate song and dance acts. . . . Rather than offering a taste of the richness and folk-passion of Russian music and dance, *Estrada* turns out to be a cheap parody of the worst in an American plasticized pop culture, with a Russian translation." — Leah D. Frank, *New York Theatre Review (11-77, p. 41)*

Comedy with Music

Victor Borge

A musical entertainment by Victor Borge. Presented by the Edgewood Organization, Inc., Lewis Friedman and John W. Ballard, executive directors; Dean Lenz and Allison McLeod, associate producers; production designed by Neil Peter Jampolis; production stage manager, Don Judge. Imperial Theatre, 249 West 45th Street.

Victor Borge has been presenting variations on *Comedy with Music* on Broadway since he opened there in 1953 with one called *Comedy in Music,* which ran for 849 performances. In the present version, he utilizes two main props, a large grand piano, on which he plays from time to time, and a singer named Marylyn Mulvey, whom he plays off, regularly interrupting her in her attempts at operatic arias and burlesquing the opera form.

Soon after entering, Borge reproves the laughter in the audience with the advice that, "If everybody's going to laugh individually, we'll never get out of here," frets over the fact that no one has marked the middle C on the piano, recalls Lyndon Johnson lifting a dog by his ears ("the dog's ears, of course") and engages in a particularly entertaining rendition of the "Moonlight Sonata," based upon fragments of the score that have become scattered and disorganized.

Opened October 3, 1977, for a limited engagement
Closed November 26, 1977

Starring Victor Borge; with Marylyn Mulvey

REVIEWS

"Returning to the New York stage after 13 years, Victor Borge is like an old singer whose musicianship remains, but whose voice is gone. Mr. Borge is still a comedian of grace and civility. His timing is precise and light. The kindness that always overhung the ferocity of his comical stage entanglements remains. . . . But the conversation has grown tired. There are some wonderful moments but they don't last. . . . He goes into the kind of routines that made him an enormous success a generation ago. . . . Some of the material is new and some is not, but most of it lacks energy. . . . Some of the charm remains, but Mr. Borge is limping badly, but it is his own two legs he is using, and for these times that is something." Richard Eder, *The New York Times (10-4-77, p. 49)*

"It was as if he'd just gone out for a loaf of bread and reappeared none the worse for wear. In fact he seems the better. . . . He was mellow and delightful and perhaps this is the time to catch up with him. . . . Yes, Borge can be corny. But he is also a droll and merry man, certainly an original and more or less the model of a type that's going out of style — the genuinely urbane, the wise and witty. . . . He is what is meant by a class act." — Martin Gottfried, *New York Post (10-4-77, p. 53)*

"Like Jack Benny, he possesses a sense of timing so acute that many seconds can pass in a breathless silence, after which the very first word he utters is often sufficient to bring down the house. . . . I recommend him with all my heart." — Brendan Gill, *The New Yorker (10-17-77, p. 93)*

"Victor Borge remains not only the funniest solo performer in the theater but also the funniest solo performer in my files." — Walter Kerr, *The New York Times (10-15-77, p. D 5)*

"All the lights on Broadway glow a little brighter now that one of the master funnymen of the age is back. . . . The timing is impeccable, the professionalism unflawed." — T. E. Kalem, *Time (10-17-77, p. 96)*

"He continues to be a master of tidy timing, sly inflections, and lukewarm, predictable comedy, rarely, very rarely, shot through with a flash of superior wit. If this is enough for you, fine; personally, I would prefer it drastically pruned and confined to a nightclub." — John Simon, *New York (10-17-77, p. 124)*

THE CAST

Claude. . . . . Randall Easterbrook
Berger. Michael Hoit
Woof. Scott Thornton
Hud . . . . Cleavant Derricks
Sheila . . . . Ellen Foley
Jeanie . . . . Iris Rosenkrantz
Dionne . . . . Alaina Reed
Crissy . . . . Kristen Vigard
Shopping Cart Lady. . . . . Michael Leslie
Mothers. . . . . Annie Golden
                                        Louis Mattioli
                                        Perry Arthur
Fathers. . . . . James Rich
                                        Eva Charney
                                        Martha Wingate
Principals. . . . . Carl Woerner
                                        Michael Leslie
                                        Linda Myers
Tourist Couple . . . . Perry Arthur
                                        Carl Woerner
General Grant. . . . . Carl Woerner
Abraham Lincoln . . . . Linda Myers
Sergeant . . . . Byron Utley
Parents . . . . Lori Wagner, James Rich
Tribe. . . . . Perry Arthur, Emily Bindiger, Paul Binotto,
   Eva Charney, Loretta Devine, Doug Katsaros,
   Michael Leslie, Louis Mattioli, Linda Myers,
   Raymond Patterson, James Rich, James Sbano,
   Deborah Van Valkenburgh, Lori Wagner, Doug Wall,
   Martha Wingate, Carl Woerner, Charlaine Woodard.

Book and lyrics by Gerome Ragni and James Rado; music by Galt MacDermot. Presented by Michael Butler, in association with K. H. Nezhad; directed by Tom O'Horgan; choreography by Julie Arenal; scenic designer Robin Wagner; lighting by Jules Fisher; costumes by Nancy Potts; sound by Abe Jacob; musical direction by Denzil A. Miller, Jr.; vocal direction by Patrick Flynn; assistant choreographer, Wesley Fata; associate producer, George Milman; production stage manager, J. Galen McKinley. Biltmore Theatre, 261 West 47th Street.

More than any other, *Hair*, which was first produced in 1967, was the musical that embodied the rebellion and rootlessness of the youth of the sixties.

Its 1977 revival, a tenth anniversary production, makes no attempt to "update" or alter the original, and is re-created by the original director, Tom O'Horgan, and most of the same designers. It remains more a concert, with some 30 songs, than a traditional "book" musical, with a plot involving Berger and Claude, who live with Sheila in the East Village, then the home of hippies. The trio has a modestly complicated romantic relationship. Claude is drafted, but does not want to go to Vietnam, but lacks the courage to flee, so ends up a war statistic.

Hair's claim to fame, however, is its songs, including such numbers as "Aquarius," "Hair," "Frank Mills," and "What a Piece of Work Is Man."

Opened October 5, 1977
Closed November 6, 1977

Hair

The "Colored Spade" number

REVIEWS

"Its message — liberation, joy, pot and multiform sex, the vision of youth as a social class of its own and, in short, the notion that there can be flowers without stalks, roots or muck to grow in — has faded. It is too far gone to be timely; too recently gone to be history or even nostalgia. Its revival at the Biltmore Theatre has no particular occasion to it and so it must stand or fall quite baldly upon its merits. It falls, or rather, it sags. Its virtues remain, but 10 years after its first appearance they look much feebler than they must have seemed at the time. Its glow is forced; its warmth becomes sentimentality and worse, sententiousness." — Richard Eder, *The New York Times (10-6-77, p. C 22)*

"Today, of course, *Hair* looks terribly dated, as any theatre related to passing fashion must. Its outright disregard of structure and form make it painfully without cohesion or stage purpose. It can hardly pay attention to itself." — Martin Gottfried, *New York Post (10-6-77, p. 29)*

"0 for a depilatory to rid us of this unwanted stage (worse than face or body) *Hair!* . . . And what a crew of graceless-looking no-talents O'Horgan has assembled this time round! . . . The staging seems to have become yet more overdone and offensive. . . . The music, in fact, hurts." — John Simon, *New York (10-24-77, p. 85)*

"*Hair* is deader than King Tut and the relics that were buried with him." — T. E. Kalem, *Time (10-17-77, p. 94)*

"You can't go home again, as Thomas Wolfe said, and you can't grow *Hair* again, as seems clear from the Broadway revival." — Jack Kroll, *Newsweek (10-17-77, p. 117)*

"Why on earth should anyone have wished to bring back *Hair*? . . . It is simply there, poor *Hair*, on the cluttered stage of the Biltmore, all feverishly abustle and all, alas, lifeless." — Brendan Gill, *The New Yorker (10-17-77, p. 94)*

Jessica Tandy and Hume Cronyn

The Gin Game

By D. L. Coburn. Presented by the Shubert Organization; directed by Mike Nichols; setting by David Mitchell; costumes by Bill Walker; lighting by Ronald Wallace; production supervisor, Nina Seely. Produced by Hume Cronyn and Mike Nichols; originally presented by the Long Wharf Theatre. John Golden Theatre, 252 West 45th Street.

The Gin Game takes place in an old-age home where two people who have recently met engage in a series of gin rummy games. Weller is the pro and, in introducing the game to Fonsia, finds himself more than meeting his match as he loses hand after hand. Obviously, it is not a situation he finds congenial, and he turns from initial annoyance to fury to obscenity to throwing over the table.

In Act 2, it emerges that both Weller and Fonsia are on welfare, though her son lives in the same town, not in Denver as she had earlier indicated. Yet, he will not come to visit her. Both, the one the embodiment of cantankerousness, the other a fairly typical prude who all her life has driven away those she most wished to keep, are lonely not because of the divorce and estrangement suffered in their marriages but because of their temperaments. In a sense, the playwright suggests, they have always been lonely if not always alone, unable to rectify the flaws or characteristics that have made them so. In the end, it is left to the audience to decide whether they will be reconciled after a particularly furious outburst.

Opened October 6, 1977

THE CAST

Fonsia Dorsey . . . . Jessica Tandy
Weller Martin . . . . Hume Cronyn

REVIEWS

"[An] extremely intelligent and immaculately performed play. . . . Ultimately, perhaps, the device is a trifle small in scope, too neat, too predictable — once we have seen it working — to quite suffice for the weight of the play's emotions. But it is generally workable, and accomplishes most of what it is trying to do. . . . Undoubtedly the performances of Hume Cronyn and Jessica Tandy, and the seamless direction of Mike Nichols, are so mesmerizing that they make a sober evaluation of the play difficult in any quick judgment." — Richard Eder, *The New York Times (10-7-77, p. C 2)*

"One suspects that none of the pensioners are quite so feeble as the play. As dramatic carpentry, *The Gin Game* is made of balsa wood, while the performances of Hume Cronyn and Jessica Tandy rival the sturdiest oaks. Their artistry is compelling, and they supply the play with its only bracing vigor." — T. E. Kalem, *Time (10-17-77, p. 94)*

"If *The Gin Game* were any slighter it would be solitaire, and that's surprising since the play combines the established talents of Jessica Tandy, Hume Cronyn and director Mike Nichols. It's difficult to understand what drew them to D. L. Coburn's new (and first) play. Not that it's unlikable. There is almost too little to like or dislike about the play." — Martin Gottfried, *New York Post (10-7-77, p. 46)*

"It is a pleasant piece greatly aided by the charming performances of Jessica Tandy and Hume Cronyn, and by Mike Nichols' canny direction. It is nicely written and sympathetic in feeling." — Harold Clurman, *The Nation (10-29-77, p. 445)*

"Mr. Coburn is telling us about a couple of miserable inmates of an old people's home, whose plight he observes with an astringent clarity and about whom, at the same time, he manages to be very funny. . . . The Cronyns are among the most gifted actors alive, and they play together not merely with great professional cunning but with a sort of family zest." — Brendan Gill, *The New Yorker (10-17-77, p. 93)*

"Some plays are plays; others, merely vehicles. *The Gin Game* . . . is resolutely of the latter kind. . . . The play is brittle enough without the added burden of pretentiousness. . . . It is staged, however, with almost indecent (because wasted) expertise by Mike Nichols, and acted to individual and joint near perfection." — John Simon, *New York (10-24-77, p. 85)*

"*The Gin Game* is not sentimental; neither is it really touching. It is dry, sometimes droll, sometimes acrid, necessarily repetitive, scrupulously honest. . . . Because its stars are superb, it deserves your admiring attention." — Walter Kerr, *The New York Times (10-16-77, p. D 5)*

The Night of the Tribades

Max von Sydow and Werner Klemperer

THE CAST

Siri von-Essen-Strindberg. . . Bibi Andersson
August Strindberg . . . . . . .Max von Sydow
Viggo Schiwe . . . . Werner Klemperer
Marie Caroline David . . . . . .Eileen Atkins
Photographer . . . . Bill Moor

By Per Olov Enquist. Presented by Burry Fredrik, Irwin Meyer and Stephen R. Friedman, in association with William Donnell; translated by Ross Shideler; directed by Michael Kahn; setting by Lawrence King; costumes by Jane Greenwood; lighting by John McLain; associate producers, Sally Sears and Marilyn Strauss; production stage manager, Suzanne Egan. Helen Hayes Theatre, 210 West 46th Street.

"Tribades" is a synonym for lesbians and Enquist, a Swedish writer, constructs his play around what is purported to be an authentic rehearsal of his fellow countryman August Strindberg's play *The Stronger,* which had its first performance in 1889, at which time the dramatist's wife, Siri, played·one of the roles.

The Stronger is incorporated into Enquist's ambitious text, as are other elements of Strindbergiana. There are five characters: Strindberg, Siri, an actor who admires her and has volunteered his assistance as director, an alcoholic whom Strindberg claims to have seen making love to Siri and a photographer who enters at the end and utters only eighteen words.

Strindberg has come to the rehearsal of his play, but cannot remain as a spectator for very long. He argues about Siri's readings and about virtually everything else, and during the course of the rehearsal the audience becomes aware of the tensions that have torn apart the Strindbergs' marriage, in particular his hysterical suspicion of women.

Opened October 13, 1977
Closed October 22, 1977

REVIEWS

"Those three fine actors . . . are not simply miscast and dubiously directed. . . . As Per Olov Enquist's play about August Strindberg unravels upon the stage . . . they are virtually bushwacked." – Richard Eder, *The New York Times (10-14-77, p. C 3)*

"The play ran to two hours of indecipherable talk and a sluggish physical display." – Martin Gottfried, *New York Post (10-14-77, p. 44)*

"Cleverly plotted and continuously entertaining . . . the play is a specimen of the current fad for mingling fact and fiction. . . . It isn't an easy play to act, and we have reason to be grateful for the presence of Max von Sydow as Strindberg, Bibi Andersson as Siri, and Eileen Atkins as Marie Caroline David. Werner Klemperer, as Siri's admirer, is either miscast or misdirected." – Brendan Gill, *The New Yorker (10-24-77, p. 143)*

"Under Michael Kahn's direction, the gifted performers never make organic contact, even though Max von Sydow tries mightily to make the mechanical emotional seizures that Enquist gives Strindberg into something moving and harrowing." – Jack Kroll, *Newsweek (10-24-77, p. 85)*

"Admirable and unfailingly perceptive . . . a play that stretches the mind, bares the nerves, challenges the ear, braces the imagination." – T. E. Kalem, *Time (10-24-77, p. 123)*

"The play has every tense but the present. . . Both in the writing and the production, things do not hang together as well as they should; still, *The Night of the Tribades* is far more deserving of a night out than anything else the supposedly serious theater on Broadway can currently offer." – John Simon, *New York (10-31-77, p. 93)*

Some of My Best Friends

Gavin Reed and Ted Knight

THE CAST

Andrew Mumford . . . . Ted Knight
Albert . . . . Gavin Reed
Irving Buxbaum . . . . Lee Wallace
Lawrence Mumford . . . . Bob Balaban
Dorothy Mumford . . . . Alice Drummond
Sari . . . . Trish Hawkins
Baby . . . . Ralph Williams
Delivery Boy and Urchins . . . . Joseph Scalzo

By Stanley Hart. Presented by Arthur Whitelaw, Jack Schlissel and Leonard Soloway; associate producers, Donald Tick and Martin Markinson; directed by Harold Prince; designed by Eugene Lee; lighting by Ken Billington; costumes by Franne Lee; production stage manager, Ben Strobach. Longacre Theatre, 220 West 48th Street.

The hero of *Some of My Best Friends* is a former business tycoon who has learned to talk with birds, dogs, potted trees and infants; with, in other words, the pure of heart. It is a gift he suddenly acquired while in a sanitarium after refusing to talk with anyone following his realization that there is more to life than material success. When his wife and very staid son arrive, there is a certain degree of interaction and, in the end, Andrew Mumford does decide he must again take on the responsibilities of a human being. He'll return home and return to making money.

As conceived by playwright Hart and directed by Harold Prince, dog, tree and baby are portrayed by adult humans, in a play that has certain resemblances to the classic American farce *You Can't Take It with You.*

Opened October 25, 1977
Closed October 29, 1977

REVIEWS

"This is his first play to be done professionally in New York, and there is not a speck of beginner's luck in it. . . . It's not the blandness of the message that makes the play about as tasty as boiled squash, though, but the blandness of the method. . . . *Friends* seems to be a notion that struggled to become a play and failed, lacking as it does, density, characters, conflict or one single line that is either witty or graceful. . . . Of the actors playing real people, all seem more or less confounded by their material." — Richard Eder, *The New York Times (10-26-77, p. C 20)*

"Adds a new dimension to the concept of disaster. It is a creative form of theatrical suicide, a magic show that closes right before your eyes." — Martin Gottfried, *New York Post (10-26-77, p. 58)*

"There's merely an idea for a play in *Some of My Best Friends*. . . . Stanley Hart's farce-fantasy brings a few smiles and a chuckle or two, but no hearty laughs. It has a wacky quality, but lacks real humor. . . . The insurmountable trouble . . . is the play itself. It does virtually nothing with what must have seemed a promising basic premise." — *Variety (11-2-77, p. 82)*

"Least said, soonest mended: One of the worst shows I have seen in my career as a reviewer." — Brendan Gill, *The New Yorker (11-7-77, p. 105)*

"This stew is from the kitchens of three cooks: the lame, halt, and blind. . . . This show bores from within." — Leo Shull, *Show Business (11-3-77, p. 6)*

Dracula

Ann Sachs, Alan Coates and Frank Langella

Dramatized by Hamilton Deane and John L. Balderston from Bram Stoker's novel *Dracula*. Presented by Jujamcyn Theaters, Elizabeth Ireland McCann, John Wulp, Victor Lurie, Nelle Nugent and Max Weitzenhoffer; directed by Dennis Rosa; scenery and costumes designed by Edward Gorey; scenery supervised by Lynn Pecktal; costumes supervised by John David Ridge; lighting designed by Roger Morgan; production supervisor, Ben Janney; production stage manager, Charles Kindl. Martin Beck Theatre, 302 West 45th Street.

Dracula has been particularly lauded for the gray-on-gray sets and costumes of Edward Gorey, who conceived the production and whose vision dominates it. The first set is a huge drawing room, a single massive pen drawing actually, complete with library, fireplace and a large wall painting. Act 2 is set in the heroine's bedroom, dominated by a towering silver-colored bed, topped by bat wings. Bats, in fact, are the motif of the evening, complete to those who come soaring onstage from time to time, and bats as fasteners on the patients' pajamas.

The present *Dracula* offers a Dracula with a difference: handsome, glamorous, approaching the tragic. All Bram Stoker's major conflicts are there: good vs. evil, God vs. Satan, wolves howling outside the door of the sanitarium where Lucy Seward's father, who operates it, a scientist friend versed in the supernatural and Lucy's fiance are struggling to rescue her from the clutches of Count Dracula, who has been surviving on blood for five centuries.

Dr. Van Helsing and Dracula are, of course, the main contenders, and worthy foes they make, battling through to the well-known end. The present production mainly adheres to the original work, though it perhaps makes more bows toward obvious humor than toward terror.

Opened October 20, 1977

14

Ann Sachs and Frank Langella

THE CAST

Lucy Seward . . . . .Ann Sachs
Miss Wells, maid . . . . .Gretchen Oehler
Jonathan Harker . . . . .Alan Coates
Dr. Seward . . . . Dillon Evans
Abraham Van Helsing . . . . Jerome Dempsey
R. M. Renfield . . . . .Richard Kavanaugh
Butterworth . . . . .Baxter Harris
Count Dracula . . . . .Frank Langella

Frank Langella

Dillon Evans and Alan Coates (standing);
Jerome Dempsey and Ann Sachs (seated)

REVIEWS

"There are many good things to be said about *Dracula* . . . it is elegant, taut, only very faintly camped-up, and visually stunning — it also tends to be bloodless. There is a surface perfection to the production. It comes in the sets and costumes by Edward Gorey, some extraordinary lighting by Roger Morgan, and a flawless command of movement and timing by the director, Dennis Rosa. The acting, on the other hand, though polished is not generally very interesting." — Richard Eder, *The New York Times (10-21-77, p. C 3)*

"This is ghoulish fun in the grand manner. . . . Productions are not usually identified with their designers but Gorey dominates this one, sets its tone and propels it. . . . It is action indeed and theater on the super scale, pure escape and great fun." — Martin Gottfried, *New York Post (10-21-77, p. 40)*

"Edward Gorey's set for *Dracula* is an eye-blinker. . . . In the performance of Frank Langella as a demonic force from the nether world, there is also a doomed lyrical romanticism. . . . The rest of the cast is exemplary, and the sounds of baying offstage hounds are ear-tingling. But the show belongs first, last, and almost always to Gorey and Langella." — T. E. Kalem, *Time (10-31-77, p. 93)*

"The producers and the director, Dennis Rosa, have camped up the proceedings ferociously. . . . It is all like having two fingers shoved into our solar plexus while being commanded to laugh." — John Simon, *New York (11-7-77, p. 75)*

The Act

Liza Minnelli and Company

A musical with book by George Furth, music by John Kander, lyrics by Fred Ebb. A Feuer and Martin Production, presented by the Shubert Organization; directed by Martin Scorese; choreography by Ron Lewis; scenery by Tony Walton; lighting by Tharon Musser; costumes by Halston; sound by Abe Jacob; musical direction by Stanley Lebowsky; orchestrations by Ralph Burns; arrangements by Ronald Melrose; choral arrangements by Earl Brown; Miss Minnelli's hairstyle by Sydney Guilaroff; production stage manager, Phil Friedman. Majestic Theatre, 245 West 45th Street.

Although it often seems more related to a nightclub act than to the legitimate theatre, *The Act* is at least nominally the saga of one Michelle Craig, who becomes a movie star who is totally dependent on her producer-husband. When they split up over her fling with a young and shallow superstud, her career goes rapidly down the drain, only to be resurrected in the Las Vegas nightclub act that gives the show its minimal form. There is a happy ending, together with a reunion of husband and wife and reconciliation of Michelle and her daughter.

The principal songs include "Shine It On," "Turning," "Little Do They Know," "Arthur in the Afternoon," "The Money Tree," "City Lights" and "My Own Space."

Opened October 29, 1977
Closed July 1, 1978

THE CAST

Lenny Kanter . . . . .Christopher Barrett
Michelle Craig. . . . . Liza Minnelli
Nat Schreiber . . . . .Arnold Soboloff
Dan Connors . . . . Barry Nelson
Arthur. . . . . Roger Minami
Charley Price . . . . Mark Goddard
Molly Connors . . . . Gayle Crofoot
The Boys. . . . . Wayne Cilento, Michael Leeds,
        Roger Minami, Albert Stephenson
The Girls . . . . .Carol Estey, Laurie Dawn Skinner

Liza Minnelli and Roger Minami

REVIEWS

"It is an act, and a splendid one. On the other hand, it is a little less than its pretensions imply. Theatrical though it is as a performance, it is indifferent musical theater. It displays the breathtaking presence of Liza Minnelli, and her command of a force that is the emotional equivalent of what good coloratura achieves in top form. . . . Its pace and staging were polished and imaginative. What is mainly lacking in *The Act* is a book. . . . As a result, *The Act* is a first-rate cabaret show expanded for theater, rather than theater itself." — Richard Eder, *The New York Times (10-31-77, p. 39)*

"This is a striking and intense show with size and muscle and marvelous dances and a wonderful star performance by Liza Minnelli. . . . Though well-constructed in a cinematic style, Furth's [book] is a soggy, skimpy and unaffecting story. . . . *The Act* is too uncertainly focused and uninvolving to be a great show, but this is an ambitious and big time musical with terrific entertainment values and stage excitement." — Martin Gottfried, *New York Post (10-31-77, p. 32)*

"[The] breathlessly hardworking cast aside, there isn't much of interest to be observed." — Brendan Gill, *The New Yorker (11-7-77, p. 103)*

"Liza is a tornado of energy, and that has a hypnotic appeal. . . . As a show, *The Act* does not deserve it. The book is dental floss inserted with tedious hygienic monotony so as to clear a space for the molar crunch of song." — T. E. Kalem, *Time (11-14-77, p. 61)*

"A personal triumph for Liza Minnelli in an overblown formula musical." — *Variety (11-2-77, p. 82)*

Liza Minnelli

An Almost Perfect Person

Colleen Dewhurst

By Judith Ross. Presented by Burry Fredrik and Joel Key Rice; directed by Zoe Caldwell; set and lighting by Ben Edwards; costumes by Jane Greenwood; production stage manager, Peter Lawrence. Belasco Theatre, 111 West 44th Street.

Irene Porter, a New York widow, is encountered on the night of and day following her unsuccessful run for Congress. Keeping the proverbial stiff upper lip after her defeat, which an inaccurate television report momentarily seems to have turned into a victory, she goes to bed first with her campaign media specialist, then with its treasurer.

In between, the indomitable Ms. Porter discovers that her campaign is $75,000 in debt, courtesy of a media blitz she did not approve. But it is just as quickly in and out of debt as Irene Porter is in and out of bed and two of the trio promise to live happily ever after. Or at least until the next election.

Opened October 27, 1977
Closed January 29, 1978

THE CAST

Irene Porter . . . . .Colleen Dewhurst
Dan Michael Connally . . . . George Hearn
Jerry Leeds . . . . Rex Robbins

REVIEWS

"Using *An Almost Perfect Person* as a vehicle for Colleen Dewhurst is like fitting out a kiddy-cart with a jet engine. Miss Dewhurst is generally magnificent in this confused mite of a comedy, and magnificence is always something to give thanks for. But she is too much for it. Even while she is salvaging it from total mediocrity she is also shaking it to pieces. . . . It is a trifle, whose three characters are three sets of remarks — some of them quite funny — held together by clothes." — Richard Eder, *The New York Times (10-28-77, p. C3)*

"It is what's called touching all the bases and not getting a hit. . . . Yet it is interesting and intelligent for much of its time, at least until it collapses altogether in the second act. . . . For all this, the play has an earnestness about it and its characters have strength. . . . Then again, the whole play is inconsistent. It doesn't even seem sure whether it is a comedy, a drama or an article. It has wholesale lapses in craft and still it manages to play for most of its time." — Martin Gottfried, *New York Post (10-28-77, p. 44)*

"*An Almost Perfect Person* is a small comedy but not an unappealing one. I admired the set and the lighting, by Ben Edwards; the costumes, by Jane Greenwood; and the direction, by Zoe Caldwell, who knows a thing or two about making a play march." — Brendan Gill, *The New Yorker (11-7-77, p. 104)*

"An old-fashioned sex comedy, contemporary in its endorsement of a woman's right to sleep with whomever she wants, but dated in its underlying feeling that sex is basically something cute. What gives this slight work its interest is that Irene is played by Colleen Dewhurst." — Howard Kissel, *Women's Wear Daily (10-28-77, p. 10)*

"Zoe Caldwell has directed the proceedings with such absolute authority, and the star and her two colleagues perform with such secure and sassy briskness that *you* feel a shade dense not to be getting the hang of it. But the fact of the matter is that the kindnesses of the couch and the cruelties of electioneering have absolutely nothing to do with each other and can't be made to hook up. . . . Even with the irresistible Miss Dewhurst . . . this is finally one instance of bedfellows making strange politics." — Walter Kerr, *The New York Times (11-6-77, p. D 3)*

Bully

James Whitmore as Teddy Roosevelt

By Jerome Alden. Presented by Don Saxon and Kevin Brown in association with Kathy Raitt; the George Spota/Four Star International Production; directed by Peter H. Hunt; setting and costumes by John Conklin; lighting by Peter H. Hunt; associate producer, Dan Lieberman; production stage manager, Martha Knight. Forty-sixth Street Theatre, 226 West 46th Street.

The scene is Theodore Roosevelt's room at Sagamore Hill, in which are arrayed a variety of buffalo and elk heads. As Alden's one-man play opens, Roosevelt has retired as President and is visibly restless over the behavior of his successor, William Howard Taft, as well as his own relative inactivity.

In the course of the play he advocates his famous doctrine of the Strenuous Life and lectures on the need for conservation; relates how the teddy bear was inspired by him and defends his tactics in pressing the Panama Canal, declaiming "I took Panama." Brief scenes touch upon the death of his first wife and his entry into politics; his achieving of the Presidency and efforts to recapture the Republican Party. He is also seen playing with his sons and reminiscing with his wife. All, of course, are imaginary encounters on stage, as Whitmore evokes their spirit and calls upon his and the audience's imagination.

Opened November 1, 1977, for a limited engagement
Closed November 6, 1977

With: James Whitmore

REVIEWS

"Mr. Whitmore's newest re-creation — that of Theodore Roosevelt — does not succeed. The figure of the first President Roosevelt has historical interest, of course, but not enough to seize us across a stage. . . . *Bully* seems disjointed and distant, and a good deal of it is plain boring. . . . The theatricality of the grand moments seems overdone." — Richard Eder, *The New York Times (11-2-77, p. C 17)*

"This 'play,' as it optimistically calls itself, only adds that [Roosevelt] was a pompous bore. . . . Ordinarily, any play, no matter how bad, deserves a break but I can't in all good conscience wish any to such merchandising of the theater." — Martin Gottfried, *New York Post (11-2-77, p. 56)*

"Whitmore proves himself to be a magician on the stage. . . . Director Peter Hunt deserves credit for helping create a one-character show that is filled with the ghosts of many other characters. So does set designer John Conklin." — Christopher Sharp, *Women's Wear Daily (11-2-77, p. 65)*

"Whitmore's playing has admirable energy and considerable conviction, and the lack of finesse appears to be due primarily to Alden's script and Peter H. Hunt's direction, which stresses physical movement and vocal monotony." — *Variety (11-9-77, p. 64)*

"A compelling portrait of TR [which] should not be missed by anyone with even a slight interest in the man, the period, or the history of the U.S. Presidency." — P. Gregory Speck, *Show Business (11-3-77, p. 22)*

Golda

THE CAST

Allon, Menachem, D.P. . . . . James Tolkan
Lior, Father, American, D.P., Cabinet Member . . Richard Kuss
Dayan (Moshe), D.P. . . . . Ben Hammer
Elazar ("Dado"), D.P. . . . . Nicholas La Padula
Galili, D.P. . . . . Harry Davis
Cabinet Member, T.V. Interviewer, British Commandant
    Bearded Man . . . . Sam Schacht
Golda Meir . . . . Anne Bancroft
Lou, D.P. . . . . Vivian Nathan
Dinitz (Simcha), D.P., Cabinet Member . . . . . Zack Matalon
Mother, Sarile, D.P. . . . . Frances Chaney
Golda as a Child, Sarile as a Child, Ruthie . . Justine Litchman
Sister, Arab Woman, Adolescent Grandchild,
    American Girl, D.P. . . . . Alice Golembo
Body Guard, Arab, Adolescent Grandson,
    T.V. Crew, Cabinet Member, D.P. . . . . Eric Booth
Morris, D.P. . . . . Gerald Hiken
"Arab" Escort, Bar-Lev (Chaim), D.P. . . . . . . Ernest Graves
Arab, Adolescent Grandson, T.V. Crew,
    Army Messenger, D.P. . . . . Phillip Cates
Arab Woman, Clara as a Young Girl, D.P. . . Corinne Neuchateau
King Abdullah, Ben-Gurion ("B.G."),
    Religious Minister, D.P. . . . . Sam Gray
Gideon, Modke . . . . Josh Freund
Grandson, D.P. . . . . Michael Brown
Menachem as a Boy, Nahum . . . . Glenn Scarpelli
Clara, D.P. . . . . Rebecca Schull
D.P., Israeli Citizens. . . . . David C. Jones, Robert Levine
D.P. . . . . Judy Unger

By William Gibson. Presented by the Theatre Guild; directed by Arthur Penn; scenery and costumes by Santo Loquasto; lighting and projections by Jules Fisher; visuals by Lucie D. Grosvenor; general manager, Victor Samrock; produced by Philip Langner, Armina Marshall and Marilyn Langner; production stage manager, Andre St. Jean. Morosco Theatre, 217 West 45th Street.

William Gibson, whose earlier works include *Two for the Seesaw* and *The Miracle Worker*, draws what he terms a "partial portrait" of the indomitable Israeli leader Golda Meir, based largely upon her own book *My Life*. He follows her from her childhood and persecution in Russia, through the various stages of her marriage, her role in the founding of Israel and the tensions and tragedies of the 1973 Yom Kippur War, among many other events. There is relatively little attempt to establish characters, apart from Mrs. Meir herself, and *Golda* thus emerges more as a portrait of a woman surviving disasters, seeking American support, urging on her generals and recalling the disasters that have beset the Jews through the ages and thus impelled them to fierce determination.

Opened November 14, 1977
Closed February 16, 1978

Anne Bancroft

REVIEWS

"[It] has authentic material for a dramatic monologue about the public struggles and confrontations of former Prime Minister Golda Meir of Israel. But it has been padded out with scenes that attempt to dramatize these events by trotting in wispy and one-dimensional figures that represent her associates. . . . William Gibson's script makes the further mistake of trying to flesh out Mrs. Meir's private life. . . . Miss Bancroft [gives an] extraordinary portrait of a leader who possessed strength amid confusion. . . . *Golda* is to be remembered for the spectacle of an actress overwhelmed by the character she plays, and yet able to master it almost completely. But it is also to be remembered as a very partial and superficial portrait of a historical figure and its history." — Richard Eder, *The New York Times (11-15-77, p. 53)*

"*Golda* isn't a play. It is an assignment, for the author and for the audience." — Martin Gottfried, *New York Post (11-15-77, p. 55)*

"*Golda* isn't a play, and I doubt if it's a partial portrait. . . . It is a comic-strip version of one of the most formidable women of our time, executed in crude, stick colors, and with words issuing in balloons from the mouths of the chief characters." — Brendan Gill, *The New Yorker (11-28-77, p. 81)*

"It's a story that should be a feast, but instead it's served up as canapés — a knish here as Golda negotiates with King Abdullah of Jordan, some chopped liver there as she comes to the U.S. to raise millions for Israeli arms." — Jack Kroll, *Newsweek (11-28-77, p. 80)*

"*Golda* is a conscientious, reverential, monumental bore. The real Golda Meir should sue." — T. E. Kalem, *Time (11-28-77, p. 103)*

"A work like this, in which every character other than Golda is a mere stick figure, does not add to our understanding of anything. . . . It cheapens everything it touches, however pious the underlying sentiments may be. Or did someone merely think that because so many New York theatergoers are Jewish, a play like this has to sell like *latkes*?" — John Simon, *New York (12-5-77, p. 138)*

The Merchant

By Arnold Wesker. Presented by the Shubert Organization, John F. Kennedy Center for the Performing Arts, Roger Berlind and Eddie Kulukundis, in association with SRO Productions; directed by John Dexter; setting and costumes by Jocelyn Herbert; lighting by Andy Phillips; lighting supervised by Andrea Wilson; production stage manager, Brent Peek. Plymouth Theatre, 236 West 45th Street.

The British playwright Arnold Wesker draws upon Shakespeare's *The Merchant of Venice* and other sources to present a distinctly different view of Shylock, Antonio, Portia and other familiar characters. His Shylock is kindly, talkative and a cultured bibliophile, and has been a devoted friend of Antonio for many years. Portia is depicted not as a brilliant law student, but as a beautiful heiress to a depleted fortune who is amenable to following her late father's wishes by taking the suitor who chooses the modest-appearing jewel casket, but clearly indicates he will have to toe the mark once he weds her. In the original play's most famous scene, in the courtroom, Wesker entirely omits Portia's celebrated plea on the "quality of mercy" and Shylock's "hath not a Jew eyes?" speech is delivered by the politically ambitious young Venetian Lorenzo as a patronizing comment rather than as a defense. Shylock eventually is stripped of his possessions but, rather than being forced to embrace Christianity, is allowed to emigrate to Palestine.

Opened November 16, 1977
Closed November 19, 1977

THE CAST

Shylock Kolner. . . . . Joseph Leon
Antonio Querini . . . . .John Clements
Portia Contarini . . . . Roberta Maxwell
Nerissa . . . . Gloria Gifford
Jessica Kolner. . . . . .Julie Garfield
Rivka Kolner . . . . Marian Seldes
Abtalion da Modena. . . . . Boris Tumarin
Tubal di Ponti. . . . . .John Seitz
Solomon da Mendes. . . . . .Angela Wood
Bassanio Sanudo . . . . .Nicolas Surovy
Graziano Sanudo. Riggs O'Hara
Lorenzo Pisani . . . . Everett McGill
Moses of Castelazzo . . . . Lieb Lensky
Doge of Venice . . . . .William Roerick
Servant . . . . .Rebecca Malka
Venetians. . . . . Russ Banham, Mark Blum,
Philip Carroll, James David Cromar,
Brian Meister, John Tyrrell

Roberta Maxwell

REVIEWS

"It is provocative, generally intelligent and sometimes strained or confused. Its writing has moments of ferocious brilliance and wit; on the other hand, its dramatic structure is weak and its dramatic impact fitful and uncertain. . . . The production does not help. The set is drab, John Dexter's staging is blocky and unimaginative, and though the acting is generally good it does not have the extra weight and artfulness to run when Mr. Wesker falters." — Richard Eder, *The New York Times (11-17-77, p. C 18)*

"A theoretical and argumentative play with little life force of its own. Its own definitions of anti-Semitism are superficial. Its characters and events exist only to disagree with Shakespeare. John Dexter, who in the past has done so well by Wesker, has done him little service this time." — Martin Gottfried, *New York Post (11-17-77, p. 53)*

"I admired the many ingenuities of *The Merchant,* but I tired at last of the amplitude with which Wesker spun them out and showed them off to us. . . . The production was an admirable one." — Brendan Gill, *The New Yorker (11-28-77, p. 81)*

"*The Merchant,* I am afraid, is to *The Merchant of Venice* what lumpfish is to caviar, or a hot-water bottle to the Gulf Stream." — John Simon, *New York (12-5-77, p. 142)*

"Shakespeare has been intellectualized and emasculated. . . . Wesker's numbingly loquacious writing is an inescapable letdown from Shakespeare's eloquent verse." — *Variety (11-23-77, p. 120)*

Chapter Two

Anita Gillette, Ann Wedgeworth,
Cliff Gorman and Judd Hirsch

THE CAST

George Schneider .... Judd Hirsch
Leo Schneider........................ Cliff Gorman
Jennie Malone...................... Anita Gillette
Faye Medwick .... Ann Wedgeworth

REVIEWS

"Mr. Simon's effort, quixotic but hedged, to escape the confinement of his own talents. Instead of using pain to secure the jokes, he goes mainly for the pain and it is the jokes that are the safety-anchor. . . . Mr. Simon has abandoned his comic control without quite being able, or perhaps willing, to substitute it with something else. *Chapter Two* is dropsical from the effort to do too many things at once – it is nearly three hours long. It is swollen with unworkable contradictions. . . . Herbert Ross directs so as to get every bit of pace he can out of the dialogue, but he is unable to make the whole divided play cohere." – Richard Eder, *The New York Times (12-5-77, p. 52)*

"Neil Simon's *Chapter Two* stormed into the Imperial Theatre last night on waves of applause that sounded like the clatter of massed celestial typewriters. . . . This time he is touching deeper – with a mocking, dancing delicacy he is walking barefoot on the heart. The heart is his own. . . . *Chapter Two* is always funny. Indeed for most of the time it is downright hilarious, but more than ever before, the torrent of laughter has an undertow of real feeling. . . . A lovely, whimsical, touching and, once in an important while, moving play." – Clive Barnes, *New York Post (12-5-77, p. 20)*

"The play ends happily – a pact Simon always keeps with his audience. When will he choose to keep the compact he seems to want to make with himself – to plunge hip-deep-bold instead of toe-deep-scared into the consciousness stream of the real Neil Simon?" – T. E. Kalem, *Time (12-19-77, p. 96)*

"In the world of Simon says, rhythm is everything, and Herbert Ross's direction has perfect pitch and cadence. The four actors make up the most winning ensemble of any Simon play." – Jack Kroll, *Newsweek (12-19-77, p. 86)*

"The cast helps a good deal to sustain the basic hoax of the play. . . . Herbert Ross's direction is everything it needs to be." – Harold Clurman, *The Nation (12-24-77, p. 699)*

"Though there are plenty of funny lines, it's true that the emotion the play intends to evoke is one of rueful poignancy." – Brendan Gill, *The New Yorker (12-12-77, p. 91)*

"Simon . . . tries to handle drama as if it could be constructed out of one-liners, only sticking in laments where the laughs would normally go. . . . The acting is basically accomplished. . . . Herbert Ross's directorial hand moves as easefully through the dimensions of the play as if it had three." – John Simon, *New York (12-19-77, p. 102)*

"In addition to having the bright, funny lines and situations you expect from a Simon comedy, it has, in its lovers, two of the most attractive characters Simon has yet placed on a stage. . . . You should enjoy it. Despite its split personality, it is, in many ways, Simon's most mature work." – Douglas Watt, *Daily News (12-5-77, p. 23)*

By Neil Simon. Presented by Emanuel Azenberg; directed by Herbert Ross; scenery by William Ritman; costumes by Noel Taylor; lighting by Tharon Musser; production stage manager, Charles Blackwell. Imperial Theatre, 245 West 45th Street.

George Schneider is a successful writer recently widowed and still mourning for his beloved wife. When he returns from a European trip unsuccessfully designed to let him forget and begin a new life, he is immediately besieged by his press agent brother's attempts to get him back in the swing of things. Especially the sexual swing.

George acknowledges that "Chapter Two" of his life is about to begin. It will, however, be a hesitant, even reluctant beginning as brother Leo sets up dates for him and generally tries to order his life.

Jennie Malone has also recently returned to New York, rebounding from a Mexican divorce. She, too, is being encouraged – by her actress friend Faye – to re-enter the dating if not necessarily the mating game. This twain obviously *is* destined to meet, which they do after a series of often confusing phone calls. Though they marry, George is not really over the death of his first wife and inevitably takes out his guilt on Jennie, then walks out on her, only to return shortly. Has he reconciled his past with his present? Will they live happily ever after? It is left for the audience to decide.

Opened December 4, 1977

Saint Joan

Robert LuPone, Lynn Redgrave and Tom Aldredge

THE CAST

Robert de Baudricourt	Roy Cooper
Steward	Armin Shimerman
Joan	Lynn Redgrave
Bertrand de Poulengey	Peter Van Norden
Court Page	Pendleton Brown
Archbishop of Rheims	Tom Aldredge
Monseigneur de la Tremouille	Tom Klunis
Gilles de Rais, Bluebeard	Kenneth Gray
Captain La Hire	Ed Setrakian
The Dauphin, later Charles VII	Robert LuPone
Duchess de la Tremouille	Gwendolyn Brown
Dunois, Bastard of Orleans	Joseph Bova
Dunois' Page	Stephen Lang
Richard de Beauchamp, Earl of Warwick	Philip Bosco
Chaplain de Stogumber	Robert Gerringer
Peter Cauchon, Bishop of Beauvais	Paul Shyre
Warwick's Page	Armin Shimerman
The Inquisitor	Paul Sparer
Canon John D'Estivet	John Rose
Canon de Courcelles	Stephen Lang
Brother Martin Ladvenu	Nicholas Hormann
Executioner	Jim Broaddus
English Soldier	Roy Cooper
A Stranger	Peter Van Norden

Court Ladies, Courtiers, Soldiers, and Monks . . Jim Broaddus, Pendleton Brown, Kenneth Gray, Sarah-Jane Gwillim, Nicholas Hormann, Stephen Lang, John Rose, Armin Shimerman, Peter Van Norden

By George Bernard Shaw. Presented by Circle in the Square, Theodore Mann, artistic director, Paul Libin, managing director; directed by John Clark; scenery by David Jenkins; costumes by Zack Brown; lighting by John McLain; wigs and hairstyles by Paul Huntley; production stage manager, Randall Brooks. Circle in the Square Theatre, Broadway and West 51st Street.

Shaw's 1923 play is a fundamentally unsentimental approach to the exploits of Joan of Arc, saint and warrior. He depicts her as a girl of naïveté in political and religious matters, but genius in military ones, a peasant girl with tomboyish traits, but great dignity in a world corrupted by conspiring and grasping politicians. Among them are the petulant Dauphin, jealous generals, a fearful Archbishop and the fanatical Grand Inquisitor. The play's most famous scene is perhaps the one between Warwick and Cauchon in which Shaw offers his interpretation of Joan as a victim in the struggle between the Church and increasingly nationalistic European states. In an epilogue, which is actually a dream sequence, Joan learns that the twentieth century is to be as alien to her honesty as were the Middle Ages.

Opened December 15, 1977
Closed February 19, 1978

REVIEWS

"Starts weakly, almost purposelessly, and proceeds uncertainly for quite a while. And then it begins to gain strength, and to acquire such movement, variety and exhilaration that by the time it finishes it has become a decided achievement, though just short of a triumph. . . . Lynn Redgrave's Joan is admirable in many ways. . . . What she lacks is the irrational contagion." — Richard Eder, *The New York Times* (12-16-77, p. C 3)

"This is not a favorite play of mine, and even the production apart from the sumptuously appropriate costumes by Zack Brown, is not destined for any particular record book. But you must see Miss Redgrave. Her performance already haunts me." — Clive Barnes, *New York Post* (12-16-77, p. 34)

"In the disastrous revival . . . Lynn Redgrave proves woefully incapable. . . . She has the inspiring warmth of an undraped mannequin in a store window. . . . Only Philip Bosco as the English Earl of Warwick conveys nobility in voice and bearing." — T. E. Kalem, *Time* (12-26-77, p. 71)

"Lynn Redgrave . . . has evidently thought hard about the role and makes her way through it with admirable valor, but seems, nevertheless, temperamentally at odds with it." — Brendan Gill, *The New Yorker* (1-2-78, p. 47)

"She is a touching Joan at times and a curiously unmoving and unimpressive one at others." — *Variety* (12-21-77, p. 74)

"She is not inspired, only insistent; intelligent, certainly, but with an intelligence you develop at Oxford, not among oxen and sheep." — John Simon, *New York* (1-9-78, p. 61)

A Touch of the Poet

THE CAST

Mickey Maloy. . . . . Barry Snider
Jamie Cregan . . . . Milo O'Shea
Sara Melody. . . . . Kathryn Walker
Nora Melody . . . . Geraldine Fitzgerald
Cornelius Melody . . . . Jason Robards
Dan Roche. . . . . Walter Flanagan
Paddy O'Dowd . . . . Dermot McNamara
Patch Riley . . . . .Richard Hamilton
Deborah (Mrs. Henry Harford). . . . . .Betty Miller
Nicholas Gadsby . . . . .George Ede

Kathryn Walker, Jason Robards
and Geraldine Fitzgerald

By Eugene O'Neill. Presented by Elliott Martin, by arrangement with the John F. Kennedy Center for the Performing Arts; directed by José Quintero; setting and lighting by Ben Edwards; costumes by Jane Greenwood; production stage manager, Mitch Erickson; casting consultant, Marjorie Martin. Helen Hayes Theatre, 210 West 46th Street.

Con Melody is the drunken proprietor of a run-down Massachusetts inn. He, however, sees himself as a gentleman, a former officer who served with the Duke of Wellington against Napoleon, a claim that is highly suspect, as is his contention that he is the son of a prosperous innkeeper. The merits of his claims aside, he nonetheless has succeeded in imposing them on his wife, daughter and drinking companions.

It is his daughter Sara who eventually is responsible for destroying Con's illusion when she falls in love with and seduces the son of a wealthy family, who humiliate her father by offering him money to prevent his daughter's marriage. He goes into a rage and, after attacking the family's home, is briefly jailed. His previously affected gentility now destroyed, he becomes the shanty Irishman he always in truth was.

Opened December 28, 1977
Closed April 30, 1978

REVIEWS

"José Quintero's production . . . has authority and a good deal of splendor to it. But misses part — only part, but a very important part — of the play's power. . . . Mr. Robards . . . is a performer of genuine magnetism and stature. . . . But whether it is a lack of energy or of his own vision, or of Mr. Quintero's, he fails in the entire first part of the play to make us believe in the touch of the poet that O'Neill was writing about. . . . Geraldine Fitzgerald gives a stunning performance as Nora." — Richard Eder, *The New York Times (12-29-77, p. C 13)*

"The play has a style, a manner and an energy — and Quintero, Robards and their company find them right down to the work's bitter, cynical core. This is a play to be seen, an evening to be remembered." — Clive Barnes, *New York Post (12-29-77, p. 27)*

"The present revival is like a tidal wave that seems to purge almost every defect of the play." — T. E. Kalem, *Time (1-9-78, p. 68)*

"What Robards cannot convincingly achieve is personal grandeur. I am not sure that José Quintero as director has wholly understood the play." — Harold Clurman, *The Nation (1-21-78, p. 60)*

"José Quintero has kept his cast in constant, nervous motion, which is not to say he has succeeded in bringing them all to life." — Brendan Gill, *The New Yorker (1-9-78, p. 59)*

Cold Storage

Len Cariou and Martin Balsam

By Ronald Ribman. Presented by Claire Nichtern and Ashton Springer in association with Irene Miller; directed by Frank Corsaro; set and costume design by Karl Eigsti; lighting design by William Mintzer; production stage manager, Clint Jakeman. Lyceum Theatre, 149 West 45th Street.

Two men, Joseph Parmigian and Richard Landau, meet on the roof garden above the cancer ward of a Manhattan hospital. Parmigian, who is an Armenian fruit dealer, is well aware he has the disease and treats it ironically, indulging in a form of banter that has put off the other patients and left him virtually isolated. Landau, on the other hand, wears a fancy Bloomingdale's robe. He is an investment adviser in the fine arts, has a wife and family he wants to return to. He is there for tests and exploratory surgery and still trying to convince himself he does not have cancer.

Parmigian will have none of that. He teases and badgers the other man, taunting and insulting him. His goading and ribaldry, his incessant talking, turn from being merely coarse and funny, deliberately shocking, to something else. He begins to probe the other man's past. It is a difficult, touchy process, but what finally emerges is the story of a boy whose mother, father and sister died in the Holocaust, a boy who had been saved by them at the sacrifice of their own lives. His survival is for him a source of guilt, something that has hung over him through all the ensuing years. Eventually, thanks to the taunting of Parmigian, he must respond and acknowledge, thereby exorcising, his demon.

Opened December 29, 1977
Closed June 4, 1978

THE CAST

Richard Landau . . . . Len Cariou
Miss Madurga . . . . Ruth Rivera
Joseph Parmigian. Martin Balsam

REVIEWS

"Graceful, intelligent and worthwhile. Its dramatic action is slight. Essentially it is less a play than a dramatic dialogue, and, in a sense, it is less a dramatic dialogue than the demonstration of a witty and touching therapy conducted on stage. . . . Mr. Ribman's writing is precise and chilling. . . . The actors, Martin Balsam and Len Cariou, have pretty nearly solved two opposite problems. . . . The play declines considerably when Landau's taciturnity is finally explained, and exorcised. . . . Mr. Ribman may have spent himself before he stopped writing, but he provided enough to allow two fine actors to exercise and stretch, to move and convince us." — Richard Eder, *The New York Times (12-30-77, p. C 3)*

"The play is funny, assertive and entertaining. The brilliance of the play is not simply that it laughs all our way to the grave, but more that it requires us to examine basic views on death. The performance that, rightly, is going to have everyone talking is Martin Balsam's grandiloquent, seedy eloquence as the greengrocer. . . . Yet just as interesting is Len Cariou's controlled, menaced and menacing art dealer. . . . Frank Corsaro's direction is soft and intimate." — Clive Barnes, *New York Post (12-30-77, p. 25)*

"If *Cold Storage* had a second act up to its first, it would be one hell of a play. . . . At his worst, [Ribman will] drive you up the slipperiest wall in no time; at his best . . . he can keep you laughing and thinking simultaneously. . . . As Parmigian, Martin Balsam gives a stunning performance. . . . Len Cariou is compelling as Landau." — John Simon, *New York (1-23-78, p. 68)*

"Ribman writes with wit and grace and an unusually eloquent command of language. But if his two characters were hanging out at the Port Authority terminal waiting for a bus to Trenton, instead of languishing in a cancer ward in expectation of death, we would probably tune out impatiently on their slender drama." — Marilyn Stasio, *Cue (1-21-78—2-3-78)*

"It is simply one of the best plays of the year. . . . The event is a powerful display of acting prowess." — Christopher Sharp, *Women's Wear Daily (12-30-77, p. 20)*

"Having said so much in disapprobation, I must take care to emphasize how interesting each of the two acts is on its own terms. I must also emphasize how well the play is acted, by Martin Balsam and Len Cariou; they command the stage like superb rival armies, and I divide the laurels of victory equally between them." — Brendan Gill, *The New Yorker (1-16-78, p. 68)*

Do You Turn Somersaults?

Mary Martin and Anthony Quayle

THE CAST

Lidya Vasilyevna. . . . . Mary Martin
Rodion Nikolayevich . . . . Anthony Quayle

REVIEWS

"If *Do You Turn Somersaults?* was intended as a vehicle for Mary Martin's return to Broadway after 10 years, she should have taken a bus. . . . Its general condition is torpor. Sometimes it ascends into winsomeness. . . . Miss Martin does not give a bad performance, but it is not often a very interesting one. Her specialty is cheerfulness and against this single ground-bass note she performs variations. . . . Mr. Quayle is equally competent. . . . But neither performer can really survive the succession of stilted, trite scenes and leaden lines that Mr. Arbuzov gives them. . . . Edwin Sherin's direction seems competent. . . . The answer to *Do You Turn Somersaults?*, I'm afraid, is: 'Not until I have left the theater.'" — Richard Eder, *The New York Times (1-10-78, p. 29)*

"The story is so sweetly, even saccharinely obvious, that it gives itself away at its first blush. It has no resistance at all to predictability. Yet it is a pleasant predictability and, most important of all, a credible predictability. . . . Edwin Sherin's direction is sleek at its best and only occasionally slick. . . . Oliver Smith's scenery works like magic. . . . The performances are just what you would expect, what you would hope for. . . . *Somersaults* is not a great play, but oddly satisfying and handsomely presented." — Clive Barnes, *New York Post (1-10-78, p. 19)*

"A sorry little windup mechanism of a play. . . . Mr. Arbuzov is a Neil Simon shorn of one-liners; his views are sentimental, and his sentimentality appears to spring not from a deeply held personal conviction but from some literary source, such as the table of contents of a five-pound box of chocolates." — Brendan Gill, *The New Yorker (1-23-78, p. 45)*

"An interesting, rather mysterious work. . . . The problem is that Arbuzov is too quiet, too ingratiating. . . . Directed by Edwin Sherin, Martin and Quayle give splendid, indeed adorable performances." — Jack Kroll, *Newsweek (1-23-78, p. 87)*

"A slight, sentimental comedy. I think it only fair, however, to state that Arbuzov . . . had something more in mind . . . a cagey satire on Soviet conformism." — Harold Clurman, *The Nation (1-28-78, p. 92)*

"Another feeble play by the Soviet playwright. . . . The acting is most endearing in its slightly self-indulgent way. . . . The star-struck, sentimental, or senescent should enjoy this play; for the others the somersault will turn into a pratfall." — John Simon, *New York (1-23-78, p. 69)*

By Aleksei Arbuzov; translated by Ariadne Nicolaeff. Presented by the Kennedy Center in association with Cheryl Crawford; directed by Edwin Sherin; scenery by Oliver Smith; costumes by Ann Roth; lighting by Ken Billington; incidental music by Charles Gross; production stage manager, Paul A. Foley. Forty-sixth Street Theatre, 226 West 46th Street.

Do You Turn Somersaults?, which has been produced by fifty theatres in the Soviet Union, takes place in August 1968 on the Riga coast. Lidya Vasilyevna, a woman in her sixties who has symptoms of arteriosclerosis, has just come to stay at a sanatorium. There she meets a staff physician named Rodion Nikolayevich, who is slightly older and also has a heart problem.

Rodion has called Lidya to see him in order to remonstrate with her concerning the many complaints that have been received from other patients about her frequently outlandish behavior. She, for instance, wakes her fellow patients in the morning by bursting into song and also has been known to sneak through a window to go walking in the garden at midnight. Predictably, Lidya causes Rodion to fall in love with her. Not only that, but even to dance the Charleston.

Opened January 9, 1978
Closed January 21, 1978

The November People

Cameron Mitchell and Jan Sterling

By Gus Weill. Presented by Shelly Beychok and Jim D'Spain; directed by Arthur Sherman; set design by Kert Lundell; lighting by Thomas Skelton; costumes by Joseph G. Aulisi; production stage manager, Alan Hall. Billy Rose Theatre, 208 West 41st Street.

It is a Sunday in November and Mitch, a former state official, has just been released after spending 18 months in prison for "taking kickbacks in the biggest scandal the state has ever known." His wife has invited several of his cronies and others to a homecoming celebration. There is one major hitch: a gubernatorial election is to be held on the following Tuesday and the last person any of those involved in it, in particular the Governor himself, want to be seen with is Mitch.

As a result, the "party" winds up entirely a family affair. Among those in attendance are Brian, who has an appointment as the Governor's assistant press secretary, and his increasingly estranged wife, a younger mentally disturbed son and Mitch's loyal wife. The play pivots on the elder son and whether he will decide to sacrifice what remains of his integrity to save the Governor's scalp by offering a bribe to the man who is about to indict him. If he does not, he and his wife may yet get together again.

Opened January 14, 1978
Closed January 14, 1978

THE CAST

Mitch . . . . .Cameron Mitchell
Mary. . . . . Jan Sterling
Donny (their younger son) . . . . John Uecker
Brian (their older son) . . . . .James Sutorius
Kathleen (Brian's wife). . . . . Pamela Reed

REVIEWS

"Just as the losing head of a political ticket can damage his running mates, everyone connected with this effort shares in the defeat, including such professionals as Arthur Sherman, the director, and Kert Lundell, the designer. . . . Faced with the emptiness of *The November People*, one can only wonder how the play ever reached Broadway." -- Mel Gussow, *The New York Times (1-16-78, p. C 25)*

"When Gus Weill's play gets under way someone is singing 'Happy Days are Here Again.' They were not. *The November People* is a nowadays unusual example of that happily endangered species, the 24-carat Broadway flop, the kind of play so obviously inept that you wonder idly how anyone could have imagined it to have a breathing chance on Broadway." – Clive Barnes, *New York Post (1-16-78, p. 16)*

"The play [is] as convoluted and turgid as the politics it describes. . . . Weill writes earnestly and with an occasional suggestion of literary style. But he shows almost no knowledge of stagecraft, including the delineation of character in theatrical terms. He simply plants his people on stage and forces speeches upon them. . . . The actors, under Arthur Sherman's foursquare direction, go about melodramatic but curiously lifeless business as though they fully believed in it. . . . Kert Lundell has run up a cheap-looking skeletal set walled-in by towering and unpleasant red-textured flats. Joseph G. Aulisi has provided suitable costumes and Thomas Skelton has done the lighting." – Douglas Watt, *Daily News (1-16-78, p. 23)*

"All the characters in *November People* are corrupt except one – who's deranged. The play itself . . . isn't in much better shape. . . . It's all laborious hokum and Arthur Sherman has compounded matters by staging the performance in stilted slow-motion. Cameron Mitchell at least has admirable intensity as the lying prodigal who fancies himself a blarney artist. . . . The whole project is a waste of everyone's time, effort and money." – *Variety (1-18-78, p. 94)*

Lou Jacobi and Rosemary Murphy

Cheaters

By Michael Jacobs. Presented by Ken Marsolais, Philip M. Getter and Leonard Soloway; directed by Robert Drivas; scenery by Lawrence King; costumes by Jane Greenwood; lighting by Ian Calderon; production supervisor; Larry Forde; associate producers, Donald Tick and Martin Markinson; production stage manager, Larry Forde. Biltmore Theatre, 261 West 47th Street.

Monica, who is married to Sam, is having an affair with Howard, who is married to Grace. Michelle, who is the daughter of Grace and Howard, is living with Allen, who is the son of Monica and Sam. The complication — or at least one of them — is that Michelle wants to get married and Allen doesn't.

The two older couples have never formally met — at least not as couples. Howard and Grace invite Monica and Sam to dinner in order to straighten out the problems between their offspring. Various complications, confrontations and duplicity ensue as the by now six characters fumble their ways toward a conclusion in an Englewood, New Jersey, livingroom.

Opened January 15, 1978
Closed February 11, 1978

THE CAST

Monica . . . . Rosemary Murphy
Howard . . . . Lou Jacobi
Sam . . . . Jack Weston
Grace . . . . Doris Roberts
Michelle . . . . Roxanne Hart
Allen . . . . Jim Staskel

REVIEWS

"Very empty indeed. It has a strong cast . . . and it ties lead weights to their feet. . . . It is a prematurely aged attempt to construct the kind of laugh mechanism that Neil Simon has developed. It is as dismal as a dissertation; its jokes all but carry footnotes of origin. . . . Mr. Jacobi has a stock blusterer's role, but he improves it where he can. . . . Miss Murphy finds nothing good to do with her part. . . . Lawrence King's sets trundle in and out sideways, inducing sea-sickness. Robert Drivas is the director and I have no idea whether he does it well or badly; it must be like directing a Mickey Mouse watch." — Richard Eder, *The New York Times (1-16-78, p. C 27)*

"This is the kind of simple sex comedy that almost eludes criticism, and it is also a genre of theater that you either like very much indeed or scarcely notice. . . . It is superbly staged. . . . In a way, this is TV style acting. Intentionally there are no characters or ideas, only caricatures and attitudes. . . . The thing to do with this kind of play is to get it moving fast and handsomely — and this is what the director Robert Drivas accomplishes marvelously. With strong assistance from the accurately observed and amusingly stylized scenery by Lawrence King and costumes by Jane Greenwood, Mr. Drivas paces the play and rounds up the laughs most adroitly. Mind you he has the cast to do it." — Clive Barnes, *New York Post (1-16-78, p. 15)*

"Robert Drivas has staged this distasteful nonsense as bravely and inventively as circumstances permit." — Douglas Watt, *Daily News (1-16-78, p. 25)*

"Mr. Jacobs writes not like a man in his twenties, but like a man in his seventies . . . and in doing so he risks being dismissed as the most uninteresting new playwright of the year. . . . And yet [it] is almost always moderately funny and rises from time to time to welcome heights of hilarity." — Brendan Gill, *The New Yorker (1-30-78, p. 71)*

"Since the characters are stereotypes out of traditional husband-wife cartoon comics, the slam-bang performances . . . are probably in order. . . . Robert Drivas has staged the rumpus without troubling about subtleties. . . . The overall impression is of a slightly bawdy, misplaced edition of a television show." — *Variety (1-18-78, p. 94)*

James Earl Jones and Burt Wallace

Paul Robeson

THE CAST

Paul Robeson . . . . James Earl Jones
Lawrence Brown . . . . Burt Wallace

By Phillip Hayes Dean. Presented by Don Gregory; directed by Lloyd Richards; original staging by Charles Nelson Reilly; scenery by H. R. Poindexter; lighting by Ian Calderon; costumes by Noel Taylor; by arrangement with Carmen F. Zollo; production stage manager, Phil Stein. Lunt-Fontanne Theatre, 205 West 46th Street; Booth Theatre, 222 West 45th Street.

In his controversial new play, Phillip Hayes Dean traces the even more controversial career of a man who has, for many, become a torment to the conscience of America. He shows, in episodic form, the young Robeson, who was the son of an escaped slave and a schoolteacher; Robeson at Rutgers, where he became an all-American football player and member of Phi Beta Kappa; Robeson as the brilliant Columbia Law School graduate who, because of his race, was doomed to work in the back offices of a prestigious law firm. The audience views him meeting his wife, Essie, then his triumphs as an actor and singer (in such works as Eugene O'Neill's *The Emperor Jones,* Jerome Kern's *Show Boat* and, later, in *Othello.)*

On the more specifically political side are scenes of Robeson in Europe, where he encounters a group of Nazi thugs; in the Soviet Union, with which he came to have something of a love-hate relationship; confronting President Truman on the issue of civil rights and defying the House Un-American Activities Committee.

Opened January 19, 1978
Closed April 30, 1978

REVIEWS

"James Earl Jones is a commanding, and where possible a transforming presence in *Paul Robeson.* But the one-character play devised by Phillip Hayes Dean out of the life of the singer, actor and political activist, defies transformation. Rarely does it achieve a dramatic texture. For most of its considerable length . . . it is essentially an acted-out narrative; a kind of travelogue through Mr. Robeson's biography. . . . We have not been shown the unique human character of the man sufficiently to be able to sense what is happening to him, as he trudges through history like a left-wing March of Time." — Richard Eder, *The New York Times (1-20-78, p. C 3)*

"Dean has written some good plays but this isn't one of them. . . . Jones is a powerful actor, a man who can easily suggest the physical and spiritual size of Paul Robeson. But even he can't singlehandedly body forth this life in oblique flashes. . . . And though Jones has a commanding voice, he's no singer and he's accompanied rather blandly by Burt Wallace at the piano. There's little that director Lloyd Richards can do to help matters." — Jack Kroll, *Newsweek (1-30-78, p. 66)*

"In fairness to Dean's work, witness a recent attempt to depict a white of heroic proportions onstage. If ever there was a trivialization of one of the world's heroines, consider the stage portrait of Golda Meir in *Golda.* . . . Playwright Dean . . . tried to humanize Robeson, and to some extent, he succeeds. . . . Unfortunately, the format . . . resembles a 25th-reunion class yearbook, a précis of achievements. . . . Jones falters as a singer but is formidable in all else." — T. E. Kalem, *Time (1-30-78, p. 68)*

"A skimpy and yet intolerably protracted narrative, written by Phillip Hayes Dean in a glib, unconvincing, and often unprepossessing documentary style. James Earl Jones, who plays Robeson, was bound to fail, but he has failed honorably." — Brendan Gill, *The New Yorker (1-30-78, p. 71)*

"I did enjoy much of Phillip Hayes Dean's *Paul Robeson.* . . . One leaves the theater convinced of and impressed by Robeson's magnitude. This is due in no small measure to James Earl Jones. . . . Jones invests his part with all anyone could ask for." — John Simon, *New York (2-6-78, p. 76)*

"Aside from some dull and overextended passages in the second part of the evening, I was gripped not only by virtue of Jones's excellence as an actor (and the director Lloyd Richards's able handling of the material) but by this perhaps inadequate outline of a great man." — Harold Clurman, *The Nation (2-11-78, p. 154)*

On the Twentieth Century

John Cullum and Madeline Kahn

Book and lyrics by Betty Comden and Adolph Green; music by Cy Coleman; based on plays by Ben Hecht, Charles MacArthur and Bruce Millholland; presented by the Producers Circle 2, Inc., Robert Fryer, Mary Lea Johnson, James Cresson and Martin Richards, in association with Joseph Harris and Ira Bernstein; directed by Harold Prince; musical numbers staged by Larry Fuller; scenic design by Robin Wagner; costumes designed by Florence Klotz; lighting design by Ken Billington; musical director, Paul Gemignani; orchestrations by Hershy Kay; production stage manager, George Martin. St. James Theatre, 246 West 44th Street.

Based on several earlier productions, notably plays by Ben Hecht and Charles MacArthur and Bruce Millholland, *On the Twentieth Century* also was a highly successful movie in the 1930s. A Broadway producer named Oscar Jaffee, who has just had a series of flops, the most recent of them a total bomb called *The French Girl* (about Joan of Arc), is heading back to New York, heavily in debt, his long unpaid press agent and manager in tow.

Who can save Oscar Jaffee? Why, Lily Garland, of course. Lily, the girl he made a star on Broadway and who has gone on to huge success in Hollywood, the girl with whom he was, and still is in love. But will she? Will her opportunistic young flame and leading man let her come to Oscar's rescue? In an effort to enlist her aid, Oscar boards the Twentieth Century Limited, hoping for one last windfall, but fearing bankruptcy. Charlatan that he is, he has contrived to get the stateroom next to Lily's.

Meanwhile, one Letitia Primrose, theoretically a millionairess with an interest in the arts and a penchant for posting stickers admonishing sinners to "Repent," turns up. "Inspired" by her religious mania, Oscar conceives of a play about Mary Magdalene, starring no less than Lily Garland, who is initially enraptured — especially when he reveals a check for $200,000, courtesy of Miss Primrose. But the latter is not what she seems; rather, in the words of one number, "She's a Nut," and about to be hauled back to the institution from which she has escaped. True to the musical comedy genre, however, Oscar and Lily do get together, presumably to live happily ever after — or at least until the next round of Broadway backbiting.

Opened February 19, 1978

THE CAST

Priest	Ken Hilliard
Bishop	Charles Rule
Stage Manager	Ray Gill
Joan	Maris Clement
Wardrobe Mistress	Carol Lurie
Actor	Hal Norman
Owen O'Malley	George Coe
Oliver Webb	Dean Dittman
Porter	Keith Davis
Porter	Quitman Fludd III
Porter	Ray Stephens
Porter	Joseph Wise
Congressman Lockwood	Rufus Smith
Conductor Flanagan	Tom Batten
Train Secretary Rogers	Stanley Simmonds
Letitia Primrose	Imogene Coca
Redcap	Mel Johnson, Jr.
Anita	Carol Lugenbeal
Oscar Jaffee	John Cullum
Max Jacobs	George Lee Andrews
Imelda	Willi Burke
Maxwell Finch	David Horwitz
Mildred Plotka/Lily Garland	Madeline Kahn
Otto Von Bismark	Sal Mistretta
Bruce Granit	Kevin Kline
Agnes	Judy Kaye
Hospital Attendents	Sal Mistretta, Carol Lurie
Dr. Johnson	Willi Burke

Female Singers . . . Susan Cella, Maris Clement, Peggy Cooper, Karen Gibson, Carol Lugenbeal, Carol Lurie, Melanie Vaughan, (Swing—Linda Poser)

Male Singers . . . . Ray Gill, Ken Hilliard, David Horwitz, Craig Lucas, Sal Mistretta, Hal Norman, Charles Rule, David Vogel, (Swing—Gerald Teijelo)

Imogene Coca

The Chorus

REVIEWS

"It is funny, elegant and totally cheerful. Its elegance is not that of a perfectly integrated and organized piece of musical theater. It has rough spots, flat spots and an energy that occasionally ebbs. . . . The authors' material, a unique marriage of civilized wit and wild humor, is closely blended with a strong score by Cy Coleman and the inspired scenic design of Robin Wagner. . . . Miss Comden, Mr. Green, Mr. Coleman, Mr. Prince and their dazzling crew have brought back what seemed dead or at least endangered: the comedy in musical comedy." —Richard Eder, *The New York Times (2-20-78, p. C 18)*

"It is about a train, about show business, about the '30s and about perfect." — Clive Barnes, *New York Post (2-20-78, p. 17)*

"Watching this two-hour show train rumble by is about as much fun as getting stranded on a station platform. But it does have razzle-dazzle aplenty." — T. E. Kalem, *Time (3-6-78, p. 75)*

"It has pizzazz and razzle-dazzle, bursts of energy and invention, music and laughter, and good, expensive production values." — John Simon, *New York (3-6-78, p. 90)*

"It adds little value to the original play or distinction to a thus-far meager Broadway musical season." — *Variety (2-22-78, p. 92)*

Deathtrap

John Wood

By Ira Levin. Presented by Alfred de Liagre, Jr., and Roger L. Stevens; directed by Robert Moore; scenery by William Ritman; costumes by Ruth Morley; lighting by Marc B. Weiss; production stage manager, Philip Cusack. Music Box Theatre, 239 West 45th Street.

Once Sidney Bruhl was a writer of hit thrillers for Broadway. Now, however, he is burnt-out: the last hit occurred some 18 years ago. Even so, he lives in posh surroundings in Connecticut, with a wife who has a heart condition and surrounded by posters from his past.

Into his present comes a script by one of his young disciples, a play clearly destined for success. It occurs to Sidney that he could kill the young man, Clifford, and claim the play as his own. It all seems to be in jest, however, at least until the bodies begin to turn up. First, there is the wife possessing the weak heart. With that, Clifford moves in and they go through the motions of collaboration, regularly interrupted by a woman possessing ESP, who pops in from next door with dire predictions. The play, incidentally, is also called *Deathtrap* and offers more than sufficient parallels with the one Levin actually has written: "two acts, one set, five characters, a juicy murder in Act I, unexpected developments in Act II, sound construction, good dialogue, laughs in the right places, highly commercial."

Opened February 26, 1978

THE CAST

Sidney Bruhl . . . . John Wood
Myra Bruhl. . . . . Marian Seldes
Clifford Anderson . . . . Victor Garber
Helga ten Dorp . . . . .Marian Winters
Porter Milgrim . . . . Richard Woods

REVIEWS

"Levin has written a complicated mechanism that keeps reversing and turning upon itself, and that pretty well consumes itself long before it ends. . . . There are some amusing lines, particularly at the beginning. . . . And Mr. Wood, who has the only really useful part in the play, makes the most of it. . . . He attacks the part with energy and verve, and he is always worth watching, but even he goes under eventually in the play's incessant, busy mechanisms. Miss Seldes, Victor Garber, who plays the student, Richard Woods, as the lawyer, and Miss Winters never get a chance to emerge from them. The problem is the play, and it is insurmountable." — Richard Eder, *The New York Times (2-27-78, p. C 15)*

"A most agreeable thriller — handsomely funny, totally undemanding, often thrill-graspingly surprising. The ending is somewhat weak — but if you know a play of this type that does not have a weak ending, I would be fascinated to know about it. . . . A perfectly good way to spend an unserious evening and this partly because as its playwright hero, John Wood is giving a very serious performance." — Clive Barnes, *New York Post (2-27-78, p. 20)*

"*Deathtrap* is like a ride on a good rollercoaster, when screams and laughs mingle to form an enjoyable hysteria. . . . It's extremely well directed by Robert Moore and skillfully acted by four-fifths of the cast. The lone exception is John Wood, who's not skillfull — he's dazzling and mesmerizing." — Jack Kroll, *Newsweek (3-13-78, p. 93)*

"A congenial successor [to *Sleuth*] — literate, amusing, booby-trapped with scarifying surprises. . . . John Wood is stupendous." — T. E. Kalem, *Time (3-13-78, p. 75)*

"Although Wood deploys a prodigal excess of technique, the result is not convincing, merely faintly unappetizing. . . . Robert Moore's direction is competent, and there are solid production values. But I wish that Levin, instead of writing a play about how one writes, or doesn't write, a mystery play, had written such a play. Or abstained." — John Simon, *New York (3-13-78, p. 72)*

The Water Engine

By David Mamet. Presented by the New York Shakespeare Festival, Joseph Papp, producer, Bernard Gersten, associate producer; directed by Steven Schachter; scenery by John Lee Beatty; costumes by Laura Crow; lighting by Dennis Parichy; music by Alaric Jans; production stage manager, Jason La Padura. Public Theatre/Cabaret, 425 Lafayette Street. Plymouth Theatre, 236 West 45th Street.

Mr. Happiness, a brief curtain-raiser to *The Water Engine,* features a radio giver of advice to the lovelorn who dispenses conventional wisdom and conservative morality with a sort of prissy outrage that belies the possibility of any genuine emotional involvement.

The Water Engine itself takes place in a radio studio that is broadcasting a series labeled "A Century of Progress." The time is 1934 and the second year of the Century of Progress Exposition is being observed by WCMJ Radio in New York. The episode to be broadcast on this particular show involves a young inventor who has developed a machine that will run on water. He takes his idea to a crooked patent lawyer who turns him over to the mysterious Oberman and interests that want to buy his invention in order to destroy it. None of that for our hero. His lab is wrecked, his sister is kidnapped and he himself is abducted after a vain attempt to tell his story to a newspaper reporter.

As the broadcast continues, the audience sees a soundman creating his effects and actors going from mike to mike as they portray various characters in the radio drama. In the end, the young inventor discovers the inevitable: he cannot beat the system except perhaps after his death. Both he and his sister are killed, but he has managed to send his plans off to the son of a friendly neighborhood candy-store owner. Perhaps justice will triumph after all.

Opened January 7, 1978, at the Public Theatre
Closed February 11, 1978
Opened March 6, 1978, at the Plymouth Theatre
Closed March 19, 1978

THE CASTS

Mr. Happiness

Mr. Happiness. . . . . .Charles Kimbrough

The Water Engine

Charles Lang (An Inventor). . . . . Dwight Schultz
Rita (His Sister) . . . . .Patti LuPone
Morton Gross (A Lawyer). . . . . .David Sabin
Lawrence Oberman (A Lawyer) . . . . Bill Moor
Mrs. Varec (A Woman from Upstairs) . . . . . Barbara Tarbuck
Mr. Wallace (Proprietor of a Candy Store) . .Dominic Chianese
Bernie (His Son) .Michael J. Miller
Dave Murray (A Reporter for the *Daily News*) . .Colin Stinton
Sound Effects Man . . . . Eric Loeb
Announcer. . . . . .Paul Milikin
Musician . . . . Alaric Jans
Lily La Pon . . . . .Patti LuPone

Bill Moor, Patti LuPone,
Dominic Chianese and Barbara Tarbuck

REVIEWS

"*Mr. Happiness* is slick and fairly routine, and makes an unfortunate addition to a complex and quite beautiful work. . . . We are drawn into the story of Charles Lang [in *The Water Engine*]. Dwight Schultz's awkward, naive and visionary playing of the role helps; so do the marvelous villains provided by David Sabin and Bill Moor. . . . It is the disquieting static arranged by Mr. Mamet that makes this frail melodrama flower into something more interesting." — Richard Eder, *The New York Times (3-7-78, p. 42)*

"It looks somewhat forlorn and mildly lonely. . . . It was funny in a cabaret setting, but simply not important enough to be taken seriously as comedy, or whatever, in a theater." — Clive Barnes, *New York Post (3-7-78, p. 21)*

"A clever and charming piece of work, a kind of esthetic toy that conceals a deep seriousness under a seductively playful exterior. . . . Everything is orchestrated with perfect touch and tone by Steven Schachter." — Jack Kroll, *Newsweek (1-16-78, p. 69)*

"Mr. Mamet's play is a synthetic that doesn't work. Its ponderous irony and its foolishness are poor substitutes for his usual original humor or his usual subtle tension." — Edith Oliver, *The New Yorker (1-16-78, p. 69)*

"The entire cast acts adroitly; the production values, under Steven Schachter's direction, are fine, but whatever may be true of tomorrow's combustion engine, you cannot run a stage play on the thin, watery inspiration that may just barely sustain a piece of radio drama." — John Simon, *New York (1-30-78, p. 60)*

Timbuktu!

A musical fable based on *Kismet*. Music and lyrics by Robert Wright and George Forrest, from themes of Alexander Borodin and African folk music; book by Luther Davis, based on the musical by Charles Lederer and Luther Davis, from the play by Edward Knoblock. Presented by Luther Davis; directed, choreographed and costumed by Geoffrey Holder; scenery by Tony Straiges; lighting by Ian Calderon; sound by Abe Jacob; musical direction, supervision, arrangements and incidental music by Charles H. Coleman; additional orchestrations by Bill Brohn; produced in association with Sarnoff International Enterprises, William D. Cunningham and the John F. Kennedy Center for the Performing Arts; production stage manager, Donald Christy. Mark Hellinger Theatre, 237 West 51st Street.

The locale of *Timbuktu!*, which is closely based on the *Kismet* of about a quarter of a century ago, has been altered primarily to turn it into what is becoming an increasingly popular genre: the all-black version of the formerly "white" show. Three of the earlier collaborators, Robert Wright, George Forrest and Luther Davis, who is also the producer, have switched the site from the Orient to Mali and employ an all-black cast.

Timbuktu!'s plot remains essentially the same, that of a lovestruck emperor, the beautiful daughter of a poor but scheming bazaar poet and the wife of the Wazir, who takes up with the poet. The show's principal songs include "Baubles, Bangles and Beads," "Stranger in Paradise," "Night of My Nights," "And This Is My Beloved" and "Sands of Time."

Opened March 1, 1978

Melba Moore in the "Baubles, Bangles and Beads" scene

34

THE CAST

The Chakaba (Stiltwalker)............Obba Babatunde
Beggars.....Harold Pierson, Shezwae Powell, Lewis Tucker
Hadji....................................Ira Hawkins
Marsinah, Daughter of Hadji............Melba Moore
Witchdoctor......................Harold Pierson
Child............................Deborah Waller
M'Ballah of the River................Daniel Barton
Najua, Bodyservant to Sahleem-La-Lume....Eleanor McCoy
The Wazir..........................George Bell
Chief of Police..................Bruce A. Hubbard
Sahleem-La-Lume....................Eartha Kitt
The Three Princesses of Baguezane......Deborah K. Brown
Sharon Cuff, Patricia Lumpkin
Munshi, Bodyservant to the Mansa........Miguel Godreau
The Mansa of Mali...................Gilbert Price
Orange Merchant...................Obba Babatunde
Birds of Paradise.........Miguel Godreau, Eleanor McCoy
Antelopes............Obba Babatunde, Luther Fontaine
Woman in the Garden................Shezwae Powell
Zubbediya.........................Vanessa Shaw
The Citizens of Timbuktu....Obba Babatunde, Gregg Baker,
Daniel Barton, Joella Breedlove, Deborah K. Brown,
Tony Carroll, Sharon Cuff, Cheryl Cummings, Luther
Fontaine, Michael F. Harrison, Dyane Harvey, Marzetta
Jones, Jimmy Justice, Eugene Little, Patricia Lumpkin,
Joe Lynn, Tony Ndogo, Harold Pierson, Ray Pollard,
Shezwae Powell, Ronald Richardson, Vanessa Shaw,
Louis Tucker, Deborah Waller, Renee Warren.

Eartha Kitt

Melba Moore

REVIEWS

"Even with its better tunes based on themes on Aleksandr Borodin, the *Kismet-Timbuktu!* score is a dull one. And that even spiced up for this new version, the lyrics are soggy and almost totally lacking in wit. . . . As for the production, it seemed skimped. . . . All in all, despite Miss Kitt and Mr. Hawkins, it was a lackluster show." — Richard Eder, *The New York Times (3-2-78, p. C 15)*

"It is a lot better than the more sensitive among you might feel. But, for that matter, it is a great deal worse than the more optimistic among you might have hoped. It has a great visual production, a stupid book, a travesty of a score, three good performances . . . and a dazzling conception, direction and costuming by Geoffrey Holder." — Clive Barnes, *New York Post (3-2-78, p. 29)*

"*Timbuktu!* displays Geoffrey Holder's talents as a director, choreographer, and designer of costumes, and I am only sorry that he didn't write the book, the music, and the lyrics, because, his handiwork aside, it is a terrible show." — Brendan Gill, *The New Yorker (3-13-78, p. 56)*

"Geoffrey Holder, who has staged the entire piece, dances and all, with more sweep and boldness than distinction, and with emphasis on his characteristic West Indian vein, also has costumed the show. . . . Costuming being Holder's strongest accomplishment, there are some lovely, as well as grotesquely effective moments. . . . *Timbuktu!* is a gaudy bore with a pearl named Melba bobbing about in it." — Douglas Watt, *Daily News (3-2-78, p. 61)*

Hello, Dolly!

Carol Channing and Cast

Book by Michael Stewart; music and lyrics by Jerry Herman; based on *The Matchmaker* by Thornton Wilder. Presented by James M. Nederlander and the Houston Grand Opera; directed by Lucia Victor; original production directed and choreographed by Gower Champion; dance and incidental music arrangements by Peter Howard; settings designed by Oliver Smith; costumes by Freddy Wittop; lighting by Martin Aronstein; production supervised by Jerry Herman; musical direction by John L. DeMain; associate producer, Robert A. Buckley; choreographed by Jack Craig; production stage manager, Pat Tolson. Lunt-Fontanne Theatre, 205 West 46th Street.

When it was originally produced, during the 1963-64 season, *Hello, Dolly!* ran for 2,844 performances, which made it one of the all-time hits of the American musical theatre.

Thornton Wilder's source was a German comedy by Johann Nestroy, *Einen Jux Will Er Sich Machen* (loosely translated, "He Wants to Have a Good Time"), which was presented at the New York City Center by the Vienna Burgtheatre during the 1967-68 season. It became, however, distinctly the creation of Gower Champion when it was turned into a Broadway musical, a showcase for Carol Channing as Mrs. Dolly Gallagher Levi, who is intent on getting her romantic ways.

Dolly's principal songs include "It Takes a Woman," "Before the Parade Passes By," "The Waiters' Gallop," "Hello Dolly!," "It Only Takes a Moment" and "So Long Dearie."

Opened March 5, 1978
Closed July 9, 1978

THE CAST

Mrs. Dolly Gallagher Levi	Carol Channing
Ernestina	P. J. Nelson
Ambrose Kemper	Michael C. Booker
Horse	Carole Banninger, Debra Pigliavento
Horace Vandergelder	Eddie Bracken
Ermengarde	K. T. Baumann
Cornelius Hackl	Lee Roy Reams
Barnaby Tucker	Robert Lydiard
Minnie Fay	Alexandra Korey
Irene Molloy	Florence Lacey
Mrs. Rose	Marilyn Hudgins
Rudolph	John Anania
Judge	Bill Bateman
Court Clerk	Randolph Riscol

Townspeople, Waiters, etc. . Diane Abrams, Carole Banninger, JoEla Flood, Marilyn Hudgins, Deborah Moldow, Janyce Nyman, Jacqueline Payne, Debra Pigliavento, Theresa Rakov, Barbara Ann Thompson, Richard Ammon, Bill Bateman, Kyle Cittadin, Ron Crofoot, Don Edward Detrick, Richard Dodd, Rob Draper, David Evans, Tom Garrett, Charlie Goeddertz, James Homan, Alex MacKay, Richard Maxon, Randy Morgan, Randolph Riscol, Mark Waldrop.

Swing Dancers . . . . .Coby Grossbart, Bubba Rambo

John Anania, Eddie Bracken and Carol Channing

Carol Channing

REVIEWS

"You can't bathe twice in the same flood. . . . Freshness is entombed in this Mandarin-like project. Musicals have no business being reverent. . . . Essentially, *Hello, Dolly!* has become *Hello, Again, Dolly!*" — Richard Eder, *The New York Times (3-6-78, p. C 15)*

"Channing owns the property, and she walks around it with a self-effacing authority. Herman's score is bold, brash and brassy. . . . Miss Channing is a sweet outrage. . . . Eddie Bracken provides the cantankerous half-millionaire his own flavor." — Clive Barnes, *New York Post (3-6-78, p. 17)*

"It looks as fresh as the paint on the star's animated face. . . . Oliver Smith's original set designs . . . are of inestimable value to the evening, as are Freddy Wittop's cascade of costumes, the whole artfully lighted by Martin Aronstein." — Douglas Watt, *Daily News (3-5-78, p. 21)*

"Jerry Herman's score has a kind of hearty, community-sing artlessness that once, in 'It Only Takes a Moment,' manages to rise higher. Gower Champion's original staging cum choreography was fluent, frolicsome, and full of perky Champion gimmicks." — John Simon, *New York (3-20-78, p. 89)*

"If there had been any doubt about the basic quality of *Hello, Dolly!,* this revival removes it. With Carol Channing starring in her original title role, the musical is spectacular entertainment." — *Variety (3-8-78, p. 104)*

Runaways

The Cast

Written, composed and directed by Elizabeth Swados. Presented by the New York Shakespeare Festival, Joseph Papp, producer, Bernard Gersten, associate producer; settings by Douglas W. Schmidt and Woods Mackintosh; costumes by Hilary Rosenfeld; lighting by Jennifer Tipton; production stage manager, Gregory Meeh. Public Theatre/Cabaret, 425 Lafayette Street. Plymouth Theatre, 236 West 45th Street.

Runaways was evolved by its 27-year-old author-composer-director out of countless interviews conducted with New York City school kids and runaways and it is essentially their story, sometimes in their own words, structured by her. It is a story of pain and bewilderment, at times slightly obvious ("It looks as if this child has got a broken heart"), at others buoyant. It is, in a sense, the *Hair* of the late seventies (and even has a song entitled "Where Are Those People Who Did *Hair*?")

Ms. Swados assembled her company primarily from among the teenagers with whom she worked on it, then added a handful of professionals. Number follows upon number, with an underlying current that reflects disenchantment with parents ("They just pretended that I wasn't there") and a need to get away, to escape from a world they neither made nor see the reason for. But there is also an innocence, at times a naivete even, an air of bravado and amused defiance and opportunism in what Ms. Swados describes as "a collage about the profound effects of our deteriorating families."

Opened March 9, 1978, at the Public Theatre
Opened May 6, 1978, at the Plymouth Theatre

THE CAST

Hubbell	Bruce Hlibok
A. J.	Anthony Imperato
Jackie	Diane Lane
Lidia	Jossie De Guzman
Melinda	Trini Alvarado
Nikki Kay Kane	Nan-Lynn Nelson
Manny	Randy Ruiz
Eddie	Jon Matthews
Sundar	Bernie Allison
Roby	Venustra K. Robinson
Lazar	David Schechter
Eric	Evan Miranda
Iggy	Jonathan Feig
Deidre	Karen Evans
EZ	Leonard (Duke) Brown
Luis	Ray Contreras
Mex-Mongo	Mark Anthony Butler
Jane	Kate Schellenbach
Interpreter for Hubbell	Lorie Robinson
Piano and Toy Piano	Judith Fleisher
String Bass	John Schimmel
Congas, Timbales, Bongos, Bells Siren and Others	Leopoldo F. Fleming
Trap Set, Triangle, Glass and Ratchet	David Sawyer
Saxophones and Flutes	Patience Higgins
Guitar	Elizabeth Swados

REVIEWS

"An inspired musical collage. . . . There are moments of joyfulness and youthful exuberance, but basically this is a serious contemplative musical with something important to say about society today. . . . The musical takes a harsh and uncompromising look at the world of runaways, but it is written and performed with great compassion. . . . Miss Swados . . . steps right into the front line of popular American theatrical composers. . . . *Runaways* is a triumph. It is an eloquent and mature vision, a musical that touches our hearts." — Mel Gussow, *The New York Times (3-10-78, p. C 3)*

"*Runaways* is probably more of a theater piece, rich and complex, than a musical, pure and simple, but it is a statement of power, brilliance and honesty. Its impact lingers in the mind long after its music is forgotten. It shouts for the unhappy, and bruises with the bruised. In the year 1978 it is perfectly essential seeing." — Clive Barnes, *New York Post (3-10-78, p. 28)*

"An immensely affecting show. To call it far and away the best musical of the season is to insult it. *Runaways* seizes your heart, plays with your pulse, dances exuberantly across the line that separates entertainment from involvement." — Jack Kroll, *Newsweek (3-27-78, p. 74)*

"Decent, appealing, enjoyable without being extraordinary. . . . The music, in all conceivable pop, folk, and ethnic modes, is fair to excellent. . . . Her lyrics . . . have their raw beauty. . . . The performances are, at the very least, engaging; in many cases, enchanting." — John Simon, *New York (3-27-78, p. 70)*

Mark Anthony Butler (foreground) and the Cast

"Too eclectic a work and too concerned with artifice at the expense of dramatic verity to strike more than an occasional spark." — Douglas Watt, *Daily News (3-10-78, p. 5)*

"The show raises the spirits. For some reason, however, it lacks the absolute authenticity, the firsthand quality, of *A Chorus Line.* . . . About Miss Swados' gifts there can be no question." — Edith Oliver, *The New Yorker (3-20-78, p. 88)*

The Cast, featuring Bernie Allison in foreground

The Effect of Gamma Rays on Man-in-the-Moon Marigolds

Shelley Winters

By Paul Zindel. Presented by Courtney Burr and Nancy Rosenthal; associate producers, William King and Charles Blum; production associate, Blossom Horowitz; directed by A. J. Antoon; setting and costumes by Peter Harvey; lighting by Ian Calderon; music by Richard Peaslee; production stage manager, Murray Gitlin. Biltmore Theatre, 261 West 47th Street.

When it opened in 1970 off-Broadway, *The Effect of Gamma Rays on Man-in-the-Moon Marigolds* won the Pulitzer Prize and the Drama Critics' Circle award as the best American play of the season. It also ran for many months. The Broadway revival did not.

Zindel portrays a domineering and disturbed mother who is also an alcoholic. She has two daughters, one of whom has a inclination toward science and the promise of succeeding in it, the other something of a slut. The daughter who is leaning toward science has developed something involving the effect of gamma rays on man-in-the-moon marigolds and her mother is called upon to go to her school to witness her daughter's expected triumph. Tillie, the daughter, wins her award, but only she seems likely to emerge from their forlorn world. "I hate this world," exclaims the mother.

Opened March 15, 1978
Closed March 26, 1978

THE CAST

Tillie.............................. Carol Kane
Beatrice......................... Shelley Winters
Ruth................................ Lori Shelle
Nanny........................... Isabella Hoopes
Janice Vickery .... Lolly Boroff

REVIEWS

"Whatever charm it may have possessed for its time is just about gone. . . . It is far less than half alive. . . . Shelley Winters' performance as Beatrice is oversized, and banishes whatever subtlety or reflection may be in the part. . . . Much of the fault lies with A. J. Antoon, the director. He has failed to guide Miss Winters' energy; and he has allowed Lori Shelle as Ruth, and Lolly Boroff in a small part as one of the science-show competitors, to overact unrestrainedly." — Richard Eder, *The New York Times* (3-15-78, p. C 25)

"An effective play successfully deals with half-truths as if they were for real. . . . Beatrice is not the kind of role Shelley Winters should play — it stresses too much her natural flamboyance and too little her plaintive poetry, yet although the balance is wrong, both attributes make their effect." — Clive Barnes, *New York Post* (3-15-78, p. 49)

"An uneasy revival. . . . Today, it seems far too literary in its construction and meagre in its emotions." — Brendan Gill, *The New Yorker* (3-27-78, p. 95)

"The quite unnecessary Broadway revival makes a most depressing shambles. Under A. J. Antoon's astoundingly obvious and leaden direction, two of New York's worst actresses, Shelley Winters and Carol Kane, reduce the troublingly beautiful principal roles to inanity." — John Simon, *New York* (3-27-78, p. 71)

"All we have is a superb performance by Shelley Winters in the main role. Nothing else on stage comes close to her level of craftsmanship, and the lack of support she has . . . only leaves an overall production that is tediously dutiful." — Christopher Sharp, *Women's Wear Daily* (3-16-78, p. 8)

13 Rue de l'Amour

Patricia Elliott, Bernard Fox and Louis Jourdan

By Georges Feydeau; adapted and translated by Mawby Green and Ed Feilbert. Presented by Circle in the Square, Theodore Mann, artistic director, Paul Libin, managing director; directed by Basil Langton; scenery and costumes by Zack Brown; lighting by John McLain; wigs and hairstyles by Paul Huntley; production stage manager, James Bernardi. Circle in the Square Theatre, 51st Street West of Broadway.

A doctor named Moricet lusts after Leontine, who inconveniently is married to Duchotel. Duchotel manages to take off on frequent "hunting trips," where he is making out with the wife of a friend, Birabeau, who is totally unsuspecting.

Although no one actually hides under a bed, this is a typical Feydeau farce, with familiar quick exits and entrances, closets to take refuge in and most of the characters winding up at least moderately frantic.

Entitled *Monsieur Chasse* in the original, this is Feydeau at his most recognizable, though, by most standards, not Feydeau at his absolute best.

Opened March 16, 1978
Closed May 21, 1978

THE CAST

Marie . . . . Jill P. Rose
Tailor . . . . Jim Broaddus
Duchotel . . . . Bernard Fox
Moricet . . . . Louis Jourdan
Leontine . . . . Patricia Elliott
Jean-Pierre . . . . Richard Pilcher
Birabeau . . . . Laurie Main
Madame Spritzer . . . . Kathleen Freeman
Inspector of Police . . . . Ian Trigger
First Policeman . . . . Jim Broaddus
Second Policeman . . . . John Shuman

REVIEWS

"A real accomplishment. It has some beautifully springy and agile performances, a well-managed direction, and quite enough fun in it to be thoroughly worth seeing. What it does not do, and perhaps cannot be expected to do, is to manipulate the crazy but precise clockwork of the original. . . . The combustion is pretty good but there are some lumpy and undigested bits left over." — Richard Eder, *The New York Times* (3-17-78, p. C 3)

"The production, both in its direction and adaptation, has been given an awe-inspiring heaviness — the effect is like lead daffodils waving valiantly in a sea of jelly." — Clive Barnes, *New York Post* (3-17-78, p. 30)

"The play fails because it has been miscast; even the director appears to have been miscast." — Brendan Gill, *The New Yorker* (3-27-78, p. 95)

"Basil Langton has picked some interesting players, and he has directed some suitably fancy business at a condignly punishing pace. But he has, to my mind, committed one very serious mistake: allowing his characters to disport themselves as if they knew they were in a farce." — John Simon, *New York* (4-3-78, p. 80)

"Comes creditably close to the Feydeau tempo and spirit, but it is difficult to orchestrate an arena stage to that crescendo of forbidden doors being opened and closed on which Feydeau depends." — T. E. Kalem, *Time* (3-27-78, p. 96)

Dancin'

The Company in "Dancin' Man"

Presented by Jules Fisher, the Shubert Organization and Columbia Pictures; directed and choreographed by Bob Fosse; scenery designed by Peter Larkin; costumes designed by Willa Kim; lighting designed by Jules Fisher; sound designed by Abe Jacob; music arranged and conducted by Gordon Lowry Harrell; orchestrations by Ralph Burns; associate producer, Patty Grubman; hair styles by Romaine Greene; production stage manager, Phil Friedman. Broadhurst Theatre, 235 West 44th Street.

Dancin' terms itself "an almost plotless musical," and the only thing to question about that is the inclusion of the word "almost." There is not even a real theme, just dance after dance. As if to take this one step further, Fosse also does not use an original score, but rather draws upon the music of, among many others, Bach, George M. Cohan, Neil Diamond, Johnny Mercer, John Philip Sousa, Cat Stevens and Edgard Varese.

Among the highlights are an early number called "Recollections of an Old Dancer," based on Jerry Jeff Walker's "Mr. Bojangles," "Dancin' Man," to the music of Johnny Mercer and Harry Warren, in which the entire company comes on in boaters and white suits to do a soft-shoe, and "Fourteen Feet," danced to Cat Stevens's "Was Dog a Doughnut," in which seven dancers open by nailing all their shoes to the floor and show just how much dancing can be done with the rest of the body, albeit with the assistance of phosphorescent lines on their costumes and some lighting that makes them seem a bit more like eels than humans.

Opened March 27, 1978

With: Gail Benedict, Sandahl Bergman, Karen G. Burke, Rene Ceballos, Christopher Chadman, Wayne Cilento, Jill Cook, Gregory B. Drotar, Vicki Frederick, Linda Haberman, Richard Korthaze, Edward Love, John Mineo, Ann Reinking, Blane Savage, Charles Ward

The "Percussion" number

REVIEWS

"There must be hundreds of thousands of footsteps in *Dancin'*. They twinkle and flash, they have fire and sometimes force, but only occasionally do they make this gaudy production really move.... At its strongest, *Dancin'* has the qualities of a spectacular recital rather than an integrated musical show. It has a few marvelous numbers, and a good many weak ones, but the strength remains in compartments and doesn't manage to spill over.... Precision and style mark the evening at its best; but too frequently they are in the service of very little. The hollowness shows; it becomes a gaudy and elaborate mask covering nothing; a deification of emptiness." — Richard Eder, *The New York Times (3-28-78, p. 48)*

"The sixteen young performers whom Mr. Fosse has brought together and forged into a company can sing as well as dance, and in their exceptional zest and discipline they give off, individually and together, an authentic radiance.... I've never seen a show more effectively lighted than *Dancin'*." — Brendan Gill, *The New Yorker (4-10-78, p. 91)*

"The missing 'g' in the title of Bob Fosse's joyous, audacious show stands for his genius, his guts in daring to make a giant claim for popular dance as something worth looking at and admiring in its own right.... It's the sheer joy of *Dancin'* that makes it a great show." — Jack Kroll, *Newsweek (4-10-78, p. 62)*

"If I had just one word to describe Bob Fosse's new musical I would probably choose 'tremendous.' Given another I might have casually selected 'fantastic.' It is that kind of musical. It opened last night, and with any justice at all, it should run for as near forever as forever can be.... What Fosse has done is to create a new theatrical form — and his sheer originality could well be overlooked in the impact of the actual show.... Oddly enough all of these dancers sing magnificently. But that is intended just as a bonus. What the kids in *Dancin'* do is dance. And how superlatively they dance. They are so alive, so brilliant, so up to the very moment of the beat, so simply decent with the dance.... It is glorious." — Clive Barnes, *New York Post (3-28-78, p. 45)*

"What Bob Fosse proves in *Dancin'* is that regardless of driving energy, exquisite symmetry of motion and flawless execution, a musical bereft of a book is stillborn.... Justice would not be served if any of the dancers were to be called anything less than marvelous.... Ann Reinking is terpsiglorious." — T. E. Kalem, *Time (4-10-78, p. 94)*

"If you're alive, see *Dancin'*. If you're not, get up and go anyway.... *Dancin'* is Bob Fosse at his lustrous and unstinting best and, perhaps, the most stylish musical you'll ever witness." — Douglas Watt, *Daily News (3-28-78, p. 23)*

"*Dancin'* is dazzlin'.... [It] captured the first-nighters with its opening moments and had them applauding every number, in some cases cheering. The show is the smash hit of the season." — *Variety (3-29-78, p. 84)*

Ann Reinking and Gregory B. Drotar

A History of the American Film

A production number

By Christopher Durang; music by Mel Marvin. Presented by Judith Gordon and Richard S. Bright; directed by David Chambers; musical staging by Graciela Daniele; set designed by Tony Straiges; costumes by Marjorie Slaiman; lighting by William Mintzer; sound by Lou Shapiro; musical direction by Clay Fullum; orchestrations by Robert M. Freedman; production stage manager, Ron Abbott. ANTA Theatre, 245 West 52nd Street.

Durang parodies and satirizes dozens of American films, from the silents to *The Exorcist* and *Earthquake*. A pianist provides accompaniment as a bouncing ball caroms along on top of the words of a popular song and the cast, portraying the movie audiences of old, sits down facing the actual audience.

From that point on, Durang and his director, David Chambers, reel through a series of scenes in which the members of the cast parody various movie types. Principal and most obvious among them are those based on Jimmy Cagney, Humphrey Bogart, James Dean and Marlon Brando, Henry Fonda, Jimmy Stewart, Gregory Peck, Anthony Perkins and Bette Davis. Among the movies are *Casablanca, The Snake Pit, The Public Enemy, The Grapes of Wrath* and *Citizen Kane.*

Opened March 30, 1978
Closed April 16, 1978

With: Maureen Anderman, Gary Bayer, Walter Bobbie, Jeff Brooks, Bryan Clark, David Cromwell, David Garrison, Ben Halley, Jr., Swoosie Kurtz, Kate McGregor-Stewart, Joan Pape, April Shawhan, Brent Spiner, Eric Weitz, Mary Catherine Wright

REVIEWS

"*A History of the American Film* is not so much title as disguise for the large and mostly very funny carnival that opened last night at the ANTA Theatre. It is no history; it is hysteria. . . . Sometimes it stalls or bogs down, but it always gets going again. . . . All the performers are first-rate. . . . It includes too much. Some of it is parody that does no more than make itself recognizable, as if simply identifying Jimmy Stewart, for instance, were enough. But far more is authentic, inspired and possessed comedy." — Richard Eder, *The New York Times (3-31-78, p. C 3)*

"There is a deliberate nonsense to this, showing its players as the unconscious shadows of that silver screen, which is always amusing but never entirely satisfying. It is a play with many echoes but few resonances. . . . The concept is amusing but at the end — and the end is particularly weak — you might feel that you have been told a long story with more accuracy than pertinence. . . . It is certainly beguiling. David Chambers has directed it with flair and finesse, and the musical numbers, staged by Graciela Daniele, are superbly effective. The decor, by Tony Straiges . . . looks decently opulent and the costumes by Marjorie Slaiman fit like an accent." — Clive Barnes, *New York Post (3-31-78, p. 32)*

"[Looks] for all the world like a gussied-up varsity show with real actors. . . . It wastes the talents of some perfectly good actors. . . . David Chambers' apt direction, Tony Straiges' garish scenery, Marjorie Slaiman's vulgar costumes, William Mintzer's expert lighting and Clay Fullum's smart conducting do everything conceivable to abet the author's fell design." — Douglas Watt, *Daily News (3-31-78, p. 3)*

"A puffed-up travesty of a big Broadway show. . . . The works don't work: Broadway greed has destroyed the delicate balance of a delicately balanced idea. The play has become smartass instead of smart." — Jack Kroll, *Newsweek (4-10-78, p. 63)*

Jesus Christ, Superstar

A musical in two acts, with music by Andrew Lloyd Webber and lyrics by Tim Rice. Presented by Hal Zeiger; directed by William Daniel Grey; choreography by Kelly Carroll; musical direction by Peter Phillips. Longacre Theatre, 220 West 48th Street.

When it opened on Broadway in October 1971, the original production of *Jesus Christ Superstar* ran for 711 performances. The present revival is a somewhat scaled-down version. Among its 24 numbers, the best-known include "What's the Buzz?," "Everything's All Right," "Hosanna," "I Don't Know How to Love Him" and "Superstar."

This version of *Superstar* did not invite press coverage. The trade paper *Variety,* however, reported as follows: "Compared to the original lavish Broadway production staged by Tom O'Horgan, this mini-version, direct from a road tour, is disappointing. . . . Performances range from competent to dismal. . . . Kelly Carroll has provided adequate choreography, and Peter Phillips' musical direction is appropriately loud" (12-7-77, p. 82).

Opened November 23, 1977
Closed February 12, 1978

THE CAST

Judas Iscariot	Patrick Jude
Jesus of Nazareth	William Daniel Grey
Mary Magdalene	Barbara Niles
Priests, Apostles	Doug Lucas, Richard Tolin
Caiaphas	Christopher Cable
Annas	Steve Schochet
Simon Zealotes	Bobby London
Peter	Randy Martin
Pontius Pilate	Randy Wilson
Soldiers, Tormentors	D. Bradley Jones, George Bernhard
Soul Girls	Freida Ann Williams, Pauletta Pearson, Claudette Washington
Maid by the Fire	Celeste Hogan
Apostles	David Cahn, Ken Samuels, Lennie Del Duca
King Herod	Mark Syers

Stages

By Stuart Ostrow. Presented by Edgar Bronfman and Stuart Ostrow; directed by Richard Foreman; settings by Douglas W. Schmidt; costumes by Patricia Zipprodt; lighting by Pat Collins; incidental music by Stanley Silverman; sound by Roger Jay; production stage manager, D. W. Koehler. Belasco Theatre, 111 West 44th Street.

Stages is divided into five sections: "Denial," "Anger," "Bargaining," "Depression" and "Acceptance." In each of them Stuart Ostrow, best known as the producer of such Broadway hits as *Pippin* and *1776*, shows a man who is approaching old age and for varying reasons receives some intimation of it.

In the first section he is depicted as a playwright whose most recent play has received a mediocre reception; in the second as fighting against the blacklisting of the fifties. Next he appears as a millionaire who is having difficulties with his much younger wife, as a very ill man and as the proprietor of a haberdashery.

The play's best moments (it closed after one performance) come in the two concluding "stages," where the normally avant-garde director Richard Foreman utilizes his approach to humor to a greater extent than in the previous segments.

Opened March 19, 1978
Closed March 19, 1978

With: Jack Warden, Roy Brocksmith, Philip Bosco, Diana Davila, Lois Smith, Tom Aldredge, Max Wright, Caroline Kava, Gretel Cummings, William Duell, Brenda Currin, Ralph Drischell, Howland Chamberlin, Manuel Martinez

REVIEWS

"Lugubrious vaudeville; a sedate and portentous effort at fusing the theatre of the absurd with the theatre of the sentimental. . . . It is an unlikely marriage of talents, and like some other unlikely marriages, unconsummated. . . . Douglas Schmidt's white vinyl sets provide an appropriately uncomfortable home for the gathering, and Stanley Silverman has provided music, mostly other people's." — Richard Eder, *The New York Times (3-20-78, p. C 15)*

"Nothing became Stuart Ostrow's new play *Stages* so much as its final curtain. . . . It is one of those plays where it would be a relief to escape into a blizzard." — Clive Barnes, *New York Post (3-20-78, p. 18)*

"Jack Warden gives an admirable but futile performance as the tortured actor. As for the hapless supporting players, they are hereby accorded the privilege of no remark." — *Variety (3-22-78, p. 122)*

"The play was so bad that even Richard Foreman's direction, which consists of applying certain antiquated and tiresome avant-garde devices arbitrarily to any material that comes to hand, was a welcome relief." — John Simon, *New York (4-3-78, p. 81)*

Diversions & Delights

Vincent Price as Oscar Wilde

By John Gay. Presented by Roger Berlind; Franklin R. Levy and Mike Wise; directed by Joseph Hardy; setting and lighting by H. R. Poindexter; lighting executed by Barry Arnold; costumes designed by Noel Taylor; production stage manager, David Clive. Eugene O'Neill Theatre, 230 West 49th Street.

A program note describes *Diversions & Delights* as "being an evening spent with Sebastian Melmouth on the 28th day of November, 1899."

The scene is a concert hall on the Rue de la Pepinier in Paris and Oscar Wilde, no longer the flamboyant figure of yesteryear, the celebrated playwright and wit, is showing the effects of the various afflictions that overtook him both in prison and subsequently, among them an inner ear infection that at times affects his equilibrium. He is here to deliver an imaginary lecture, and opens with some of his most caustic gibes, from time to time taking a moment to sip from a bottle of absinthe. He is in a velvet jacket, wears a flowing tie and has a grossly overpainted face. "I am," he says, "a towering scandal." It is an announcement made with no little pleasure. Tossing off such lines as one about Shaw being "a man without an enemy in the world; and none of his friends liked him," he is bent on shocking, bent on patronizing. "Women," he notes, "look like public buildings."

In the second half of the program, he descends to self-pity, reflecting on his love for Lord Alfred Douglas and the latter's "betrayal" of him. He has, it seems, scheduled the evening to help to pay off his debts. He was soon to die, and the play ends with a muted "that is all."

Opened April 12, 1978
Closed April 22, 1978

Starring: Vincent Price

REVIEWS

"Mr. Price gives a most delicate and touching performance. . . . The format of a lecture serves very well as long as Wilde is masking his wounds with quips. Mr. Gay was less wise in using it for the kind of direct anguish and self-revelation that Wilde reserved for material not to be published during his life. . . . Mr. Price's performance is often moving in this second half . . . but the material fights the dramatic framework. It drags, and loses color and contrast." — Richard Eder, *The New York Times (4-13-78, p. C 19)*

"Essentially an amusing, witty, at times moving, one-man show. . . . The idea is contrived, and no amount of the hero demonstrating the pain of his terminal ear infection, or drinking . . . will take away from the contrivance. . . . [Mr. Price's] sense of timing during all these anecdotes and excerpts, stories and even poems, is absolutely impeccable. . . . Joseph Hardy's direction . . . has clearly been most helpful, and together director and actor, working on Gay's patchwork quilt of a script, have come up with many diversions and much delight." — Clive Barnes, *New York Post (4-13-78, p. 38)*

"Price, who has been directed by Joseph Hardy, gives a thoroughly professional performance. . . . But a performance of what? No real figure emerges from this outpouring of epigrams, other writings and recollections. . . . H. R. Poindexter has designed a small, old-fashioned false proscenium to frame the action, and he has lighted it well." — Douglas Watt, *Daily News (4-13-78, p. 73)*

"The show turns out to be a highly enjoyable one. . . . Mr. Price admirably conveys Wilde's intelligence and his persistent misuse of that intelligence; he makes him, ill and alone and bereft of his talent, an affecting figure." — Brendan Gill, *The New Yorker (4-24-78, p. 93)*

"There is nothing duller than a dull one-man show, and the show at the Eugene O'Neill Theatre about Oscar Wilde is pretty dull." — Christopher Sharp, *Women's Wear Daily (4-14-78, p. 14)*

The Cast

The Mighty Gents

THE CAST

Rita . . . . .Starletta DuPois
Frankie . . . . .Dorian Harewood
Tiny . . . . .Brent Jennings
Lucky . . . . .Mansoor Najee-Ullah
Eldridge. . . . . Richard Gant
Zeke . . . . Morgan Freeman
Braxton. .Howard E. Rollins, Jr.
Father. . . . . Frank Adu

By Richard Wesley. Presented by James Lipton Productions and the Shubert Organization and Ron Dante; directed by Harold Scott; music by Peter Link; setting by Santo Loquasto; costumes by Judy Dearing; lighting by Gilbert V. Hemsley, Jr.; production stage manager, David Taylor. Ambassador Theatre, 215 West 49th Street.

Ten years ago, the members of the Mighty Gents roamed the streets of Newark, swaggering, drinking, making love, dancing, fighting. Ten years ago, they were something.

But a decade has passed and the adventures and hopes have given way to the malaise of the black ghetto. Their future is past. Now, they spend their time lounging around aimlessly, drinking and making ritualized attempts to capture once more the highs of the past.

The principal character is Frankie, the former gang leader, who is on the brink of despair, and decides on one final effort to break out; the alternatives being joining the winos like Zeke, who appears from time to time, or going the way of the small-time crook Braxton. Frankie's last fling, his last grasp for self-esteem, is bound to end in disaster.

Opened April 16, 1978
Closed April 23, 1978

REVIEWS

"The best moments are harshly musical. Although the score itself is secondary, the play's brief scenes and recitations are like sardonic ballads in a street opera about hopelessness. . . . There is both wit and desolation in the street scenes that show Frankie and his three fellow-Gents lounging, brooding, clowning and quarreling. . . . Dorian Harewood is very good as the tormented and finally rebellious Frankie. And as Zeke, the broken-down wino . . . Morgan Freeman gives a spectacular performance. . . . The direction by Harold Scott is sharp and crisp." — Richard Eder, *The New York Times (4-17-78, p. C 17)*

"Electric. . . . The visually rewarding setting by Santo Loquasto is nothing but carpeted ramps and stairs. . . . The actors, caught in Gilbert V. Hemsley's lighting, are spotlighted like jewels on black velvet. The acting is nothing short of superb. . . . A fascinating play." — Clive Barnes, *New York Post (4-17-78, p. 53)*

"A small, pleasing work of art in immaculate order; with the lilting clarity and economy of a ballad, it carries us unswervingly from first word to last. . . . Harold Scott has directed — and, in effect, choreographed — this touching ballad with a sure sense. . . . The cast itself is exemplary." — Brendan Gill, *The New Yorker (4-24-78, p. 93)*

"*The Mighty Gents* numbs rather than moves you. . . . It sounds heartless to say we've seen and heard all this before, but we have. . . . Only the acting moves you with the power of its veracity." — Jack Kroll, *Newsweek (5-1-78, p. 74)*

"Wesley is a talented writer and his play has power and poignancy." — Harold Clurman, *The Nation (5-6-78, p. 549)*

"Da"

Brian Murray, Barnard Hughes, Richard Seer and Mia Dillon

By Hugh Leonard. Presented by Lester Osterman, Marilyn Strauss and Marc Howard; the Hudson Guild Theatre Production, Craig Anderson, producer; directed by Melvin Bernhardt; set design by Marjorie Kellogg; costume design by Jennifer von Mayrhauser; lighting design by Arden Fingerhut; general manager, Richard Horner; production stage manager, Edward R. Fitzgerald. Morosco Theatre, 217 West 45th Street.

Recipient of most of the season's "best play" awards, *"Da"* originated at the off-Off Broadway Hudson Guild Theatre, from where it moved to Broadway.

Charlie, a middleaged writer, returns to Dublin to attend the funeral of his father, the "Da" of the title. To make peace with him; to make peace with himself.

This is Leonard's most obviously autobiographical play, far more so than such other works as *The Au Pair Man* and *Stephen D.*

Charlie sits at the kitchen table — remembering, regretting, trying to exorcise his demons. The house is empty and he begins to dispose of fragments from the past. As he sorts through his father's papers, he destroys a great deal more than he retains. He is, perhaps, attempting to destroy much of his own past; perhaps to destroy the domination of his father.

Leonard moves between past and present, between images and illusions to reality, showing Charlie as a young man, contending with his present self and attempting to rid himself of the ghost that is his father. Yet, he does not really wish to rid himself of him. They are irrevocably linked, tied by bonds that he only intellectually believes he wishes to shed.

Charlie refers to his father as a "malignant, lopsided old liar," but believes only some of that — if any. Despite his disparagement of the old gardener, a man replete with bluster and typical Irish blarney, his son cannot avoid one fact: His father almost unquestionably led a far happier and, in its way, more fulfilled life than he has.

Charlie is depicted in his teens, trying to rendezvous with the local prostitute, known as the Yellow Peril; seen applying for a job as a clerk. When he returns in the spring of 1968 and the funeral is over, he is revisited by his dead father and by a boyhood chum named Oliver. Both serve to open up the past — for Charlie and for the audience. It is a past that he must, in the end, both flee from and recognize. His father will not let him do otherwise.

Opened May 1, 1978

THE CAST

Charlie Now	Brian Murray
Oliver	Ralph Williams
Da	Barnard Hughes
Mother	Sylvia O'Brien
Young Charlie	Richard Seer
Drumm	Lester Rawlins
Mary Tate	Mia Dillon
Mrs. Prynne	Lois de Banzie

Richard Seer, Barnard Hughes and Brian Murray

Brian Murray and Barnard Hughes

REVIEWS

"A beguiling play. . . . Warmly but unsentimentally, it concerns itself with paternity, adolescence, the varieties of familial love and the tricks and distortions of memory. In a class with the best of Sean O'Casey, it is steeped in Irish language, laughter and atmosphere, but it rises above ethnicity. . . . Gently and quietly, the play enfolds our emotions and rewards our empathy. It will make you laugh, and, when a senile Da momentarily mistakes his son for his prospective father-in-law, it should make you cry. . . . Led by the astute, scrupulous staging of Melvin Bernhardt, the actors never falter. . . . Barnard Hughes' portrayal of Da must be considered a high point of his career. . . . Brian Murray is wonderfully expressive, his face a frieze of seemingly contradictory impulses. . . . Da is a humane and honest memory play in which, with great affection and humor, we are invited to share the life of a family." — Richard Eder, *The New York Times (5-2-78, p. 46)*

"There are some plays that are totally attractive, even lovable. Such a play is Hugh Leonard's *Da*. . . . It is just the best Irish play we have had in years. . . . Brian Murray and Barnard Hughes are both giving the best performances of their considerable careers. . . . It is a stab to the heart. Yet somehow it is a stab that laughs. . . . The decor by Marjorie Kellogg is accurate, workable but not imaginative. Bernhardt has not taken a step wrong. Murray and Hughes are brilliant together." — Clive Barnes, *New York Post (5-2-78, p. 63)*

"[An] Irish comic gem. . . . Heading the list is Da himself, of course, in a richly humorous and unforgettable performance by Barnard Hughes. But beautifully balancing this performance is Brian Murray's as the middle-aged son. . . . Melvin Bernhardt's staging remains ideal for this charming, immensely entertaining and really quite perceptive comedy. . . . Da is a joyous, admirably composed play in which Hughes has the role of a lifetime, with Murray the keenest of straight men." — Douglas Watt, *Daily News (5-2-78, p. 25)*

"Director Melvin Bernhardt gives the play a kind of tart sweetness, and the cast is warm and winning, notably Brian Murray and Lester Rawlins. That excellent veteran, Barnard Hughes, makes the most of Da." — Jack Kroll, *Newsweek (5-15-78, p. 56)*

"Da — charming, exasperating, staunch, stubborn, once in a while pathetic, but almost always humorous — is quite a fellow to write a play about, and Mr. Leonard has written a fine play about him. . . . The production, under Melvin Bernhardt's direction, is as good as any I've seen privately or professionally this year." — Edith Oliver, *The New Yorker (3-27-78, p. 96)*

"A fascinating blend of comedy and pathos. It's also delightful entertainment and unquestionably a popular success." — *Variety (5-3-78, p. 90)*

"A charming, mellow, saucy, and bittersweet boulevard comedy, but from a boulevard whose dreams are not entirely housebroken and have a bit of untamable Hibernian wildness left fluttering in them." — John Simon, *New York (4-10-78, p. 74)*

Ain't Misbehavin'

Based on an idea by Murray Horwitz and Richard Maltby, Jr. Presented by Emanuel Azenberg, Dasha Epstein, the Shubert Organization, Jane Gaynor and Ron Dante; conceived and directed by Richard Maltby, Jr.; associate director, Murray Horwitz; orchestrations and arrangements by Luther Henderson; vocal arrangements by William Elliott and Jeffrey Gutcheon; sets by John Lee Beatty; costumes by Randy Barcelo; lighting by Pat Collins; music supervision and pianist, Luther Henderson; musical numbers staged by Arthur Faria; production stage manager, Richard Evans. Originally produced by the Manhattan Theatre Club. Longacre Theatre, 220 West 48th Street.

Ain't Misbehavin', which began as a cabaret revue earlier in the season at the off-Off Broadway Manhattan Theatre Club, went on to capture virtually every "best musical" award when it transferred to Broadway at the end of the season.

It is made up of well over two dozen numbers either by Thomas (Fats) Waller or with which he is otherwise associated. Waller was, of course, one of the great jazz pianists of our time; he died in 1943.

Its principal numbers include: "Ain't Misbehavin'" (1929), "Honeysuckle Rose" (1929), "I've Got a Feeling I'm Falling" (1929), "The Ladies Who Sing with the Band" (1943), "Lounging at the Waldorf" (1936), "Mean to Me" (1929), "Your Feet's Too Big" (1936), "Fat and Greasy" (1936), "Black and Blue" (1929) and "It's a Sin to Tell a Lie" (1933).

Opened May 9, 1978

Starring: Nell Carter, Andre De Shields, Armelia McQueen, Ken Page, Charlaine Woodard

Nell Carter, Andre De Shields and Armelia McQueen

REVIEWS

"A whole cluster of marvels. No self-respecting audience could let it go on without interrupting it continually, and if the audience at the Longacre Theatre, where it opened last night, was self-respecting to start off, it ended up in a state of agitated delight. . . . If the five performers, all of them talented and three of them magnificent, ever flagged in holding the stage, there was always the piano." — Richard Eder, *The New York Times (5-10-78, p. C 19)*

"A joyous celebration. . . . You will find giggles galore at the show, which struts and parades with glee. . . . [It] is basically gorgeous. . . . This really is Fats Waller on Broadway. It is a memorial that breathes. It is a testament to a curious genius. . . . It involves a fine veteran jazzman on piano, Luther Henderson, a good orchestra, and five performers, three women, two men, who will sweep your heart away. . . . Maltby has put the show together with great finesse. The musical numbers have been staged with a special fizz by Arthur Faria. . . . It is quite simply a Broadway show that you will never forget." — Clive Barnes, *New York Post (5-10-78, p. 49)*

Nell Carter and Ken Page

Andre De Shields and Company

"[It] celebrates the Falstaffian Waller, and it does so with irresistible joy, gladness and energy. It is blazingly entertaining, and if the blaze leaves some embers of irony, Fats would have been the first to appreciate that. . . . John Lee Beatty's set, Randy Barcelo's costumes and Pat Collins's lighting evoke a Harlem cabaret circa the 1930s. Inside this cozy space, five human dynamos perform two dozen or so of Waller's songs, accompanied superbly by pianist Luther Henderson leading a six-piece combo." — Jack Kroll, *Newsweek (5-22-78, p. 71)*

"The delicious songs by Waller and his friends, suggestively lighted by Pat Collins, continue their joyous renaissance under Richard Maltby Jr.'s canny and easeful staging, with Arthur Faria's fetching mini-choreography. . . . Allow me to rave incontinently about the cast of five that works together as nimbly and wickedly as five fingers in a piece of sleight of hand." — John Simon, *New York (5-22-78, p. 111)*

"There is more animation in the occasion than in anything ever devised by the producers of our film cartoons. And a lot more vitality. . . . Good as the songs may be, they would not affect us as they do if it were not for the five actors who deliver them — and the man at the piano and musical supervisor, Luther Henderson. They and Arthur Faria, who staged the numbers, and the director, Richard Maltby, Jr., make a more integrated ensemble than anything now on a New York stage." — Harold Clurman, *The Nation (5-27-78, p. 645)*

Angel

Fred Gwynne and Don Scardino

THE CAST

Helen Gant	Donna Davis
Ben Gant	Joel Higgins
Mrs. Fatty Pert	Patti Allison
Mrs. Snowden	Grace Carney
Eugene Gant	Don Scardino
Eliza Gant	Frances Sternhagen
Will Pentland	Elek Hartman
Florry Mangle	Rebecca Seay
Mrs. Clatt	Justine Johnston
Jake Clatt	Gene Masoner
Mr. Farell	Billy Beckham
Miss Brown	Jayne Barnett
Laura James	Leslie Ann Ray
W. O. Gant	Fred Gwynne
Dr. Maguire	Daniel Keyes
Joe Tarkington	Rex David Hays
Reed McKinney	Carl Nicholas
Tim Laughran	Norman Stotz
Madame Victoria	Patricia Englund

A musical, with book by Ketti Frings and Peter Udell, from Ketti Frings' *Look Homeward Angel,* based on the novel by Thomas Wolfe; music by Gary Geld; lyrics by Peter Udell. Presented by Philip Rose and Ellen Madison; associate producers, Karen Wald, Norman Main; directed by Philip Rose; setting by Ming Cho Lee; lighting by John Gleason; costumes by Pearl Somner; hair designs by Patrick D. Moreton; orchestrations by Don Walker; musical direction and dance arrangements by William Cox; choreography by Robert Tucker; production stage manager, Steve Zweigbaum. Minskoff Theatre, 45th Street, West of Broadway.

Angel is based on Ketti Frings' 1957 Pulitzer Prize-winning adaptation of Thomas Wolfe's novel, first published almost five decades ago.

It takes place primarily in a boardinghouse operated by Eliza Gant, who goes about catering to her summer boarders and accumulating money for her real estate ventures, but at the sacrifice of giving appropriate attention to her husband and children. The husband is an alcoholic stonecutter and Eliza is attempting to sell his shop during much of the play. He will have none of that and seventeen-year-old Eugene, apparently based on Wolfe, serves as a reluctant go-between. He wants to go away to college, but his mother resists. As the musical progresses, Eugene falls in love with one of the boarders, an "older woman," and experiences the death of his older brother, Ben, from tuberculosis. All the while, the need to depart becomes ever more pressing.

Opened May 10, 1978
Closed May 13, 1978

REVIEWS

"A damp and oppressive amalgam of bathos. It has lyrics of the consistency of cornbread soaked in milk, a whole collection of indifferent performances and a score of sufficient banality to furnish a number or two for the piped music on airplanes waiting to take off.... *Angel* has no feeling to it, only slickness, and the oddities are flattened out into marshmallows, and these are hooked together in awkward and absurd transitions. . . . It is putting things too strongly to call *Angel* a disaster. It is a desert." – Richard Eder, *The New York Times (5-11-78, p. C 17)*

"The songs hardly helped, although probably they hardly hurt either. . . . It is far from a disaster — there are some perfectly nice things here, not least three exquisitely poised performances from Frances Sternhagen, Fred Gwynne and Don Scardino. . . . It was just the show that didn't work." – Clive Barnes, *New York Post (5-11-78, p. 39)*

"A simple, old-fashioned, and occasionally touching musical comedy. . . . Alas, [Gary Geld and Peter Udell] proved to be masters of banality, both in melody and in prosody. . . . The acting of the large cast was, in most cases, admirable." – Brendan Gill, *The New Yorker (5-22-78, p. 91)*

"A profoundly inept musical, and condignly directed by Philip Rose. Rather than having invested in this flop, the angels should have looked homeward." – John Simon, *New York (5-29-78, p. 77)*

Working

The Cast

A musical from the book by Studs Terkel. Adapted and directed by Stephen Schwartz; dances and musical staging by Onna White. Presented by Stephen R. Friedman, Irwin Meyer, in association with Joseph Harris; settings by David Mitchell; costumes by Marjorie Slaiman; lighting by Ken Billington; musical direction and vocal arrangements by Stephen Reinhardt; orchestrations by Kirk Nurock; dance and incidental music by Michele Brourman; songs by Craig Carnella, Micki Grant, Mary Rodgers/Susan Birkenhead, Stephen Schwartz, James Taylor; associate director, Nina Faso; associate to Mrs. White, Martin Allen; production stage manager, Alan Hall. 46th Street Theatre, 226 West 46th Street.

Based upon Studs Terkel's book of the same title, *Working* shows the joys, hopes, problems and frustrations of "average" people in varying walks of life.

They are primarily blue-collar workers: waitresses, firemen, mill hands, steelworkers, a parking-lot attendant, call girls, meter readers, a hockey player, a newsboy, a retired clerk.

Among the songs are: James Taylor's "Millwork," "Nobody Tells Me How" (with music by Mary Rodgers and lyrics by Susan Birkenhead) and "Fathers and Sons" by Stephen Schwartz.

Opened May 14, 1978
Closed June 4, 1978

With: Brad Sullivan, David Langston Smyrl, Patti LuPone, Steven Boockvor, Lynne Thigpen, Rex Everhart, Arny Freeman, Matthew McGrath, Bobo Lewis, Lenora Nemetz, David Patrick Kelly, Joe Mantegna, Matt Landers, Susan Bigelow, Robin Lamont, Terri Treas and Bob Gunton

REVIEWS

"By and large, Stephen Schwartz's idea of making a musical out of Mr. Terkel's chronicle of men and women talking about their work is out of focus. Despite the talents involved, the show lacks a workable form and combines elements that don't agree. . . . There are a few characters who do achieve dramatic intensity. Mr. Schwartz, whose conception may be faulty but whose direction is magnificent, uses them very well. . . . David Mitchell's set, a series of high red girders with city and work scenes projected between them, is effective. Onna White's dances are fairly unimaginative. . . . In general the songs are musically uninteresting and what is worse, trite and sentimental in their lyrics." — Richard Eder, *The New York Times* (5-15-78, p. C 15)

"Some people will find such stories very comforting. But more people — especially the people who go to the theater — might find them a trifle banal. . . . It is a very, very talky musical. It is a personal reminiscence interrupted by the occasional feeble song. . . . It was a good cast." — Clive Barnes, *New York Post* (5-15-78, p. 22)

"The message of the show is so relentlessly upbeat that we come to long for at least one ratty son of a bitch in a blue collar to step up and say vile things about his mother. . . . Most of the songs are far too sweet for their own good, and none is memorable. . . . The big cast is admirable." — Brendan Gill, *The New Yorker* (5-29-78, p. 84)

"The show's problem is that the characters are not doing their jobs but talking about them. . . . The songs are written by too many hands to possess a distinctive signature." — T. E. Kalem, *Time* (5-29-78, p. 83)

"It is a distinctly clever attempt to do the impossible, but no amount of ingenuity is worth the common sense that would have told one to desist." — John Simon, *New York* (5-29-78, p. 77)

Broadway

*Plays from Previous Seasons That Continued
to Run During the 1977-78 Season*

Agamemnon

Priscilla Smith and Jamil Zakkai

By Aeschylus; conceived by Andrei Serban and Elizabeth Swados, using fragments of the original Greek and Edith Hamilton's translation. A New York Shakespeare Festival production, presented by Joseph Papp; associate producer, Bernard Gersten; directed by Andrei Serban; music composed by Elizabeth Swados; scenery by Douglas W. Schmidt; costumes by Santo Loquasto; lighting by Jennifer Tipton; production stage manager, Julia Gillett. Vivian Beaumont Theatre, Lincoln Center, 150 West 65th Street.

Agamemnon is part of Aeschylus' *Oresteia*, which also includes *Libation Bearers* and *Eumenides*.

It is the tenth year of the Trojan War. Shortly after the opening of the play, the Chorus of Argive elders explores the confused moral background, which has involved Agamemnon's sacrifice of his own daughter, Iphigenia, prior to his sailing for Troy, where he has triumphed. Returning, Agamemnon brings with him Cassandra, a prophetess, who comments on the crimes of Troy and upon the evils in Agamemnon's family, among them the fact that Agamemnon's father, Atreus, had tricked his brother, Thyestes, into eating his own children's flesh and the adultery of Queen Clytemnestra with Thyestes' remaining son, Aegisthus. She also describes the ensuing murders of Agamemnon and of herself. Clytemnestra appears, triumphant, at the door of the palace, standing over their bodies, only to become subdued by the Chorus's statements concerning responsibility. As the play ends, the Chorus invokes Agamemnon's son Orestes, who in time will return and join with his sister, Electra, to exact vengeance on their mother and her lover.

In the Serban production, the Chorus chants in both Greek and English and the major roles of Clytemnestra/Cassandra and Agamemnon/Aegisthus are doubled by the actors, who frequently wear half-masks. Although their intent is partly to re-create the Greek theatrical form itself, Serban and Swados also introduce considerable contemporary stylization and elements from the other plays in the trilogy.

Opened May 18, 1977, for a limited engagement
Reopened in Central Park, August 2, 1977
Closed August 28, 1977

Cast: Priscilla Smith, Jamil Zakkai, George Voskovec, Diane Lane
Chorus: Stuart Baker-Bergen, Patrick Burke, Suzanne Collins, Gretel Cummings, Jerry Cunliffe, Jon De Vries, Helena D. Garcia, Natalie Gray, Kathleen Harris, C. S. Hayward, Rodney Hudson, Onni Johnson, Paul Kreppel, Paula Larke, Roger Lawson, Esther Levy, Mimi Locadio, Tom Matsusaka, Valois Mickens, Joseph Neal, William Parry, Justin Rashid, Peter Schlosser, Jai Oscar St. John, Eron Tabor, John Watson, Beverly Wideman

American Buffalo

Robert Duvall, John Savage and Kenneth McMillan

By David Mamet. Presented by Edgar Lansbury and Joseph Beruh; directed by Ulu Grosbard; designed by Santo Loquasto; lighting designed by Jules Fisher; general manager, Marvin A. Krauss; associate producer, Nan Pearlman; production stage manager, Herb Vogler. Ethel Barrymore Theatre, 243 West 47th Street.

Three men sit around in a Chicago junk shop and begin to plan to rob a man of his coin collection. One, the proprietor, is slow and bluff; the second, nicknamed "Teacher," is a loudmouthed hothead; the third and youngest is the rookie to crime and has something of a father-son relationship with the store owner. Teacher decides they should enlist another man, obviously presumed to be more adroit at the intricacies of such a caper. But he fails to arrive and it is left to the boy to tell them he will not — and to be attacked for his trouble. But these three small-time crooks can really do little beyond talk, frequently, almost obsessively, in obscenities, celebrating their own imagined (or fantasized) cleverness. That they will not succeed in their robbery is foreordained.

Opened February 16, 1977
Closed June 11, 1977

Cast: Kenneth McMillan, John Savage, Robert Duvall

Anna Christie

By Eugene O'Neill. Presented by Alexander H. Cohen, by arrangement with Gabriel Katzka and Edward L. Schuman; directed by Jose Quintero; setting and lighting by Ben Edwards; costumes by Jane Greenwood; hairstyles and makeup by J. Roy Helland; production stage manager, George Martin; associate producers, Hildy Parks and Roy A. Somlyo. Imperial Theatre, 249 West 45th Street.

The action of Eugene O'Neill's 1921 drama takes place primarily on a coal barge captained by Chris Christopherson, a hard-drinking man who years before had left his daughter Anna with relatives in the state of Minnesota. One evening, in Johnny-the-Priest's waterfront saloon, he has an unexpected reunion with her. Unfortunately, she has fallen upon hard days and become a prostitute. He invites her to join him on his next voyage and she unexpectedly takes to the sea, which he constantly refers to as "dat ole davil."

They come upon a young Irish seaman, Mat Burke, victim of a shipwreck, and rescue him. Anna and Mat fall in love but, when she discloses her past, the devout Mat is shocked. Anna consents to swear on the rosary of Mat's deceased mother that she has never loved anyone else and will now remain forever pure. As Mat and Chris leave for a trip to South Africa, she promises to be waiting for them when they return.

Opened April 14, 1977
Closed July 30, 1977

Cast: Richard Hamilton, Edwin McDonough, Vic Polizos, Ken Harrison, Jack Davidson, Robert Donley, Mary McCarty, Liv Ullmann, John Lithgow

Liv Ullmann

Annie

Reid Shelton, Andrea McArdle and Sandy Faison

A musical, with book by Thomas Meehan; music by Charles Strouse; lyrics by Martin Charnin. Presented by Mike Nichols; produced by Irwin Meyer, Stephen R. Friedman and Lewis Allen; directed by Martin Charnin; musical numbers choreographed by Peter Gennaro; settings by David Mitchell; costumes by Theoni V. Aldredge; lighting by Judy Rasmuson; musical direction and dance music arranged by Peter Howard; orchestrations by Philip J. Lang; production stage manager, Janet Beroza; based on "Little Orphan Annie," by permission of Chicago Tribune-New York News Syndicate, Inc.; produced by Alvin Nederlander Associates, Inc.-Icarus Productions, in association with Peter Crane. Alvin Theatre, 250 West 52nd Street.

Based on Harold Gray's "Little Orphan Annie" comic strip, *Annie* became the major musical hit of the season. Annie herself has been left in an orphanage, where a particularly outrageous tyrant reigns, one who happens to have a special hate for the musical's heroine. Annie, however, is rescued by the secretary of Oliver Warbucks, who has decided he would like to have an orphan spend Christmas at his home. Warbucks is, of course, a billionaire, a confidante of the President, F.D.R., who promptly calls him in for a consultation. Somewhere in between Annie's introduction and the predictable happy ending, she meets up with the dog Sandy. All but the villains seem destined to live happily ever after.

Major musical numbers include: "It's the Hard-knock Life," "Tomorrow," "N.Y.C.," "Easy Street," "You Won't Be an Orphan for Long," "Something Was Missing," "Maybe" and "A New Deal Christmas."

Opened April 21, 1977

Cast: Danielle Brisebois, Robyn Finn, Donna Graham, Janine Ruane, Diana Barrows, Shelley Bruce, Andrea McArdle, Dorothy Loudon, James Hosbein, Steven Boockvor, Donald Craig, Richard Ensslen, Raymond Thorne, Laurie Beechman, Sandy Faison, Edwin Bordo, Edie Cowan, Penny Worth, Reid Shelton, Robert Fitch, Barbara Erwin, Bob Freschi, Mari McMinn and "Sandy"

The Basic Training of Pavlo Hummel

Joe Fields and Al Pacino

By David Rabe. Presented by Moe Septee and Carmen F. Zollo; directed by David Wheeler; the Theatre Company of Boston production; scenery designed by Robert Mitchell; costumes designed by Domingo Rodriguez; lighting designed by David F. Segal; production stage manager, Patrick Horrigan. Longacre Theatre, 220 West 48th Street.

Pavlo Hummel, the hero of David Rabe's first (1971) play, is the archetypal misfit. In its opening scene, which takes place in a Vietnam whorehouse, Pavlo is killed by a handgrenade thrown by a jealous and angry sergeant. The remainder of the play is a flashback in which Pavlo, a confused and quirky kid, quixotic and eager to please, lying to his fellow trainees about his exploits as a car thief, is anxiously preparing for the proficiency test that comes at the end of his eight weeks of training, gung-ho about being a soldier, yet anything but a brutal, hard-nosed killer.

A somewhat mysterious figure, Ardell, moves in and out of Pavlo's life, adviser and observer, conscience and goad, telling him, "You black inside, I look at you. You black on the inside."

In Vietnam after a brief furlough, Pavlo rebels at being made a medic. He wants to fight — to kill — but with an odd and naive charm. He gets his wish and is thrice wounded. All the while, death goes on around him; an older soldier, both legs and one arm amputated after a landmine explosion, lies in his hospital bed beseeching visitors to kill him.

Eventually, Pavlo dies in the whorehouse, a pointless death in a long since pointless war. He has, perhaps, achieved a partial self-identity, but the what or why of that identity is never really clear.

Opened April 24, 1977
Closed September 3, 1977

Cast: Al Pacino, Tisa Chang, Gustave Johnson, Joe Fields, Jack Kehoe, Max Wright, Larry Bryggman, Lance Henriksen, Paul Guilfoyle, John Aquino, Damien Leake, Gary Bolling, Michael Dinelli, Kevin Maung, Brad Sullivan, Ron Hunter, Andrea Masters, Rebecca Darke, Don Blakely, Anne Miyamoto, Richard Lynch, Sully Boyar

Bubbling Brown Sugar

A musical revue, with book by Loften Mitchell, based on a concept by Rosetta LeNoire. Presented by J. Lloyd Grant, Richard Bell, Robert M. Cooper and Ashton Springer, in association with Moe Septee, Inc., the Media House production. Musical direction by Danny Holgate; choreography and musical staging by Billy Wilson; directed by Robert M. Cooper; settings by Clarke Dunham; lighting by Barry Arnold; costumes by Bernard Johnson; projections by Lucy D. Grosvenor and Clarke Dunham; sound by Joel S. Fichman; hair styles by Stanley James and Gene Sheppard; choral arrangements by Chapman Roberts; music and lyrics by Eubie Blake, Duke Ellington, Billie Holiday, Andy Razef, Cab Calloway, Earl (Fatha) Hines, W. C. Handy, Noble Sissle, Thomas (Fats) Waller, Alexander Roberts and Bert Williams; production stage manager, Sam Ellis. ANTA Theatre, 245 West 52nd Street.

Although its book involves a tour through the "time and space" of the Harlem of the 1920s and 30s and such locations as the Cotton Club, Small's Paradise and the Savoy Ballroom, which attracted white as well as black audiences, *Bubbling Brown Sugar* is primarily a musical revue and its reason for being, a succession of well-known songs. Among them are "Sweet Georgia Brown," "God Bless the Child," "Solitude," "Stompin' at the Savoy," "Some of These Days," "There'll Be Some Changes Made" and "Honeysuckle Rose."

Opened March 2, 1976
Closed December 31, 1977

Cast of 17, including Avon Long, Josephine Premice, Joseph Attles, Vivian Reed, Chip Garnett, Ethel Beatty and Barry Preston

California Suite

Tammy Grimes and George Grizzard

By Neil Simon. Presented by Emanuel Azenberg and Robert Fryer; directed by Gene Saks; scenery by William Ritman; costumes by Jane Greenwood; lighting by Tharon Musser; production stage manager, Philip Cusack. Eugene O'Neill Theatre, 230 West 49th Street.

California Suite is made up of four brief plays whose action takes place in suites 203 and 204 in the Beverly Hills Hotel. Almost a sequel to the playwright's highly successful *Plaza Suite* (1968), it reveals Simon's ability to be both perceptive and sensitive to the "human condition" and at the same time why he is the most popular writer of comedy in the recent history of the American theatre.

Four couples come to Simon's California suite. The first, in their forties, do scathing battle over who is to have custody of their daughter; the second has a farcical confrontation over the presence of a hooker only hours before the bar mitzvah they have come west to attend. In Act 2, a British actress and her homosexual but nonetheless loving husband suffer the travails of Hollywood's Academy Awards night and two couples from Chicago discover that traveling in pairs is far from twice the fun.

Opened June 10, 1976
Closed July 2, 1977

Cast: Tammy Grimes, George Grizzard, Jack Weston, Leslie Easterbrook, Barbara Barrie

The Cherry Orchard

Irene Worth and Raul Julia

By Anton Chekhov; new English version by Jean-Claude van Itallie. A New York Shakespeare Festival production, presented by Joseph Papp; directed by Andrei Serban; scenery and costumes by Santo Loquasto; lighting by Jennifer Tipton; incidental music by Elizabeth Swados; dance arranged by Kathryn Posin; associate producer, Bernard Gersten; production stage manager, Julia Gillett. Vivian Beaumont Theatre, Lincoln Center, 150 West 65th Street.

Although the production is by a director primarily known for his experimental work off-Off Broadway, the characters in this Lincoln Center presentation of *The Cherry Orchard* remain very much Chekhov's dreaming, self-deceiving pre-Revolutionary Russians (the play was written in 1904, almost on the eve of the first of the cataclysmic events that were to lead to the October Revolution). Madame Ranevskaya and her 17-year-old daughter Anya return to their heavily mortgaged estate after five years in France. The cherry orchard is in bloom, but it appears it will soon no longer be theirs. The merchant Lopakhin informs them that it must be sold in order to pay the interest on the estate. They will have, he says, to permit it to be cut down and have the land divided into lots to be rented to summer vacationers. Thus will both what has been the life of a family and the old order pass, to be replaced by the emergence of the newly wealthy, self-made Lopakhin; to be replaced also by the revolution that is soon to change the face of Russia and affect the future of the world.

Opened February 17, 1977, for a limited engagement
Closed April 10, 1977
Reopened June 28, 1977
Closed August 7, 1977

Cast: Raul Julia, Meryl Streep, Max Wright, Marybeth Hurt, Irene Worth, Priscilla Smith, George Voskovec, Cathryn Damon, C. K. Alexander, Ben Masters, Dwight Marfield, Michael Cristofer, Jon De Vries, William Duff-Griffin, John Ahlburg, Suzanne Collins, Christine Estabrook, C. S. Hayward, Diane Lane, Jim Siering

Chicago

A musical vaudeville, with book by Fred Ebb and Bob Fosse; music by John Kander; lyrics by Fred Ebb; based on the play *Chicago,* by Maurine Dallas Watkins. Presented by Robert Fryer and James Cresson, in association with Martin Richards, Joseph Harris and Ira Bernstein. Directed and choreographed by Bob Fosse; settings by Tony Walton; costumes by Patricia Zipprodt; lighting by Jules Fisher; musical director, Stanley Lebowsky; orchestration by Ralph Burns; dance music arranged by Peter Howard; sound by Abe Jacob; hair styles by Romaine Green; production stage manager, Phil Friedman. 46th Street Theatre, 226 West 46th Street.

The play *Chicago* became the movie *Roxie Hart* and it provides the basis for a combination cabaret show and murder case involving Roxie, an entertainer whose mechanic husband shoots a lover who has already grown tired of her. In prison, she meets another alleged murderess and in the series of farcical scenes that follow both come under the wing of the attorney Billy Flynn. *Chicago*'s chief distinction is in numbers occasionally reminiscent of some of the Brecht-Weill musicals.

Opened June 3, 1975
Closed August 27, 1977

Starring: Chita Rivera, Gwen Verdon and Jerry Orbach; features Mary McCarty and Barney Martin

Jerry Orbach and Gwen Verdon

A Chorus Line

The Chorus Line

Conceived, choreographed and directed by Michael Bennett. Presented by the New York Shakespeare Festival; Joseph Papp, producer, Bernard Gersten, associate producer. Book by James Kirkwood and Nicholas Dante; music by Marvin Hamlisch; lyrics by Edward Kleban; co-choreographer, Bob Avian; setting by Robin Wagner; costumes by Theoni V. Aldredge; lighting by Tharon Musser; orchestrations by Bill Byers, Hershy Kay and Jonathan Tunick; music coordinator, Robert Thomas; music direction and vocal arrangements by Don Pippin; production stage manager, Jeff Hamlin. Shubert Theatre, 225 West 44th Street.

Michael Bennett, who conceived *A Chorus Line,* is a young former chorus line dancer who achieved major recognition with his work as director or choreographer of such Broadway hits as *Promises, Promises, Coco, Company* and *Follies,* then felt he had to get back to what he calls, "the people," the hundreds of dancers he had worked with in earlier years. Out of his decision came many hours with dancers and many hours of tape recordings.

A Chorus Line focuses upon the "gypsies," the chorus line dancers who day after day, year after year, troop from audition to audition, rehearsal to rehearsal, show to show, for the most part unidentified and unrecognized, certainly uncelebrated by other than their peers. Yet they are individuals, and *A Chorus Line* brings them alive in all their vulnerability, epitomized in the early lyric "I Really Need This Job." On Broadway, their opportunities are rapidly diminishing as the number of shows diminishes. Some of them still dream of becoming stars, but they have a haunting fear: "What do you do when you can't dance anymore?" They are left with one even stronger reaction, however, that what they did they "did for love."

Opened May 21, 1975 (at the Public Theatre)
Opened July 25, 1975 (at the Shubert Theatre)

Featuring: Carole Bishop, Priscilla Lopez, Donna McKechnie and Sammy Williams

Equus

By Peter Shaffer. Presented by Kermit Bloomgarden and Doris Cole Abrahams, in association with Frank Milton; directed by John Dexter; scenery and costumes by John Napier; lighting by Andy Phillips; sound by Mark Wilkinson; mime by Claude Chagrin; American supervision of scenery and lighting by Howard Bay; costumes by Patricia Adshead; production stage manager, Robert L. Borod. Plymouth Theatre, 236 West 45th Street.

Equus is primarily a psychological detective story, probing the background of a young stable boy who is in love with horses, who have also become his surrogate God, a substitute for the picture of Christ that once hung above his bed. The stables are "the temple, the holy of holies." Why, then, has Alan Strang blinded six of them with a steel spike? What will psychiatrist Martin Dysart find out concerning the circumstances and the motivation? What will he find out about himself?

On another level, the play explores the nature of sanity and "normal" adjustment. Freed from his aberration, will Alan not also be deprived of his passion, become another among the ranks of the gray men? "That boy," says Dysart, "has known a passion more intense than any I felt all my life.... Passion can be destroyed by a doctor, it cannot be created."

Opened October 24, 1974
Closed October 2, 1977

Starring: Anthony Hopkins, Peter Firth, Marian Seldes, Michael Higgins, Frances Sternhagen and Roberta Maxwell

For Colored Girls Who Have Considered Suicide/ When the Rainbow Is Enuf

By Ntozake Shange. Presented by Joseph Papp and Woodie King, Jr.; a New York Shakespeare Festival production in association with the Henry Street Settlement's New Federal Theatre; associate producer, Bernard Gersten; directed by Oz Scott; scenery by Ming Cho Lee; lighting by Jennifer Tipton; costumes by Judy Dearing; choreography by Paula Moss; music for "I Found God in Myself" by Diana Wharton; production stage manager, John Beven. Booth Theatre, 222 West 45th Street.

Colored Girls started out off-Off Broadway, moved on to the Henry Street Settlement's New Federal Theatre and thence to the New York Shakespeare Festival's Public Theatre before arriving on Broadway. Its author, Ntozake Shange, is more poet than play-

The Cast, with Trazana Beverley in foreground

wright, yet her vignettes of the "colored girl" who has been "dancing on beer cans and shingles" all her life is also remarkably viable and evocative on stage.

Ms. Shange writes of the black woman who sings her song of life — "she's been dead for so long" — in a series of poems that in the theatre generally become monologues delivered by the seven young women, including the playwright, who make up the cast. They are monologues of pride and bitterness and regret; monologues of exultation and tragedy, which encapsulate the history and the present of the black woman in America.

Much of the early part of *Colored Girls* involves the revelation of initial experiences of sex, descriptions of failed loves and lovers and scorn (mixed with sympathy) for the deceptions and poses of the black male. As the evening progresses, the material becomes more personal, more clearly identified with specific human experiences rather than general situations.

At the end, the black women stand not merely enduring but in a sense triumphant. They repeat over and over again the lyrics of Diana Wharton's song, "I found God in myself and I loved her fiercely," a symbol of their unity, a testimony to their rainbow.

Opened September 15, 1976
Closed July 16, 1978

Cast: Janet League, Aku Kadogo, Trazana Beverley, Paula Moss, Rise Collins, Laurie Carlos, Ntozake Shange

Gemini

By Albert Innaurato. Presented by the Circle Repertory Company in association with PAF Playhouse; directed by Peter Mark Schifter; setting by Christopher Nowak; costumes by Ernest Allen Smith; lighting by Larry Crimmins; production stage manager, Fred Reinglas. Circle Repertory Theatre, 99 Seventh Avenue South; Little Theatre, 240 West 44th Street.

Gemini is set in the Geminiani/Lowenstein backyard in South Philadelphia. Its principal characters are Fran Geminiani, a lower-middle-class working man, and his son Francis, a Harvard student who is about to celebrate (if that is the word) his twenty-first birthday. Two of Francis's college friends, a well-to-do brother and sister, show up unexpectedly and set up their tent in the backyard.

Francis is embarrassed, ashamed of his father, ashamed also of their surroundings. He is, in addition, it turns out, thoroughly confused about whether he is homo- or heterosexual. The sister, Judith, it seems, is in love with him and he thinks that he is in love with her brother, Randy, and that is why he has been seeing Judith during his months at Harvard.

As nextdoor neighbors the Geminianis have a most unlikely duo: a blowsy Irishwoman named Bunny Lowenstein and her extremely fat and asthmatic adolescent son, whose contribution to the play's evolution is not inconsiderable.

Innaurato works out Francis's dilemma in scenes that are alternately funny and touching, amid uproar, tears, a failed suicide attempt, a birthday party that turns into a fiasco and other often raucous events. There is, however, a happy ending — much to almost everyone's surprise.

Opened March 13, 1977, for a limited engagement
Closed April 10, 1977
Reopened on Broadway, May 10, 1977

Cast: Robert Picardo, Jessica James, Reed Birney, Carol Potter, Jonathan Hadary, Danny Aiello, Anne DeSalvo

Danny Aiello, Jessica James and Robert Picardo

Godspell

Don Scardino (kneeling) as Jesus and Tom Rolfing

A musical based on the Gospel According to St. Matthew, conceived and directed by John-Michael Tebelak; music and lyrics by Stephen Schwartz. Presented by Edgar Lansbury, Stuart Duncan, Joseph Beruh and the Shubert Organization, Inc.; Charles Haid, associate producer. Lighting by Spencer Mosse; costumes by Susan Tsu; production supervision by Nina Faso; musical director, Steve Reinhardt; sound by Robert Minor. Plymouth Theatre, 236 West 45th Street.

Godspell originated at off-Off Broadway's LaMama Experimental Theatre Club and transferred to Off Broadway on May 17, 1971, thence to Broadway in the summer of 1976, making it one of the longest-running musicals in the history of the American theatre.

It involves variations on the life and parables of Jesus and, in the second act, a depiction of his crucifixion. In addition to Jesus, there are nine others in the cast, all of whom play multiple roles, doubling as apostles and other New Testament figures, and sometimes playing themselves.

The musical projects an engaging innocence and includes several by now familiar numbers, among them "Prepare Ye the Way of the Lord," "Day By Day" and "By My Side."

Opened June 22, 1976
Closed September 4, 1977

Cast: Lamar Alford, Laurie Faso, Lois Foraker, Robin Lamont, Elizabeth Lathram, Bobby Lee, Tom Rolfing, Don Scardino, Marley Sims, Valerie Williams

Grease

A musical, with book, music and lyrics by Jim Jacobs and Warren Casey. Presented by Kenneth Waissman and Maxine Fox, in association with Anthony D'Amato. Musical supervision and orchestrations by Michael Leonard; musical direction, vocal and dance arrangements by Louis St. Louis; setting by Douglas W. Schmidt; costumes by Carrie F. Robbins; lighting by Karl Eigsti; sound by Bill Merrill; hair styles created by Jim Sullivan; musical numbers and dances staged by Patricia Birch; directed by Tom Moore; production stage manager, Joe Calvan. Royale Theatre, 242 West 45th Street.

The audience enters to find a banner proclaiming "Welcome Back Rydell Class of 1959." It is the era of Jimmy Dean and Elvis Presley at his hip-swingingest; of Sandra Dee and ducktail haircuts; the time of what a shortlived Broadway play of several seasons before called the "nervous set"; a period in which "neat," "creep" and "endsville" were the current argot and the drive-in movie was experiencing its heyday.

Sandy and Danny have met during the summer, but when the new school year opens he is considerably less amorous. His friends among the Burger Palace Boys might not approve. Dances, pajama parties and even a track team enter in, but it is not until Sandy drops her very proper ways and adopts those of the "Pink Ladies" that love, in a manner of speaking, triumphs.

Opened February 14, 1972

Cast of 17, featuring Adrienne Barbeau, Barry Bostwick, Carole Demas and Marya Small

Happy End

Music by Kurt Weill; lyrics by Bertolt Brecht; original German play by Elisabeth Hauptmann; book and lyrics adapted by Michael Feingold; Chelsea Theatre Center production newly conceived by Robert Kalfin. Presented by Michael Harvey and the Chelsea Theatre Center; directed and staged by Robert Kalfin and Patricia Birch; scenic design by Robert U. Taylor; costumes by Carrie F. Robbins; lighting by Jennifer Tipton; musical direction by Roland Gagnon; associate producer, Wilder Luke Burnap; production stage manager, Mark Wright. Martin Beck Theatre, 302 West 45th Street.

Originally produced in Germany in 1929, when it was intended as a sequel to Brecht and Weill's highly successful *Threepenny Opera, Happy End* was not revived until 1958 in Munich. It has since become a standard in the European repertory.

The scene is Chicago in 1915, but a Chicago based far more on motion picture fantasy than on the reality, which Brecht had never visited. Alternating between scenes in Bill's Beer Hall and a Salvation Army mission, *Happy End* tells of gang rivalry and the attempt of a Salvation Army lieutenant nicknamed "Hallelujah Lil" to turn Bill Cracker and the other members of "The Fly's" gang away from the wages of sin and toward God. Much of the musical is satirical, complete to a predictable happy ending, which finds The Fly reunited with her long lost husband who has become a Salvation Army officer and Bill and Hallelujah Lil about to tie the knot and work for God.

Happy End's best-known songs include "The Bilbao Song," "The Sailor's Tango" and "Surabaya Johnny."

Opened April 25, 1977, at the Chelsea Theatre Center, Brooklyn
Reopened May 3, 1977, at the Martin Beck Theatre
Closed July 10, 1977

Cast: Christopher Lloyd, Benjamin Rayson, Tony Azito, John A. Coe, Robert Weil, Raymond J. Barry, Grayson Hall, Donna Emmanuel, Meryl Streep, Liz Sheridan, Joe Grifasi, Prudence Wright Holmes, Alexandra Borrie, Christopher Cara, Kristin Jolliff, Frank Kopyc, Tom Mardirosian, Martha Miller, Victor Pappas, David Pursley

Christopher Lloyd, Meryl Streep and Tony Azito

I Love My Wife

Book and lyrics by Michael Stewart; music composed and arranged by Cy Coleman; from a play by Luis Rego. Presented by Terry Allen Kramer and Harry Rigby by arrangement with Joseph Kipness; directed by Gene Saks; musical numbers staged by Onna White; scenery by David Mitchell; lighting by Gilbert V. Hemsley, Jr.; costumes by Ron Talsky; musical direction by John Miller; sound design by Lou Gonzalez; associate producer, Frank Montalvo; production stage manager, Bob Vandergriff. Ethel Barrymore Theatre, 243 West 47th Street.

The scene is Trenton, New Jersey, where a public relations man named Wally meets with a former high school classmate named Alvin, who is a furniture mover. The supposed sophisticate involves his buddy in wife-swapping, or at least attempts to. On Christmas Eve, they give it a good try, but in the words of the title song, the furniture mover decides "I Love My Wife." Apparently, they are not "today people" after all.

Among the songs are: "We're Still Friends," "By Threes," "A Mover's Life," "Love Revolution," "Sexually Free," "Lover on Christmas Eve" and "Everybody Today Is Turning On."

Opened April 17, 1977

Cast: Ilene Graff, Joanna Gleason, James Naughton, Michael Mark, Joe Saulter, John Miller, Ken Bichel, Lenny Baker

Ilene Graff and Lenny Baker

The Ice Show

Toller Cranston

Presented by Dennis Bass and Robin Cranston; produced and directed by Myrl A. Schreibman; set design by Anthony Sabatino and William H. Harris; costume design by Miles White; lighting design by D. Scott Linder; sound design by Jack Shirk; music supervision by Bill Courtney; skating consultant, Bill Turner; original music by Al Kasha and Joel Hirshhorn; choreography and staging by Brian Foley; additional choreography by Ellen Burka; production stage manager, Joe Lorden. Palace Theatre, Broadway and 47th Street.

Toller Cranston's *Ice Show* seeks to meld the world of ice skating and ice dancing with that of dance in a way previously attempted only on a more limited scale. To do so, Cranston, the former Canadian men's and world's free-skating champion and 1976 Olympic bronze medalist, has brought to Broadway a group of 15 other American and Canadian Olympians and other skating champions in a program choreographed by Brian Foley.

The Ice Show is divided into five sections: "Trilogy," skated to selections from, among others, *West Side Story, On the Waterfront* and *Nicholas and Alexandra;* "Dance Medley," to the *Charleston, Fascination, Dark Town Strutters Ball* and other dance favorites; "Russian Ode," which utilizes such songs as "The Young and the Restless," "The Warlords" and "Dream of Love"; "Toller's Ball," which draws upon *Le Prophete, Gaite Parisienne* and *Raymonda,* among others, and "Latino," which is skated to such numbers as "Habanera," "La Carioca" and a selection from *I Pagliacci.*

Opened May 19, 1977, for a limited engagement
Closed June 12, 1977

Starring: Toller Cranston, Jim Millns and Colleen O'Connor, Gordon McKellen, Jr., Ken Shelley, Wendy Burge, Candy Jones and Don Fraser, Kath Malmberg, Barbara Berezowski and David Porter, Elizabeth Freeman, Jack Courtney and Emily Benenson, Janet and Mark Hominuke

The King and I

A musical, with music by Richard Rodgers, book and lyrics by Oscar Hammerstein 2nd, based on the novel *Anna and the King of Siam* by Margaret Landon. Presented by Lee Guber and Shelly Gross; associate producer, Fred Walker; settings by Peter Wolf; costumes by Stanley Simmons; lighting by Thomas Skelton; hair styled by Werner Sherer; musical supervision by Milton Rosenstock; musical director, John Lesko; sound by Richard Fitzgerald; original choreography by Jerome Robbins; directed by Yuriko; production stage manager, Ed Preston. Uris Theatre, West 51st Street and Broadway.

Originally presented on Broadway in 1951, with the same star, Yul Brynner, *The King and I* tells of a charming English widow who takes her young son to Bangkok, where she is to give English lessons to the numerous children of the king of Siam. As she attempts to cope with his tyrannical behavior, romance predictably occurs as the king turns tender in his dealing and response to her challenge.

Among the best known musical numbers are: "I Whistle a Happy Tune," "Hello, Young·Lovers," "March of the Siamese Children," "A Puzzlement," "Getting to Know You" and "We Kiss in a Shadow."

Opened May 2, 1977

Cast: Larry Swansen, Alan Amick, Constance Towers, Jae Woo Lee, Michael Kermoyan, Yul Brynner, June Angela, Hye-Young Choi, Gene Profanato, Julie Woo, Martin Vidnovic, John Michael King

Yul Brynner

Lily Tomlin in "Appearing Nightly"

Lily Tomlin

Written and directed by Jane Wagner and Lily Tomlin. Presented by Ron Delsener; staged by George Boyd; music by Jerry Frankel; lighting by Daniel Adams; costume by J. Allen Highfill; sound by Jack Mann; stage manager, Brian Meister. Biltmore Theatre, 261 West 47th Street.

Miss Tomlin is best known for her numerous television appearances, concerts, cabaret performances and roles in such films as *Nashville,* for which she received an Academy Award nomination, and *The Late Show.* In *Appearing Nightly* she appears primarily as a standup comic, drawing upon many characterizations familiar to her admirers. Among them are a cunning street waif, a fantasy-inclined adolescent, a young woman on the road from marijuana to hard drugs, a television commercial announcer and a former athlete who has turned into a drunk.

One of Miss Tomlin's most popular television characters, that of Ernestine the telephone lady, receives only a short thirty seconds of attention and her Bobbi-Jeanine, the lounge organist, appears only as a listener.

Opened March 24, 1977, for a limited engagement
Closed June 12, 1977

With: Lily Tomlin

The Magic Show

A musical, with book by Bob Randall; songs by Stephen Schwartz; magic by Doug Henning. Presented by Edgar Lansbury, Joseph Beruh and Ivan Reitman. Directed and choreographed by Grover Dale; settings by David Chapman; costumes by Randy Barcelo; lighting by Richard Nelson; production stage manager, Herb Vogler. Cort Theatre, 138 West 48th Street.

Although it has a nominal story line about a seedy nightclub in Passaic, New Jersey, which encounters a problem when its conjuror develops too much of a taste for liquor, *The Magic Show* is mainly the occasion for some remarkable illusionist displays by Doug Henning. In the crisis, he appears from a talent agency, is seen by a major producer and clearly is destined for a glorious future. Mr. Henning saws a woman in half, burns a girl to a skeleton, changes a live dove to a live rabbit and even succeeds in a Houdini-like escape trick, and that is what makes the show the long-running hit it is.

Opened May 28, 1974

Starring: Doug Henning; features David Ogden Stiers, Anita Morris and Dale Soules

Mummenschanz

The Mummenschanz mime theatre. Presented by Arthur Shafman International, Ltd.; production supervisor, Christopher Dunlop; production stage manager, Patrick Lecoq. Bijou Theatre, 209 West 45th Street.

This unusual Swiss mime theatre, which was totally unknown in the United States until 1973, attempts to appeal to a wide age range, children through adults.

Andres Bossard, Bernie Schurch and Floriana Frassetto, who make up the troupe, formed it in 1972. They rejected the traditions of classical mime, eschewing whiteface and utilizing masks, ignoring stylized movement in favor of forms that they consider more suitable to the shapes and characters they depict. Their masks, interestingly, are likely to use toilet paper rolls and geometric shapes. In general, the members of Mummenschanz dress as fantasy figures and comment upon the human condition, blending sophistication and simplicity. In the first portion of the program this involves what Mr. Schurch describes as "about growing, building up." "The second," he says, "is more destructive. When the two men with the clay masks fall to the floor, they become earth again." The intent is "to touch as many levels as possible," through abstract techniques, a grasping for essence.

Opened March 30, 1977

With: Andres Bossard, Floriana Frassetto, Bernie Schurch

Oh! Calcutta!

Devised by Kenneth Tynan. The contributors: Jules Feiffer, Dan Greenburg; Leonore Kandel, John Lennon, Jacques Levy, Leonard Melfi, David Newman, Robert Benton, Sam Shepard, Clovis Trouille, Kenneth Tynan and Sherman Yellen. Presented by Hillard Elkins, Norman Kean and Robert Fishko; conceived and directed by Jacques Levy; music and lyrics by Stanley Walden, Robert Dennis and Peter Shickele; additional music and lyrics by Mr. Walden and Mr. Levy; choreography by Margo Sappington; music director, Mr. Walden; setting by James Tilton; lighting by Harry Silverglat; costumes by Kenneth M. Yount (supervised by Mr. Tilton); musical conductor, Michael Tschudin; sound by Sander Hacker; stage manager, David Rubinstein. Edison Theatre, 240 West 47th Street.

When *Oh! Calcutta!* opened in 1969 it was variously viewed as a show that would liberate pornography or, as Clive Barnes put it, "give pornography a bad name." It has changed only marginally in this 1976 resuscitation. For better or worse, however, attitudes have changed. Nudity as such is no longer quite the guarantee of attendance that it was in 1969.

Kenneth Tynan described the original production, done off-Broadway, as an evening of "elegant erotica," and its present virtues and defects are those of that original: too little genuine humor and too much striving for "shock" effects and a considerable, though now limited, degree of pretentiousness.

Opened October 25, 1976

With: Haru Aki, Jean Andalman, Bill Bass, Dorothy Chansky, Cress Darwin, John Hammil, William Knight, Cy Moore and Pamela Pilkenton

A scene from *Mummenschanz*

Otherwise Engaged

Carolyn Lagerfelt and Tom Courtenay

By Simon Gray. Presented by James M. Nederlander, Frank Milton and Michael Codron; directed by Harold Pinter; settings by Eileen Diss; costumes by Jane Greenwood; set supervision and lighting by Neil Peter Jampolis; production stage manager, Ben Janney. Plymouth Theatre, 236 West 45th Street.

Simon has acquired a new recording of *Parsifal* and, just as he is settling down for his Wagnerian interlude, the first of a succession of visitors bursts in — an antagonistic student who rents an upstairs flat in Simon's London house. He is soon followed in rapid order by Simon's brother, who is distraught over the likelihood that he will not get the assistant headmastership he so covets; by an overimbibing litterateur who is having difficulties with both his mistress and his former wife; by the mistress; by a middle-aged man who is convinced his young fiancee has been seduced by Simon, and, finally, by Simon's own wife.

What is Simon's attraction for them? It is clearly not simply that he is a reasonably, if reluctantly, generous and successful publisher. No, he is different from the rest of them. Ironic and detached, droll and something of a snob, he can listen and respond, but without ever really making contact with the other human being and the crisis he is undergoing; without, one suspects, making more than glancing contact with himself. By the time he finally gets to play his *Parsifal,* however, things have changed at least a little. He has not been quite able to remain inside his protective shell, fight though he does for it.

Opened February 2, 1977
Closed October 30, 1977

Cast: Tom Courtenay, John Christopher Jones, John Horton, Nicolas Coster, Lynn Milgrim, Michael Lombard, Carolyn Lagerfelt

Pippin

A musical comedy by Roger O. Hirson. Music and lyrics by Stephen Schwartz. Presented by Stuart Ostrow; directed and choreographed by Bob Fosse; scenery by Tony Walton; costumes by Patricia Zipprodt; lighting by Jules Fisher; musical direction by Stanley Lebowsky; orchestrations by Ralph Burns; dance arrangements by John Berkman; sound design by Abe Jacob; production stage manager, Phil Friedman. Imperial Theatre, 249 West 45th Street.

Michael Rupert as Pippin

Pippin, who is loosely based on Pepin, the son of Charlemagne, has "the overwhelming need to be completely fulfilled." Even though it is only the eighth century, he thinks he can do a better job of running things than his father and therefore becomes a revolutionary and kills Charlemagne while he is at prayer, at the same time beseeching "Father forgive me, I hope I can make a better world."

Almost needless to say, he cannot. Wars must be fought, taxes must be levied and nothing in the ways of men really changes very much. A disappointed Pippin brings his father back to life and heads elsewhere to look for fulfillment, still convinced that he is "Extraordinary," still seeking his "Corner of the Sky," in two of the musical's best-known numbers.

Opened October 23, 1972
Closed June 12, 1977

Starring: Ben Vereen, John Rubinstein, Eric Berry, Leland Palmer, Irene Ryan and Jill Clayburgh

Same Time, Next Year

Sandy Dennis and Ted Bessell

By Bernard Slade. Presented by Morton Gottlieb, Dasha Epstein, Edward L. Schuman and Palladium Productions; associate producers, Ben Rosenberg and Warren Crane; directed by Gene Saks; scenery by William Ritman; costumes by Jane Greenwood; lighting by Tharon Musser; hair styles by Steve Atha; stage manager, Kate Pollock. Brooks Atkinson Theatre, 256 West 47th Street.

Doris and George are both married, but not to each other. Yet they meet once a year for twenty-four years to make love in the same resort hotel near San Francisco. Over the years, both obviously change. Each has three children, but Doris progresses from a typical, if not overly bright, housewife to a shrewd businesswoman. George, on the other hand, follows the opposite course and becomes something approaching a hippie by the time of their twenty-fourth encounter. The audience views them on six of their weekends and, to some extent, sees not only the development of their lives but the social changes of the period, all viewed with wit and considerable perception.

Opened March 13, 1975

Starring: Ellen Burstyn and Charles Grodin

The Shadow Box

By Michael Cristofer. Presented by Lester Osterman, Ken Marsolais, Allan Francis and Leonard Soloway; the Mark Taper/Long Wharf Theatre production; directed by Gordon Davidson; setting by Ming Cho Lee; costumes by Bill Walker; lighting by Ronald Wallace; production stage manager, Franklin Keysar. Morosco Theatre, 217 West 45th Street.

The action of *The Shadow Box,* which received the 1977 Pulitzer Prize for drama, takes place in three cottages on the grounds of a large hospital, where three people are dying. Two realize it and in their disparate ways seem prepared to face it; the third, a senile octagenarian, may or may not recognize she is in her last lap — she insists, however, on holding on to life because of her dream: the belief that her favorite daughter, Clare, will return. Clare, however, has been dead for many years; her existence kept alive by letters written by the second daughter, who has come to the cottage to wait out her mother's last hours with her. The absent daughter is "something to hope for.... People need something to keep them going."

The wife of the first of the patients refuses to believe her husband is dying, just as she has refused to acquiesce to Joe's request that she tell their teenage son of the fact. When she asks *why* it must happen, he stolidly admits one of the things that is at the core of what Cristofer is saying not only about death but about much of life: "I don't know. Like everything else, I don't know."

Brian and his young lover, Mark, live in the second cottage. He is in the terminal stages of cancer, a failed writer who has returned to writing. They are visited by his flamboyantly alcoholic wife, a visit deeply resented by Mark but welcomed by the dying man who is attempting to sort things out.

Meanwhile, in cottage three, the ancient wheelchair-bound Felicity and her frustrated daughter Agnes, torn between telling her mother that her other daughter is long dead and permitting the old woman her hope, also sit waiting for death.

Cristofer is as much concerned about those who remain as about those who are to die. Inevitably, the questions he raises must remain unanswered — save, perhaps, for those who have also had to face them.

Opened March 31, 1977
Closed December 31, 1977

Cast: Josef Sommer, Simon Oakland, Vincent Stewart, Joyce Ebert, Laurence Luckinbill, Mandy Patinkin, Patricia Elliott, Rose Gregorio, Geraldine Fitzgerald

Geraldine Fitzgerald and Rose Gregorio

Shenandoah

Music by Gary Geld; lyrics by Peter Udell; book by James Lee Barrett, Mr. Udell and Philip Rose. Presented by Rose, Gloria and Louis K. Sher. Directed by Mr. Rose; setting by C. Murawski; lighting by Thomas Skelton; costumes by Pearl Somner and Winn Morton; orchestrations by Don Walker; musical direction by Lynn Crigler; dance arrangements by Russell Warner; choreography by Robert Tucker; production stage manager, Steve Zweigbaum. Alvin Theatre, 250 West 52nd Street.

The setting is the Shenandoah Valley during the Civil War. Charlie Anderson has six sons and a daughter. He wants to mind his own business, to remain apart from the conflict between North and South and, most important of all, to keep his sons out of the Confederate army — even if those sons, as they proclaim in a rousing song, feel that "Next to Lovin', I Like Fightin' Best." It is not to be, however. The youngest son, Robert, is kidnapped by marauding Union troops and Anderson, together with all but his oldest son, whom he leaves behind with his wife and newborn baby, starts off in search of the boy. There is a happy ending, but not before some appealing ballads, among them "Violets and Silverbells" and "Meditation," which Anderson intones over his wife's grave.

Opened January 7, 1975
Closed August 7, 1977

Starring: John Cullum; featuring Donna Theodore, Penelope Milford and Chip Ford

John Cullum as Charlie Anderson

Side by Side by Sondheim

Millicent Martin and Julie N. McKenzie

A musical entertainment, with music and lyrics by Stephen Sondheim and music by Leonard Bernstein, Mary Rodgers, Richard Rodgers and Jule Styne. Presented by Harold Prince in association with Ruth Mitchell, by arrangement with the Incomes Company Ltd.; directed by Ned Sherrin; musical director, Ray Cook; pianists, Daniel Troob and Albin Konopka; musical staging by Bob Howe; scenery by Peter Docherty; costumes by Florence Klotz; lighting by Ken Billington; scenery supervision by Jay Moore; musical supervision by Paul Gemignani; stage manager, John Grigas. Music Box Theatre, 239 West 45th Street.

This import from London, where it has been a great success, brings together a potpourri of songs by Stephen Sondheim, for most of which he has provided both the music and lyrics. The numbers include "Comedy Tonight," from *A Funny Thing Happened on the Way to the Forum,* "If Momma Was Married," from *Gypsy,* "Getting Married Today," "Company," "Barcelona" and "Marry Me a Little," from *Company,* "Broadway Baby," from *Follies,* "Anyone Can Whistle," from the show of that title, "Pretty Lady," from *Pacific Overtures* and "A Boy Like That," from *West Side Story.*

Opened April 18, 1977
Closed March 19, 1978

With: Millicent Martin, Julie N. McKenzie, David Kernan and Ned Sherrin

Your Arms Too Short to Box with God

Conceived from the Book of Matthew and directed by Vinnette Carroll; music and lyrics by Alex Bradford; additional music and lyrics by Micki Grant. Presented by Frankie Hewitt and the Shubert Organization in association with Theater Now, Inc.; settings and costumes by William Schroder; setting supervisor, Michael J. Hotopp; lighting by Gilbert V. Hemsley, Jr.; orchestrations and dance music by H. B. Barnum; choral arrangements and direction by Chapman Roberts; choreography by Talley Beatty; production stage manager, Haig Shepherd. Lyceum Theatre, 149 West 45th Street.

Delores Hall and the Cast

Vinnette Carroll's *Your Arms Too Short to Box with God,* which originated at her Urban Arts Corps and was presented as part of the Spoleto Festival prior to its Broadway opening, is set in a chapel, which the cast enters garbed in liturgical robes. A minister announces, "We're gonna have a good time." He proceeds to begin to relate the story of Christ's Crucifixion and Resurrection, freely based on the Book of Matthew. As he does, the cast/congregation changes into biblical attire to become followers, Pharisees and the people of Jerusalem in order to act out the events that follow, relying heavily upon gospel singing, rock music and dance, before returning to their original robes for a tribute to some of the great gospel singers of the past.

Musical numbers include: "Beatitudes," "We're Gonna Have a Good Time," "Do You Know Jesus? He's a Wonder," "Something Is Wrong in Jerusalem," "Be Careful Whom You Kiss" and "Give Us Barabbas."

Opened December 22, 1976
Closed

With: Salome Bey, Clinton Derricks-Carroll, Sheila Ellis, Delores Hall, William Hardy, Jr., Hector Jaime Mercado, Stanley Perryman, Mabel Robinson, William Thomas, Jr., Deborah Lynn Bridges, Sharon Brooks, Thomas Jefferson Fouse, Jr., Michael Gray, Cardell Hall, Bobby Hill, Lidell Jackson, Edna Krider, Leon Washington, Marilyn Windbush

The Wiz

Clarice Taylor

Book by William F. Brown; music and lyrics by Charlie Smalls. Based on L. Frank Baum's *The Wonderful Wizard of Oz.* Presented by Ken Harper; directed by Geoffrey Holder; setting by Tom H. John; costumes by Mr. Holder; lighting by Tharon Musser; orchestrations by Harold Wheeler; musical direction and vocal arrangements by Charles H. Coleman; dance arrangements by Timothy Graphenreed; choreography and musical numbers staged by George Faison; production stage manager, Charles Blackwell. Majestic Theatre, 247 West 44th Street.

Loosely based on *The Wizard of Oz,* this all-black musical couches the familiar story in jive talk and even introduces a voodoo element. Young Dorothy, the Scarecrow, the Tinman and the Cowardly Lion all are there, however, in a show that features extraordinary dance numbers and spectacular costumes.

Opened January 5, 1975

Starring: Stephanie Mills, Clarice Taylor, Hinton Battle, Tiger Haynes, Ted Ross and Andre De Shields

Off and
Off-Off Broadway

1977-78 Season
through May 31, 1978

The Second Greatest Entertainer in the Whole Wide World

Dick Shawn

By Dick Shawn. Presented by Kenneth D. Laub; directed by Mr. Shawn; setting by Akira Yoshimura; lighting by Marilyn Rennagel; production stage manager, Robin Brecker. Promenade Theatre, 76th Street and Broadway.

The stage of the theatre is transformed into a dingy backstage dressing room adorned with old photographs and a large pile of newspapers. A phonograph sounds offstage "Hail to the Audience" to its scratchy end. Under the pile of newspapers is Dick Shawn, the "entertainer" of the title, who is about to perform for the first time in five years.

During his 90-minute performance, Shawn prepares himself and reveals his uncertainties and fears. Will he, he wonders, fail to be funny? Is it, he suggests, really possible to do comedy? He muses upon the disappearance of such onetime luminaries as Mort Sahl, Lenny Bruce and Shelly Berman; wonders, too, who he is and perhaps even who cares. He even discusses Thanksgiving, pondering whether it wasn't established to get rid of all those turkeys because of their ugliness.

He is, in essence, a broken-down comedian trying out his lines before going on. The jokes — intentionally — are not good and proceed to get worse, even going so far as to resurrect the old chestnut: "Melancholy Baby — head like a melon; body like a collie."

In the second act, supposedly set on a Las Vegas stage, he does imitations of Sammy Davis, Frankie Laine and others, perhaps as a dream or a recollection of the dishevelled figure of the previous act, perhaps simply as mockery. But he isn't in Las Vegas at all, still in the same essentially tacky theatre, but now really about to go on.

Opened June 2, 1977
Closed August 1977

With: Dick Shawn

"What's the point? Mr. Shawn may feel that comedy is dead, but he tends to make us think that it is his fault." — Richard Eder, *The New York Times (6-3-77, p. C 3)*

"Not being a playwright, Shawn and his excellent idea are victimized by his own limitations as a craftsman of theater and the eccentricity of his personal performing style. So, Shawn's play . . . is on the one hand reserved for his personal fans and on the other fails as a dramatic event. But it fails honorably for despite much trite philosophizing and haphazard construction it rises to a peak of considerable power and Shawn himself into the performance with great energy and conviction." — Martin Gottfried, *The New York Post (6-3-77)*

"The comedian's anguish is genuine and moving. . . . His routines about politics and contemporary events are nowhere as profound as his apostrophe to the banana . . . or as funny as his savage satire on the performer he most despises. He'll work it out. He's crazy and I think I love him." — Marilyn Stasio, *Cue (6-25—7-8-77, p. 89)*

"Dick Shawn is a manic human pinwheel spinning off a shower of satiric comic sparks that shine more often than they scald. One feels that Shawn intended it just that way. . . . Shawn clearly relishes casual irreverence, pungent social commentary and the hatpin thrust that punctures hypocrisy and pomposity. . . . He can range nimbly, and with surprising freshness." — T. E. Kalem, *Time (6-13-77, p. 89)*

The Square Root of Soul

Adolph Caesar

Conceived and acted by Adolph Caesar. Presented by the Negro Ensemble Company; direction and lighting by Perry Schwartz; musical score by Jothan Callins; stage manager, Michael Nunley; Theatre de Lys, 121 Christopher Street.

Adolph Caesar, best known for his roles with the Negro Ensemble Company, has selected a group of poems and other pieces, approximately 40 of them, to depict the black experience in America through a dramatic monologue. In theory, he is a black actor awaiting a testimonial dinner for him which is about to begin.

Among the works are a folk ballad about a plantation party by Paul Laurence Dunbar, Countee Cullen's account of a lynching, Oscar Brown, Jr.'s "Forty Acres and a Mule," James Weldon Johnson's "Since You Went Away" and a selection from Joseph Walker's play *The River Niger*.

Opened June 14, 1977
Closed July, 1977

With: Adolph Caesar

REVIEWS

"He can be a good performer, sometimes wry, sometimes harsh, often moving; and he is best when he is not simply reciting the poems, but acting out some character or attitude in them. Yet the whole concept does not come off very well. Perhaps it forces things too much. An anthology of poems is one thing; a collage is another. Here they do not seem to want to stick together; the themes may be similar, but the tone and, more important, the quality, vary greatly.... There were too many occasions when Mr. Caesar's appealing efforts to [hold the evening together] only made evident the frailty of his poems." — Richard Eder, *The New York Times (6-15-77, p. C 20)*

"What can you say about an anthology after you've said it's spotty? . . . The potpourri is an indiscriminate celebration of the poetic impulse, with Caesar's love the only organizing factor. . . . The reading is marred only by the programmatic stage effects that pop up predictably throughout the evening. . . . *Square Root of Soul* offers a little something for everyone. And not much for anyone in particular." — Sylviane Gold, *New York Post (6-15-77)*

"Skillfully transformed into an exciting and moving theatre piece. . . . A fine actor with a resonant voice, Caesar commands the stage throughout." — *Variety (7-13-77, p. 66)*

Unsung Cole

Gene Lindsey, Mary Louise, Anita Morris and John Sloman

A musical entertainment conceived and staged by Norman L. Berman. Presented by the Circle Repertory Company; music and vocal arrangements by Mr. Berman; additional music and vocal arrangements by Leon Odenz; music direction by Mr. Odenz; choreography by Dennis Grimaldi; setting by Peter Harvey; costumes by Carol Oditz; lighting by Arden Fingerhut; production stage manager, Amy Schechter. Circle Repertory Theatre, 99 Seventh Avenue South.

Unsung Cole is made up of 32 rarely performed Cole Porter songs, some of which were cut from Broadway shows prior to their opening. It opens with the entire company in "Farming," from the musical *Let's Face It* and, during its two acts, moves on to include numbers from such other Porter shows as *The New Yorkers, Fifty Million Frenchmen, Red Hot and Blue, Silk Stockings, Mexican Hayride, Kiss Me, Kate* and *Anything Goes*.

Opened June 18, 1977
Closed September 4, 1977

With: Gene Lindsey, Mary Louise, Maureen Moore, Anita Morris, John Sloman

REVIEWS

"Teeters fascinatingly between delight and bareness. Without his best songs, it was Cole Porter with his right arm tied behind his back. But what a left arm he had! . . . They are sung by five performers with the help of serviceable but uninspired choreography, and acting that ranges from wooden to sparkling. And with the hindrance of the set. . . . In the second part both the material and the performances pick up." – Richard Eder, *The New York Times (6-24-77, p. C 3)*

"The songs in *Unsung Cole* tend to have first-class Porter lyrics and second-class Porter melodies. . . . Not just for die-hard Porter freaks, it is a show for all musical lovers and if not overwhelming it is certainly engaging." – Martin Gottfried, *New York Post (6-24-77, p. 38)*

"A delightful musical evening in the theatre. . . . The bright, witty lyrics that are synonymous with the Porter name come through fine and seemed to give enormous pleasure to the capacity audience. The cast . . . come through admirably. . . . Norman L. Berman, who conceived and staged the show deserves high praise, not only for his staging but for his vocal arrangements as well." – *Variety (6-29-77, p. 66)*

"*Unsung Cole* left me with a renewed sense of Porter's limitations rather than his talents. Mr. Berman has not chosen his songs altogether shrewdly. [His] staging is busy and fussy; it gets in the way. . . . But it could have been worse." – Julius Novick, *The Village Voice (7-11-77, p. 63)*

Children of Adam

The Cast

A musical in one act, with music and lyrics by Stan Satlin. Presented by John A. Vaccaro and James J. Wisner, in association with R. Anthony Zeiger; conceived and directed by John Driver; musical direction and vocal arrangements by Jimmy Wisner; setting by Ernest Allen Smith; lighting by Robert F. Strohmeier; costumes by Polly P. Smith; choreography by Ruella Frank; production stage manager, Sari E. Weisman. Chelsea Westside Theatre, 407 West 43rd Street.

Against the theme of "the span of a lifetime," six performers move from the "myth" of the Garden of Eden to the realities of adolescence, love, marriage and parenthood.

Among the more than two dozen songs (there is no dialog) are the opening of lifetime, reflected in "Mr. and Mrs. Myth"; the progression to speech, in "What's Your Name?"; a high school dance, to the music of "Move Along"; and the discovery of sex in "Sex Is Animal."

Opened August 17, 1977
Closed October 9, 1977

With: Gene Bua, Elizabeth Lathram, Karen Phillipp, Robert Polenz, Roger Rathburn, Carole Schweid

REVIEWS

"Count on this upbeat little show to be resolutely affirmative. The fact is that this is a skein of songs, innocent and amiable, but stretched porously thin as an evening's entertainment. . . . What is irritating in an otherwise innocuous evening is the lyrics, which are based on the monotonous notion that once you choose a word or a line, why change it? . . . However, the cast is fresh and likable. . . . The director lets the show sing for itself, which may not be an entirely wise decision." — Mel Gussow, *The New York Times (8-18-77, p. C 13)*

"If you're one of those people who like airline magazines, Muzak and light verse, you might want to see *Children of Adam*. It's harmless enough; the company sings well, works hard and smiles a lot; the songs are inoffensively undistinguished; the staging is slick; the cabaret ambience is pleasing. But if pap is not your cup of tea, forget it." — Sylviane Gold, *New York Post (8-18-77)*

"A welcome addition to the current off-Broadway lineup . . . a charming musical. . . . On hand to perform the tunes are six young, attractive and talented performers . . . who are equipped with the necessary vocal credentials to turn the evening of song into a celebration of life, love and human growth, which becomes an uplifting theatrical experience. Satlin's music, which is primarily sentimental (and why not), except for the rock and gospel tunes, is refreshingly melodious, and his lyrics, although simple and direct, succeed in revealing the truth of the particular situation depicted." — *Variety (8-24-77, p. 67)*

Counsellor at Law

THE CAST

Bessie Green. . . . . Kent Wilson
Henry Susskind. . . . . .Raymond Faber
Sarah Becker . . . . .Madeline Shaw
Moreti. . . . . Charles Lutz
Zedorah Chapman. . . . . . . Maxine Taylor-Morris
Goldie Rindskopf . . . . Ann Saxman
Charles McFadden. . . . . .John Neary
John P. Tedesco . . . . .Leonard Di Sesa
A Bootblack. . . . . Charles Lutz
Regina Gordon . . . . Claudine Catania
Herbert Howard Weinberg. . . . . Robert Nersesian
Arthur Sandler . . . . .Jay Diamond
Lilian LaRue . . . . Kristen Christopher
A Messenger. . . . . Hart Faber
Roy Darwin . . . . Douglas Popper
George Simon. . . . . .George Guidall
Rigby Crayfield. . . . . .George Spelvin
Cora Simon . . . . .Carolyn Lenz
Lena Simon . . . . .Joan Turetzky
Peter J. Malone. . . . . .Mel Jurdem
Hirschberg. . . . . Charles Lutz
Johann Breitstein . . . . Richard Spore
David Simon. . . . . .Glenn Alterman
Harry Becker . . . . Ian Ehrlich
Richard Dwight, Jr.. . . . . Mike Shari
Dorothy Dwight . . . . .Valentina Fratti
Francis Clark Barid . . . . .Glen McClaskey

Claudine Catania and George Guidall

By Elmer Rice. The Quaigh Theatre production, presented by Jayne Wolf and the Hotel Diplomat; directed by Will Lieberson; setting and costumes by Christina Giannini; lighting by Bill McComb; sound by George Jacobs; production stage manager, Ted Mornel. Quaigh Theatre, Hotel Diplomat, 108 West 43rd Street.

Rice's melodrama, originally produced in 1939, has its share of dramatic clichés: the poor immigrant boy who made good as a criminal lawyer and regularly turns up on the front page, the proud mother and snobbish aristocratic wife and in-laws, the faithful and loving secretary, the doomed young rebel, the crisis over the lawyer's sole and in some ways admirable ethical transgression.

The lawyer, Simon, though on occasion greedy and ruthless, self-indulgent and devious, clearly is the subject of the playwright's fond attention and almost inevitably emerges a hero, though one who has to struggle right to the end, when it becomes clear that the right people will get together and the others get their comeuppance.

Opened September 6, 1977
Closed October 16, 1977

REVIEWS

"The pleasures in watching . . . may be archaic, but they are authentic. And they are worth pointing out, not only to praise the modest but highly successful production . . . but also because they remind us of one or two useful but not always noticed facts about theater." — Richard Eder, *The New York Times (9-8-77, p. B 13)*

"Basically seedy and the company is not fully up to professional standards. . . . Director Will Lieberson has taken this essentially interesting drama and given it an energetic production with strong performances in the leading roles. George Guidall is particularly effective as the attorney." — Martin Gottfried, *New York Post (9-7-77, p. 54)*

"I raced, gasping for deliverance, out into the street after the first act, which seemed to me twice as long as *The Ring of the Nibelung* and not half so funny." — John Simon, *New York (9-26-77, p. 61)*

"In the title role of George Simon, George Guidall is a dynamic presence, exuding self-confidence, and then self-doubt. . . . Director Will Lieberson has the large cast maneuvering skillfully about the one cramped law-office set." — Miranda Hendrickson, *Show Business (9-29-77, p. 22)*

"Rather than a piece of somber social commentary, *Counsellor* is a kind of breeze. . . . Lieberson's production is sluggish. His actors weigh every moment, consider every nuance, play every word. They *act*. By the time they're finished, three and a half hours have gone by." — Terry Curtis Fox, *The Village Voice (9-19-77, p. 82)*

Christopher Bernau

The Passion of Dracula

THE CAST

Jameson . . . . Brian Bell
Dr. Cedric Seward . . . . K. Lype O'Dell
Professor Van Helsing . . . . .Michael Burg
Dr. Helga Van Zandt . . . . .Alice White
Lord Gordon Godalming . . . . K. C. Wilson
Mr. Renfield . . . . .Elliott Vileen
Wilhelmina Murray . . . . Giulia Pagano
Jonathan Harker . . . . Samuel Maupin
Count Dracula . . . . .Christopher Bernau

REVIEWS

"Eventually the lack of any definite purpose catches up with things. What is funny becomes silly; what is silly becomes boring. But for the first two acts or so, its cheerful incongruities coupled with several interesting performances keep things reasonably entertaining. . . . Mr. Bernau . . . achieves a fine balance between the awesome and the ridiculous." — Richard Eder, *The New York Times (9-30-77, p. C 3)*

"It is, first of all, not uninteresting. . . . Unfortunately, however, the authors and their director — Peter Bennett — distrusted the materials enough to turn regularly to mockery and the tongue in cheek." — Martin Gottfried, *New York Post (9-30-77, p. 52)*

"Campiness is not intrusive, however, and the play moves with the brisk tempo and sustained suspense of a good detective story." — T. E. Kalem, *Time (10-31-77, p. 93)*

"A quite stylish and unpretentious pastiche of prewar English upper-class drama. . . . Under the exceptional direction of Peter Bennett, the performance maintains that style throughout. . . . The play is very well cast." — Edith Oliver, *The New Yorker (10-10-77, p. 92)*

"A piece of winsome foolishness. . . . There is funny dialogue; excellent use of the small stage . . . and performing that is likable even when less than polished." — Alan Rich, *New York (10-17-77, p. 124)*

"A thoroughly entertaining show. Thanks to the performances of a fine cast, imaginative and intelligent staging, and a number of impressive special effects, this first presentation [of the season] of the chiller deserves a lengthy run." — *Variety (11-2-77, p. 87)*

By Bob Hall and David Richmond. Presented by the Dracula Theatrical Company, Eric Krebs, executive producer; directed by Peter Bennett; sets by Bob Hall and Allen Cornell; costumes by Jane Tschetter; lighting by Mr. Cornell; production stage manager, Andrea Naier. Cherry Lane Theatre, 38 Commerce Street.

The Passion of Dracula is loosely based on Bram Stoker's legendary novel and takes place in 1911 in the study of Dr. Cedric Seward, who operates a mental institution adjoining his house.

Dracula appears, dressed in crushed velvet evening clothes and cape and lusting for blood, preferably that of the young woman he is seeking for his bride. A young reporter has, however, fallen desperately in love with the girl and, no little aided by a Dutch psychologist who is called in to solve the mystery of what has been happening to Count Dracula's victims, proceeds to contribute his share to this admittedly camp version of the ever-popular and frequently adapted novel.

Opened September 28, 1977

The Present Tense

Jim Cyrus and Lianne Kressin

Written by the cast, Stephen Rosenfield, Haila Strauss and Ralph Buckley, and head writer Jeff Sweet; music and lyrics by Allen Cohen, Bob Joseph, Alan Menken, Muriel Robinson, Don Siegal, Jeff Sweet and Lee S. Wilkof. Presented by Roger Ailes and John Fishback, with the Comedy Club Company; directed by Stephen Rosenfield; musical director, Skip Kennon; scenery and costumes by Paul DePass; lighting by John Fishback; assistant director, Haila Strauss; associate producer, Norma Ferrer; production stage manager, Haila Strauss. Park Royal Theatre, 23 West 73rd Street.

The collaborative work of a group of young writers and composers, the Comedy Club Company, *The Present Tense* opens with a series of brief exchanges among the six performers, which relate primarily to modern social hangups. "You have to believe in something," one character insists. "I do," another responds. "What?" "Anxiety."

This is the tenor of *The Present Tense* and it is embodied in scenes involving Sarah Lawrence students, a New York labor leader who sings about the city's fiscal travails, two former radicals who have succeeded in life and a third who has not and one about an average citizen who receives a series of phone calls from President Carter who is seeking advice.

Opened October 4, 1977
Closed October 23, 1977

With: Barbara Brummel, Chris Carroll, Jim Cyrus, Lianne Kressin, Michael Nobel and Lee S. Wilkof

REVIEWS

"A series of topical skits and songs that aim at easy targets, hit a few and miss quite a few. Five of the cast range from very talented to simply agreeable. The sixth is Lee S. Wilkof. The five embellish their material, but when it runs dry, as it frequently does, they run aground. Mr. Wilkof, a genuine comic, generates his own water and walks on it. . . . It is not quite right to say that Mr. Wilkof saves the show from what it is, despite its fresh performances, an amiable mediocrity. He doesn't save it; he alternates with it, and most hilariously." — Richard Eder, *The New York Times (10-5-77, p. C 20)*

"There's nothing about this kind of intimate show that is pin-pointably out-of-date. It's just the overall approach. . . . On balance it's a pleasant enough entertainment even though the room feels like the bingo parlor of a seedy cruise liner and the show an entertainment rustled up for the overnight to Bayonne. . . . The show skips inconsistently from subject to subject. Some sketches are funny until their punch lines, some songs make no sense at all." — Martin Gottfried, *New York Post (10-5-77, p. 54)*

"In the show as a whole, a kind of cheerful self-mockery takes the place of satire . . . and although the evening is agreeable enough, it rarely takes off unless Mr. Wilkof is onstage." — Edith Oliver, *The New Yorker (10-17-77, p. 96)*

"Hopefully, the show is free enough to grow as it is performed, so that it can change or discard some of the flat moments. . . . The . . . main weakness is the tendency to end some of these acts too routinely." — Christopher Sharp, *Women's Wear Daily (10-5-77, p. 88)*

"The sketches never manage to be clever, and like balloons losing air, most suffer from chronically weak endings. . . . All six performers are personable, and Lee S. Wilkof is a standout comic." — Holly Hill, *New York Theatre Review (12-77, p. 43)*

Survival

Seth Sibanda, Selaelo Dan Maredi,
Fana David Kekana and Themba Ntinga

Written and performed by Fana David Kekana, Selaelo Dan Maredi, Themba Ntinga and Seth Sibanda. Originally directed and co-authored by Mshengu, with additional staging by Dean Irby. Presented by Clyde Kuemmerle, in association with the Negro Ensemble Company; setting by Mr. Kuemmerle; music by Mr. Maredi. Astor Place Theatre, 434 Lafayette Street.

"Our material is what ordinary people think and feel," the black creators of *Survival* state in the program. As such, the work is a collage of incidents in the lives of the black South Africans who make up the cast. It takes place in and out of jail and, they suggest, there is little difference for the black in Johannesburg, which they view as itself a prison. In one scene, for instance, a convict is released and discovers that he is so unnerved by the realities he finds outside that he allows himself to be re-incarcerated, where there is at least a degree of order. The food, however, is virtually inedible; sleep is regularly interrupted. It is only by saying "Thank you, Boss" when you are struck that it is possible to stay out of trouble.

In an effort to pass time, but also to understand their dilemma, the prisoners stage mock trials. The defendant is, of course, always guilty, even though he may not be aware of the nature of his offense. The enemy has two characteristics: he is not black and he is in power, and he prompts them to speculate "how many of those who hate us now won't one day wish that they, too, had been black."

Opened October 9, 1977
Closed

With: Fana David Kekana, Selaelo Dan Maredi, Themba Ntinga and Seth Sibanda

REVIEWS

"One could, perhaps, fault the evening for its artlessness and its familiarity, but that would overlook much more important qualities — its authenticity, its fierce commitment to humanity and its effectiveness as indictment. . . . *Survival* is a sobering plea for justice and solidarity." — Mel Gussow, *The New York Times (10-10-77, p. 35)*

"It is only sometimes artistically viable and even less often professional in terms of structure and presentation. . . . However appalling the situation in South Africa and however righteous the idea of this work, it is being presented as professional theater and it doesn't meet the standards." — Martin Gottfried, *New York Post (10-10-77, p. 18)*

"A necessary reminder of one of the world's great injustices, executed with suavity and irony, a disciplined anger and an astounding amount of humor and undistorted humanity. . . . As art, *Survival* may be amateurish; it is terribly professional as living history." — John Simon, *New York (10-24-77, p. 85)*

"It is an attractive if somewhat slick ensemble. . . . The action is fast-paced, the ensemble is loud, energetic, and engaging." — Arthur Sainer, *The Village Voice (10-17-77, p. 90)*

"*Survival* is enraging but never depressing. The performance is stylized, the songs and dances are beautiful, and that energy is contagious. The acting, as the four players quickly switch from one characterization to another, is good." — Edith Oliver, *The New Yorker (10-24-77, p. 145)*

"A mixed bag of high purpose, wit, absurdity and horror." — Christopher Sharp, *Women's Wear Daily (10-11-77, p. 18)*

Landscape of the Body

By John Guare. Presented by the New York Shakespeare Festival, Joseph Papp, producer, Bernard Gersten, associate producer; directed by John Pasquin; music and lyrics by John Guare; setting and costumes by Santo Loquasto; lighting by Jennifer Tipton; musical arrangements and incidental music by Wally Harper; production stage manager, Stephen McCorkle. Public/Newman Theatre, 425 Lafayette Street.

John Guare's play opens on the deck of a Nantucket ferryboat, where Betty, a woman entering her forties, is seen writing notes, putting them in bottles and throwing them overboard. She is joined by a man wearing a Groucho Marx mask, who turns out to be a Greenwich Village detective who has been questioning her for several months concerning the murder of her fourteen-year-old son, and seeking to trap her into a confession.

Landscape of the Body then launches on a series of episodes and songs, involving fantasy, reality and monologues — in Betty's apartment, in the police station and, eventually, back on the ferry. At one point, Betty is seen working for a travel agency run by a Cuban transvestite; at another, a character named Raulito is killed by accident when he attempts to make a deposit in his Christmas Club account at the Chase Manhattan bank. Betty turns up in pornographic movies and takes to drugs. A former Good Humor man gives Betty a thousand dollars to run away with him.

At one point early in the second act, Betty's son Bert sings a song entitled "I Used to Believe," and it, as much as anything in Guare's deliberately idiosyncratic play, suggests its theme: that everything, especially death, is unpredictable and that life's enigma must be accepted by human beings who have come to recognize their mutual dilemma.

Opened October 12, 1977, for a limited engagement
Closed November 20, 1977

THE CAST

Betty . . . . Shirley Knight
Capt. Marvin Holahan. . . . . F. Murray Abraham
Rosalie . . . . Peg Murray
Raulito . . . . Richard Bauer
Bert . . . . Paul McCrane
Donny. . . . . Anthony Marciona
Joanne . . . . Alexa Kenin
Margie. . . . . Bonnie Deroski
Durwood Peach. . . . . Remak Ramsay
Masked Man, Dope King of Providence, Bank
    Teller . . . . Raymond J. Barry

Remak Ramsay, Shirley Knight and Paul McCrane

REVIEWS

"Set about with many ingenious devices, and with some authentically moving moments in it, it remains a play of language strung upon a mediocre structure supporting a melodrama that is often banal and sometimes grisly. . . . Some of the scenes themselves are very fine. . . . Mr. Guare has some haunting images and beautifully specific language in his exploration of illusions. . . . He is magnificently served by his two principal actors." — Richard Eder, *The New York Times* *(10-13-77, p. C 17)*

"If a waiter brought you *Landscape of the Body* you'd send it back. . . . [It] is not bitchy. It is merely unpleasant and boring. . . . The style is dead and had it not been, the outrageousness of the plot would have done the trick. . . . Guare cannot be pampered any longer." — Martin Gottfried, *New York Post (10-13-77, p. 26)*

"What an odd mixture of inspired comedy, sudden horror, and plain guff. . . . The form of the play may be catch as catch can, but it is filled with surprises and theatrical resourcefulness. It is also filled with good acting." — Edith Oliver, *The New Yorker (10-24-77, p. 144)*

"The impact of *Landscape of the Body* comes from the collision between goofy whimsy and stark horror. . . . Mr. Guare has no workable idea of how to get his heroine out of what he has gotten her into. The play is too long. The playwright is unsure how to begin it and how to end it, and there are cute, self-indulgent irrelevancies scattered through the middle." — Julius Novick, *The Village Voice (10-24-77, p. 107)*

"*Landscape of the Body* . . . isn't finally satisfactory but it's a ripening nonetheless. Mr. Guare's hand is growing firmer, his jovially jaundiced eye keener, as he draws blood with his biggest laughs, turns the palpably absurd into plain common sense." — Walter Kerr, *The New York Times (10-23-77, p. D 5)*

Feedlot

Jeff Daniels, Joseph Ragno and Mark J. Soper

THE CAST

Gene Harris . . . . Mark J. Soper
Wesley. . . . . .Jeff Daniels
Billy Fred . . . . Joseph Ragno
John . . . . .James Ray Weeks
Kelly. . . . . .Edward Seamon

By Patrick Meyers. Presented by the Circle Repertory Company; directed by Terry Schreiber; setting by Hal Tine; lighting by Dennis Parichy; costumes by Laura Crow; sound by Charles London; production stage manager, Amy Schecter. Circle Repertory Theatre, 99 Seventh Avenue South.

Patrick Meyers's first play is set in the control tower of a Texas feedlot, a cattleyard, where animals are stuffed for slaughter. It is almost antiseptic and the world itself is locked outside.

There are four men, three of them cowboys and the fourth a young college student. The characters at first seem to be "types." Three have pin-ups in their lockers; the fourth photographs of dancers. But *Feedlot* soon evolves into what is essentially a two-character play, a struggle between the college boy and the most aggressive of the cowboys, a war hero who has fought in Vietnam. They are natural enemies, but, surprisingly, it is the younger man who is the aggressor, who ridicules the other, questions his virility and threatens to blow up the feedlot. There is a homosexual rape, done in darkness, which somehow seems to point toward resolution and understanding.

Opened October 13, 1977, for a limited engagement
Closed November 27, 1977

REVIEWS

"[It] has a raw muscularity and a quiet intensity. It has its unsteady moments, but it deals forcefully with some provocative subjects: heroism, cowardice, and complicity in violence; aggressive masculinity and fear of homosexuality. . . . Despite the symbolic undercurrents, the play is naturalistic. The production . . . is straightforward. Mr. Schreiber and his cast give the work a tautness that is not always audible in the writing." — Mel Gussow, *The New York Times (10-14-77, p. C 3)*

"All the actors are competent or better, with Jeff Daniels being especially good as a puckishly funny youth." — Edmund Newton, *New York Post (10-14-77, p. 47)*

"Effective on the level of tough dialogue, violent action, suspense. . . . It is greatly aided, and made nerve tingling, by the acting, especially that of Joseph Ragno as the frightening and subsequently humiliated and appeased 'villain' of the piece." — Harold Clurman, *The Nation (11-12-77, p. 506)*

"The characters are as dramatic as Texas verism can get, and the events are either exceptional or unlikely, depending on your mood. But director Terry Schreiber has skillfully created a context in which excessive personalities and unlikely events make sense." — Christopher Sharp, *Women's Wear Daily (10-17-77, p. 8)*

"Mr. Meyers need only reduce his restless exercize of a genuine ingenuity to manageable proportions. His excesses are an aspect of what is best about him: his theatrical energy, his willingness to go for broke, his love of a scene with a sting to it." — Walter Kerr, *The New York Times (11-13-77, p. D 3)*

Cockfight

Mary Alice and Gylan Kain

THE CAST

Reba . . . . Mary Alice
Sampson . . . . Morgan Freeman
Carl . . . . Charles Brown
Jesse . . . . Gylan Kain
Claudia . . . . Cynthia McPherson

By Elaine Jackson. Presented by the American Place Theatre, Wynn Handman, director, Julia Miles, associate director; directed by Woodie King, Jr.; set by C. Richard Mills; costumes by Ruth Morley; lighting by Edward M. Greenberg; production stage manager, Nancy Harrington. American Place Theatre, 111 West 46th Street.

A group of New York blacks have settled in the Bay Area of California where a converted farmhouse near San Francisco has been taken over by a young couple, Reba and Jesse. They — in particular Reba — have turned it into a not notably flourishing shop where they sell arts and crafts, fruit and puppies. Reba is enthusiastic about the project, while Jesse thinks about the book he may someday write and plays and sings in a country-western trio.

Another member of the trio, Carl, lives with — and off — them and it is with him that Jesse shares most of his ruminations. Two others appear, the sex-obsessed Claudia and her older counterpart, another country singer named Sampson, who eventually makes a play for Reba. Ms. Jackson seems, however, more interested in her feminist theme, and in the thought that "Black women bring the reality of life crashing down on black men" than in the actual fate of her characters.

Opened October 16, 1977, for a limited engagement
Closed October 30, 1977

REVIEWS

"*Cockfight* is a play not merely stuffed with a lesson but overstuffed. It also is incessantly didactic, and the lessons are of a vast and obvious ordinariness. The characters are stereotypes and not less so because it is only in the last dozen years or so that we have been made aware of what they are intended to illustrate. Miss Jackson adorns these stereotypes with a good ear for language and occasional wit. Her characters often speak well, but it is hard to advance very far dramatically with a stage full of men who are pre-defined as infantile, and a woman who is pre-defined as overanxious." — Richard Eder, *The New York Times (10-17-77, p. 39)*

"The American Place Theatre has come upon a playwright of uncertain technique but definite talent and her first major play develops from a vague, over-talkative opening act to a conclusion of considerable playability, vigor and feeling." — Martin Gottfried, *New York Post (10-17-77, p. 27)*

"Miss Jackson has quite a satiric ear and the makings of a humorist, and she may, indeed be headed in that direction. *Cockfight* is not a funny play, although there is humor in it; the heroine is, and feels herself to be, too much a victim for that, while the character of Carl is almost deformed by the dramatist's contempt for him. That of Jesse doesn't fare very well either." — Edith Oliver, *The New Yorker (10-31-77, p. 116)*

"It turns out structureless and murky. The main characters, Reba and Jesse, aren't consistent enough to illustrate a thesis; nor do they, on the other hand, have the depth and poetry of real people seen close up." — Erika Munk, *The Village Voice (11-7-77, p. 83)*

"A tedious, pointless drama. . . . A humor that depends largely on cliches provides the only relief from the choppy, mediocre script." — L. M. Evers, *Show Business (10-27-77, p. 23)*

"The play takes a heavy-handed look at the dissolution of a marriage and why the break-up is occurring, but one gets the impression that the playwright was striving for much more than what is appearing on stage. There are too many texts and sub-texts running through this work, and the result is a rambling, ponderous script." — Leah D. Frank, *New York Theatre Review (12-77, p. 44)*

You Never Can Tell

Sarah-Jane Gwillim, Rachel Gurney,
Curt Dawson and Kristie Thatcher

By George Bernard Shaw. Presented by the Roundabout Theatre Company; directed by Tony Tanner; setting by Timothy Galvin; lighting by Richard Butler; costumes by V. Jane Suttell; score by Philip Campanella; hairstyles by Paul Huntley; production stage manager, Tom Gould. Roundabout/Stage One, 333 West 23rd Street.

Shaw's 1897 comedy deals with the events that follow upon the return to England of an aging suffragette named Mrs. Clandon. She brings with her a twenty-year-old daughter and eighteen-year-old twins. In the period she has been living abroad in Madagascar, separated from her husband, she has been raising the children in a manner considered "advanced" when she left England. Now, she finds those ideas supplanted by others and her children discover they have not been properly prepared for English life. The eldest daughter, for instance, soon realizes that intelligence is no protection against the old-fashioned concept of love; the twins that their lack of inhibition is regarded as "bad manners." To add confusion, they unexpectedly meet their father, a very conservative Victorian, who insists that he now be allowed to raise the twins, much to everyone's horror. There is a happy ending of sorts, brought about by an elderly waiter and his lawyer son.

Opened October 18, 1977, for a limited engagement
Closed October 30, 1977

THE CAST

Dolly . . . . .Kristie Thatcher
Valentine. . . . . .Curt Dawson
Philip . . . . .Richard Niles
Mrs. Clandon . . . . .Rachel Gurney
Gloria. . . . . .Sarah-Jane Gwillim
Mr. Crampton. . . . . Ralph Clanton
Walter (William) . . . . Norman Barrs
M'Comas. . . . . Richard Neilson
Bohun. . . . . .David Sabin
First Waiter . . . . .Jeff Passero
Second Waiter. . . . . John Savage

REVIEWS

"Despite the Roundabout's claim that the play is 'startlingly modern,' it seems stuffily old-fashioned. . . . Miss Gurney . . . along with several other actors, brings a certain vivacity to an otherwise tedious exercise in exhumation. . . . This is minimal Shaw, with no surprises." — Mel Gussow, *The New York Times (10-18-77, p. 32)*

"One of Shaw's grandest and most expansive plays. . . . Unfortunately the Roundabout Theatre has done just about everything it could to hide its charm in the new production. . . . The fun of this play is in the playing and it calls for style and technique — a call this Roundabout production isn't remotely capable of answering." — Martin Gottfried, *New York Post (10-18-77, p. 57)*

"It has been well cast — no brilliance or star acting but everything in keeping — and the performance, under Tony Tanner's direction, trips merrily along, never impeding the script or muffing any of its points." — Edith Oliver, *The New Yorker (10-31-77, p. 118)*

"This production is very satisfying as it is directed by Tony Tanner. The cast is one of the strongest that the Roundabout has ever put together." — Christopher Sharp, *Women's Wear Daily (10-18-77, p. 42)*

Ellis Rabb

A Life in the Theatre

By David Mamet. Presented by Jane Harmon; directed by Gerald Gutierrez; incidental music by Robert Waldman; scenery by John Lee Beatty; lighting by Pat Collins; costumes by John David Ridge; production stage manager, Frank Hartenstein. Theatre de Lys, 121 Christopher Street.

Two actors, Robert and John, are seen preparing backstage for performances and on stage in bits from various plays. They "go up" on (forget) lines, suffer the embarrassment of breaking a costume fly zipper, miss entrances and generally less than shine. At first, the older Robert is the obvious mentor and John merely the subservient apprentice. But John begins to enjoy some success and there is considerable role reversal which finds the veteran becoming increasingly insecure and dependent.

Opened October 19, 1977

THE CAST

John. . . . . .Peter Evans
Robert . . . . .Ellis Rabb
Stage Manager. . . . . Benjamin Hendrickson

REVIEWS

"A short play written with humor, affection and sophistication. It is an evening of pure theater . . . featuring an exhilarating performance. by Ellis Rabb as the older of two actors. . . . Though the work has serious undertones, it is, first of all, a comedy — and Mr. Mamet's language glistens. His writing is a cross between the elegant and the vernacular, an ironic combination that is uniquely his own. . . . Ellis Rabb wears his role as if it were a tailor-made theatrical cape of many colors. He gives a grand performance." — Mel Gussow, *The New York Times (10-21-77, p. C 3)*

"Sends you out of the Theatre de Lys feeling marvelous and filled with love for the theater, for actors and for humanity in general. [It] overflows with good feeling and humanism. It confirms [Mamet's] profound abilities. It is surely the warmest (and often the funniest) play in town." — Martin Gottfried, *New York Post (10-21-77, p. 42)*

"Comforting platitudes, burlesque mishaps, greasepainted lies from among which a grinning truth now and then sallies on its deadly mission — all the love-hate of fellow actors is here in its gaudy sadomasochism, scarcely less lacerating for being platonic." — John Simon, *New York (11-7-77, p. 75)*

"Ellis Rabb can tango with words and he is a sly devil at milking an audience dry of laughter. Peter Evans' John rolls his lines like dice in a crap game he dare not lose. For Mamet, this play is a five-finger exercise, but so nimble that he often seems to be using ten." — T. E. Kalem, *Time (10-31-77, p. 94)*

"The brilliant David Mamet play . . . provide[s] devastating looks at backstage actor traumas. But it does so in such an engagingly funny and poignant way, that more universal human truths are strengthened rather than overshadowed in trivia." — *Variety (11-16-77, p. 92)*

"[A] beautiful, wonderfully theatrical play." — Howard Kissel, *Women's Wear Daily (10-24-77, p. 10)*

Naked

Nina Dova, Larkin Ford and Lucien Zabielski

By Luigi Pirandello. Presented by the Round-about Theatre Company; directed by Gene Feist; setting by Ron Antone; lighting by Robert Strohmeier; costumes by Nancy L. Johnson; sound sequences by Philip Campanella; production stage manager, Paul Moser. Roundabout/Stage Two, 302 West 26th Street.

Written in 1923, *Naked* is set in Rome in the late 1920s and attempts to portray the types of myth men create to organize their lives. Like most of Pirandello's plays, it deals with such themes as reality and illusion and the nature of identity.

A young governess named Ersilia Drei attempts to commit suicide because she has been abandoned by her lover and dismissed by her mistress, who is married to the consul at Smyrna, after the death of his child in an accident. The press makes a great deal of her saga and Ersilia quickly becomes the talk of the city. She is taken into the home of an aging novelist who pretends to have disinterested motives. In time it emerges that the baby had died while in her care as she was engaged in her romantic pursuits. The novelist takes inspiration from her plight, but, finally, she dies in a second suicide attempt.

Opened October 24, 1977
Closed December 31, 1977

THE CAST

Ersilia Drei . . . . Fran Brill
Ludovico Nota . . . . Larkin Ford
Signora Onoria . . . . .Nina Dova
Alfredo Cantavalle . . . . .Philip Campanella
Franco Laspiga .Lucien Zabielski
Grotti . . . . .Gordon Gould

REVIEWS

"It is a difficult play, talky and convoluted in argument. The Roundabout production may not be the ideal performance — but it is no disappointment. . . . Gene Feist's direction tends to rush the pace, especially in the first half. His people read their lines as if they were in a French farce. The words come across, but the flavor is lost. Matters do improve in the second half. . . . It makes for a provocative evening in the theater." — Thomas Lask, *The New York Times (10-25-77, p. 46)*

"Director Gene Feist's solution to the dilemma of a rather talky, ponderous play seems to have been 'Keep the actors moving, even if it means using every old-fashioned, stylized gesture in the book.' The result is a constant, irritating awareness of actors acting, an awareness that doesn't really let up until the final touching scene." — Edmund Newton, *New York Post (10-25-77, p. 52)*

"Brill is affecting as the governess, Gould radiates sensual magnetism as her employer lover, and Zabielski is ardent and elegant as the ex-fiancé. But the dry winy brilliance of Pirandello dominates the evening." — T. E. Kalem, *Time (11-14-77, p. 61)*

"In effect, we have half of Pirandello's play. Ersilia is a naked, tragic personality, and is presented that way, but all this Gene Feist production does is drum this portrait into our heads. . . . The Roundabout did eliminate one character in this production, and considering the wooden performances by four of the six performers here, maybe we should be grateful." — Christopher Sharp, *Women's Wear Daily (10-25-77, p. 16)*

"Gene Feist demonstrates an appreciation for the impulsiveness and ambiguity that color the action in this eloquent drama." — P. Gregory Speck, *Show Business (10-27-77, p. 27)*

Brontosaurus

Tanya Berezin

THE CAST

Antiques Dealer . . . . Tanya Berezin
Assistant . . . . Sharon Madden
Nephew. . . . . .Jeff Daniels

By Lanford Wilson. Presented by the Circle Repertory Company; directed by Daniel Irvine; lighting by Gary Seltzer; costumes by Laura Crow; music selections by Norman L. Berman; sound by Charles S. London; stage manager, Andrew Mishkind. Circle Repertory Theatre, 99 Seventh Avenue South.

A prosperous, sophisticated, middle-aged New York antiques dealer invites her young nephew, whom she hardly knows, to stay with her at her apartment. She is unmarried and he, preparing for the ministry. He tells her of a incident in his life when he thought he had been touched by the hand of God. Despite his poverty, his ascetic ways cause him to reject both her hospitality and attempts at communication. After he moves out, in favor of staying with some friends who share his attitudes toward contemporary society, the woman feels her apparently superficial lifestyle has been challenged. Not that she is too likely to change, for she is the "brontosaurus" of the title, the representative, even relic, of the past. She can, however, accept her life, despite its trivial aspects, its disappointments and its loneliness.

Opened October 25, 1977, for a limited engagement
Closed November 18, 1977

REVIEWS

"*Brontosaurus* could be — and almost is — a monologue. The third and most minor character, Miss Berezin's assistant, is largely silent, someone for the antiques dealer to look at when she is talking. The youth, potentially the second character, is undeveloped. The heroine's struggle with him is no contest. . . . Although essentially a one-character sketch, *Brontosaurus* is pungent and incisive." — Mel Gussow, *The New York Times* (10-27-77, p. C 17)

"A one-hour piece which is less a drama than a statement of or an approach to an attitude. It is gracefully, though perhaps too self-consciously, written, interesting in its suggestion of a present-day dilemma. . . . Ms. Berezin has been an impressive actress; she always makes us feel that we are in the presence of a *person*, not merely a stage instrument." — Harold Clurman, *The Nation (11-26-77, p. 571)*

"The play . . . is more of a runaway intellectual exercise than it is presentation of characters and action. . . . [It] ultimately traps itself in its own high-mindedness. Tanya Berezin does an admirable job with the aunt, but her effort is limited by the play to recital rather than acting." — Christopher Sharp, *Women's Wear Daily (10-27-77, p. 12)*

"Wilson's one-liners are often hysterically funny, as are the boy's far less frequent replies. What rankles is not the ease with which Wilson conveys his wit but the conventional use to which it is put. . . . *Brontosaurus* is what people mean whey they speak of an artist's 'right to fail.' This is a failure good enough not just to be staged, but to be seen." — Terry Curtis Fox, *The Village Voice (11-7-77, p. 84)*

Barbara Caruso and Christina Pickles

Chez Nous

By Peter Nichols. Presented by the Manhattan Theatre Club; directed by Lynne Meadow; associate director, Richard Maltby, Jr.; setting by John Conklin; costumes by Nanzi Adzima; lighting by Dennis Parichy; sound by George Hansen; associate director, Thomas Bullard; associate artistic director, Stephen Pascal; production stage manager, Maureen Lynett. Manhattan Theatre Club, 321 East 73rd Street.

Two English couples who are not exactly the best of friends have nonetheless chosen to vacation together in a converted barn in the south of France. One of the men is a successful pediatrician who has recently authored a book advocating sexual freedom, particularly for children. Their visiting friends prompt a crisis of sorts when it emerges that the first couple's newborn child is actually that of their teenage daughter, and seemingly was fathered by the other man. Nichols seems to suggest that the pediatrician has deserved it as punishment for writing his book. No one really seems overly concerned, though there is some talk about Dick, the pediatrician, and Diana, the apparent father's wife, going off together.

Opened October 26, 1977, for a limited engagement
Closed November 27, 1977

THE CAST

Dick, a pediatrician . . . . John Tillinger
Phil, an architect .Sam Waterston
Diana . . . . .Christina Pickles
Liz . . . . Barbara Caruso
Le Français . . . . Charles Mayer
Burt . . . . Jim Jansen
Zoe . . . . Linda Atkinson

REVIEWS

"[A] long session of wasted talents. . . . *Chez Nous* is endless artificial talk in an endlessly artificial situation. . . . The actors are quite wasted in this, strung out as they are on a jumbled set and with all too much to say." — Richard Eder, *The New York Times (11-7-77, p. 44)*

"The theater of this new play is marred only least by its smug and spurious moral superiority. Although the characters are very well defined and the writing polished, it has more of the magazine article than drama. Its details are the stuff of soap opera, and its ending is perfectly baffling. . . . The four central performances are excellent. . . . The overall uncertainty of tone and style make it a confused production of a confused and thematically annoying script." — Martin Gottfried, *New York Post (11-7-77, p. 55)*

"The characters in their changing relationships are not always clear or convincing; the plot sometimes seems to twist and turn for no particular reason. . . . Still, *Chez Nous* is the kind of play I like: a nice, realistic, ironic British play about articulate, 'civilized' people. . . . And there really is some fine playwriting in it, where you are led to expect cliché and given instead a couple of humane, believable, highly satisfactory small surprises." — Julius Novick, *The Village Voice (11-21-77, p. 84)*

"This is an unsteady little comedy about two English couples . . . engaged in rustication, reminiscences, a bit of adultery and ill feeling, some pontification . . . and other unessential existential speculations. . . . As I gravitated out of the theater at midpoint, I wondered why this most inept of actors [Sam Waterston] keeps getting good roles and lavish reviews instead of being booed off the stage." — John Simon, *New York (11-21-77, p. 106)*

Rum an Coca Cola

By Mustapha Matura. Presented by the Chelsea Theatre Center, Robert Kalfin, artistic director, Michael David, executive director; by arrangement with Oscar Lewenstein; directed by Donald Howarth; setting by Wolfgang Roth; costumes by Debra J. Stein; lighting by William Mintzer; steel band leader, Kurt Nurse; production stage manager, Bob Jaffe. Brooklyn Academy of Music, 30 Lafayette Avenue; Chelsea Westside Theatre, 407 West 43rd Street.

Rum an Coca Cola, by the Trinidadian playwright Mustapha Matura, depicts the strains of attempting to cope with life in a poor Third World nation.

Matura employs the image of a declining calypso singer, a deposed and now rum-soaked former king of calypso, and how he reacts and is reacted to by a young disciple named Bird as they sit near the sea and attempt to compose a new calypso for a competition. The young and eager Bird makes suggestion after suggestion, but it is up to Creator to reject or refine them. They work out a song about the Minister of Works and Communications and his adventures with another man's wife, and tension develops between them; between the man in his declining days and the younger one anxious to move ahead. Several times, they are interrupted and stop to sing distinctive versions of "Rum and Coca Cola" and "Mary Ann," which they view with contempt, as they view the decline of culture through commercialization. They do their commercial songs in a nightclub until Creator, frustrated, is beaten up and thrown out. Bird, meanwhile, meets an American girl who offers to finance them until they can complete their song. But it does more harm than good for Creator and finally prompts a violent ending.

Opened October 26, 1977, at the Chelsea Theatre
    Center, Brooklyn
Closed October 30, 1977
Opened November 2, 1977, at the Chelsea Westside
    Theatre
Closed November 20, 1977

THE CAST

Creator . . . . .Leon Morenzie
Bird . . . . Lou Ferguson
Steel Band . . . . .Kurt Nurse,
            Brian Griffith, Winston Phillips

Leon Morenzie and Lou Ferguson

REVIEWS

"By the time it ends it has foundered badly. But its first half-hour or so is brilliant, and even when it begins to go downhill Mr. Matura's gifts and the fine performances of its two actors smooth the descent." — Richard Eder, *The New York Times* (10-27-77, p. C 17)

"An absorbing and challenging play that manages to work on the story and symbolic levels consistently. . . . The play is nearly always involving and it rides a real tension created by the contrast between the two men's high spirits and the ever present tragedy of their situation. . . . Donald Howarth has directed the production with an understanding of the author's purposes and tone. . . . This is the kind of original, stimulating theater that has made Chelsea's reputation." — Martin Gottfried, *New York Post* (10-27-77, p. 45)

"A funny, deeply serious play — a good play, too. . . . The play is subtle and pervasive. . . . The acting, under Donald Howarth's masterly direction, is superb." — Edith Oliver, *The New Yorker* (11-7-77, p. 105)

"The inherent merit of the play is not in its story but in its feeling: a sweet humanity, a songlike quality of language and speech. . . . Both Leon Morenzie as the Creator and the handsome Lou Ferguson as Bird are natural, funny and winning players who authentically savor of the island soil." — Harold Clurman, *The Nation* (10-19-77, p. 540)

"There are times in the middle of the work when the story simply wanders. But there are more interesting moments in this work than there are in many more perfectly constructed new plays." — Christopher Sharp, *Women's Wear Daily* (10-28-77, p. 10)

A Man and His Women

Craig Russell as Carol Channing

Craig Russell

REVIEWS

"One or two camped-up female impersonations . . . will seem like too many to a lot of people. A whole evening of them has a more universal claim to being excessive. . . . The effects become increasingly pointless. . . . With one or two exceptions, Mr. Russell captures only the most superficial traits of gesture or voice. At best, his targets are merely recognizable, and nothing more." — Richard Eder, *The New York Times* (11-3-77, p. C 17)

"He just seems to flow effortlessly from an incoherent Peggy Lee to an implacably cheerful Dinah Shore to an exuberantly unhinged Farrah Fawcett, and so on, using a variety of gowns and multi-purpose wigs, a pitiless eye for the comical and some badly obscene gestures to bring his characters to life. It's a brilliantly calculated performance, which almost — not quite — levitates from nightclub act to legitimate theater. . . . The show probably offers as much entertainment as any Vegas act, and as much of a mental challenge. Maybe that's all you should expect." — Edmund Newton, *New York Post* (11-7-77, p. 20)

"[A] marvelous revue. . . . Russell does an amazing range of 'women.' . . . In every case the voice is perfect. . . . Russell's physical movements are not always as perfectly on target as his vocal work. . . . Though occasionally the language gets raunchy and some of the wit is scathing . . . the tone is basically healthy and good humored." — Howard Kissel, *Women's Wear Daily* (11-1-77, p. 36)

"For the most part, good clean fun; for the rest, it is good not-so-clean fun. . . . He is a gifted and personable entertainer. But what he does in his own one-man and many-women show is even more exhilarating than his movie audience might expect. . . . With his vocal pinpoint accuracy, his stinging appositeness of gesture, and a wit that bubbles, crackles, or flashes as the occasion calls for, Russell is more fun singlehandedly than all but one or two of the current Broadway attractions with all hands combining." — John Simon, *New York* (11-21-77, p. 105)

Presented by Jonathan Scharer in association with Stephen Novick; music director, Stephen Stucker; gowns by Tony Marando; sound by Bob Casey; lighting by Consolidated Edification; stage manager, Nicholas Plain. Theatre East, 211 East 60th Street.

Female impersonator Craig Russell portrays a variety of famous female performers, ranging from Anita Bryant through Carol Channing, Bette Midler, Barbra Streisand, Judy Garland, Mae West, Ethel Merman and Marlene Dietrich. Generally, they are presented in scenes or parodies of some of their better-known film or stage roles.

Mr. Russell, who is best known for his work in the Canadian film *Outrageous,* is supported by a four-man band led by Stephen Stucker at the piano.

Opened October 31, 1977
Closed January 20, 1978

Starring Craig Russell

Hot Grog

A musical, with book by Jim Wann, music and lyrics by Jim Wann and Bland Simpson. Presented by the Phoenix Theatre, T. Edward Hambleton, managing director; Daniel Freudenberger, artistic director; directed by Edward Berkeley; setting and lighting by James Tilton; costumes by Hilary Rosenfeld; musical direction by Jeff Waxman; musical staging by Patricia Birch; stage manager, James Harker. Marymount Manhattan Theatre, 221 East 71st Street.

The authors, who previously came up with the successful *Diamond Studs,* again have selected a legendary outlaw as the subject for their creative efforts. In this case it is the pirate Edward Teach, better known as Blackbeard. He and his followers are presented as a straggly, accident-prone group which tries to mull its rum by adding gunpower, but succeeds only in blowing things up. They enter into a less than happy partnership with the Governor of North Carolina, who connives with them, though tepidly objecting to their ability to find supposedly "abandoned" vessels in the middle of Charleston harbor. He winds up hanging them, which puts him in the disfavor of his daughter, Anne Bonney, who has fallen in love with one of the pirates. A duel to the death between the pirate and Anne's former fiancé, a southern policeman, ensues, but comes to a halt when she reveals that she has discovered "a perfect sand dollar."

Opened October 14, 1977, for a limited engagement
Closed

THE CAST

Anne Bonney . . . . Mimi Kennedy
Gov. Charles Eden . . . . Patrick Hines
Calico Jack Rackham . . . . Terry O'Quinn
Blackbeard, Edward Teach . . . . Frederic Coffin
Caesar . . . . John McCurry
Israel Hands . . . . Timothy Meyers
Mr. Read . . . . Mary Bracken Philips
Major Stede Bonnet . . . . Homer Foil
Savannah . . . . Rebecca Gilchrist
Jamaica . . . . Kathi Moss
Lieut. William Rhett . . . . Roger Howell

REVIEWS

"It alternates between insipid and mildly refreshing, like cider on a warm day. About an inch of cider. . . . The humor coughs as much as it bubbles, and frequently runs out. It is replaced by alternate doses of romance and solemn lyricism. The doses seem prescribed and arbitrary. The music generally lacks much character or bite. . . . The performances are mostly good." — Richard Eder, *The New York Times (10-8-77, p. 32)*

"The combination of efforts just does not go together — at least not under their auspices and not as performed by this likeable-but-rough-hewn company. All in all, it's pretty heavy stuff, and Jim Wann's confused script continually mangles its intent. . . . Edward Berkeley's direction does nothing to tie together the disparate styles." — Debbi Wasserman, *New York Theatre Review (12-77, p. 45)*

Housewife! Superstar!

Written and acted by Barry Humphries; accompanist, Iris Mason. Presented by Michael White and Arthur Cantor; lighting by Andrea Wilson. Theater Four, 424 West 55th Street.

The program identifies *Housewife! Superstar!,* written and acted by the Australian Barry Humphries, as "a reasonably amusing show." It involves primarily one Dame Edna Everage and has a certain resemblance to some of Monty Python, encompassing two hours of barbed jokes and insults which rely primarily upon ethnic prejudice, toilet functions and jabs at the audience.

As the show opens, an "eleven-fingered" Miss Mason is playing the piano with all the adroitness of an elephant. After about 15 minutes of *Warsaw Concerto,* Dame Edna (Humphries) comes on. Among the things she reveals is that she has come upon a little undiscovered restaurant in New York. It's called Chock Full of Nuts. For her, Lincoln Center is "where Abraham Lincoln was assassinated." The picture on the wall of her sister-in-law's is "The Scream by Edvard Munch." Or, on second thought, is it "The Munch by Edvard Scream"?

Housewife!, a drag show, is a form more popular in Australia and England than in the United States and relies primarily on British wit and vaudeville, not to mention a finale in which Humphries hurls dozens of gladiolas at the audience, then insists that the recipients stand up and move the flowers in unison.

Opened October 19, 1977
Closed November 20, 1977

With: Barry Humphries and Iris Mason

REVIEWS

"It is abysmal. . . . There is virtually no outrage and still less comedy. Instead, with Mr. Humphries togged out as a middle-aged housewife-comedienne, there is endless wooden hammering away at weak and lonely jokes." — Richard Eder, *The New York Times (10-20-77, p. C 20)*

"The humor is all a mixed salad of double entendre, insult, British wit, surrealism, vaudeville, Australian provincialism and farce. There are no dead spots in this production — the tension between victim and verbal assailant ensures that. Dame Edna's wit may be unfunny at times, but it never loses its bite. . . . It is clearly a show for those who harbor secret masochistic longings." — Edmund Newton, *New York Post (10-20-77, p. 45)*

"The characterization is detailed, but the character is a bore, and most — though by no means all — of the jokes are awful." —Edith Oliver, *The New Yorker (11-7-77, p. 106)*

"Every time something bitterly funny starts to emerge, it is vitiated by long trivial interchanges with the audience, and by interminable toilet stories that aren't even scatological." — Erika Munk, *The Village Voice (11-7-77, p. 83)*

Margaret Barker and Thomas Barbour

The Wayside Motor Inn

THE CAST

Ray	Drew Snyder
Frank	Thomas Barbour
Jessie	Margaret Barker
Vince	John Braden
Mark	Richard Sale
Phil	Gary Cookson
Sally	Catherine Schreiber
Andy	Wayne Tippit
Ruth	Jill Andre
Sharon	Jill O'Hara

REVIEWS

"The five vignettes are essentially ordinary, but Mr. Gurney has treated them with an accomplished humor, pathos or irony. Sometimes the treatment overcomes the ordinariness, and sometimes it does not. The most obviously striking thing about *Motor Inn* is its form. . . . More often than not, it drains life from individual vignettes. It has a stop-and-go effect, though this is minimized as much as possible by the accomplished directing of Tony Giordano." — Richard Eder, *The New York Times (11-12-77, p. 13)*

"An earnest play. . . . But it is too thoughtful, a thinking writer's play rather than an inspired one's. . . . Tony Giordano seems to have directed the production academically, as if he were teaching the playwright by putting the play on its feet. There is a distinct scent of the workshop about the production." — Martin Gottfried, *New York Post (11-11-77, p. 42)*

"Though none of the plots is especially original, the show as a whole is deftly written, and the characters and their behavior and what they say and feel are interesting and credible. The simultaneous action is always clear and very well managed by the company. . . . David Potts' good setting is appropriately disheartening." — Edith Oliver, *The New Yorker (11-21-77, p. 143)*

"Gurney is good-natured, sometimes wisely observant, and never hoity-toity. The trouble with recording cliches is that one falls into their trap. . . . A generally good cast — Margaret Barker particularly as the still positive elderly wife — does justice to their characters which, though acceptably honest in the writing, do not rise above our placid consent." — Harold Clurman, *The Nation (12-3-77, p. 604)*

"For such a sketch of a play, the acting is suitably sketchy, external but sincere and unquestionably skilled. . . . Tony Giordano's direction is deft. . . . The set by David Potts is authentic." — Tom Simpson, *Show Business (11-24-77, p. 18)*

By A. R. Gurney, Jr. Presented by the Manhattan Theatre Club, Lynne Meadow, artistic director; directed by Tony Giordano; setting by David Potts; costumes by Kenneth M. Yount; lighting by Spencer Mosse; sound by George Hansen; production stage manager, Johhna Murray. Manhattan Theatre Club, 321 East 73rd Street.

A number of people check into a motel outside Boston. Among them are a traveling salesman, who almost immediately pulls out his bottle of whisky, ice and a copy of *Penthouse* magazine, which he proceeds to enjoy as he waits to get through to his head office. An old man and his wife, on their way to visit their daughter, come in, followed by a cheerful father taking his anything but cheerful son to Harvard. Two students intent on making love follow, then a doctor who is in the midst of getting a divorce.

All the action takes place in a single large room and, in fact, constitutes a number of overlapping short plays in which all the characters go about their individual pursuits, apparently oblivious of each other's existence.

Opened November 10, 1977, for a limited engagement
Closed November 27, 1977

Uncommon Women and Others

Swoosie Kurtz and Jill Eikenberry

THE CAST

Kate Quin . . . . .Jill Eikenberry
Samantha Stewart . . Ann McDonough
Holly Kaplan . . . . .Alma Cuervo
Muffet DiNichola . . . . . Ellen Parker
Rita Altabel . . . . .Swoosie Kurtz
Mrs. Plumm . . . . .Josephine Nichols
Susie Friend . . . . . . .Cynthia Herman
Carter . . . . Anna Levine
Leilah . . . . .Glenn Close

By Wendy Wasserstein. Presented by the Phoenix Theatre, T. Edward Hambleton, managing director; Daniel Freudenberger, artistic director; directed by Steven Robman; setting and lighting by James Tilton; costumes by Jennifer von Mayrhauser; production stage manager, Tom Aberger. Marymount Manhattan Theatre, 221 East 71st Street.

Five former Mount Holyoke College students meet for a reunion six years after their graduation. Since only a relatively short time has elapsed since they were seniors together, not a great deal has changed. Ms. Wasserstein focuses, instead, on the wounds, disappointments and confusions these former members of the "Seven Sisters" elite have encountered since they ceased being members of that particular group of "uncommon women." To some extent, the college itself is caricatured, especially as it is seen through the eyes of Susie, who was not a member of the group and upholds such school traditions as folding her napkin in a floral pattern, and Carter, a bright freshman, who sits more or less catatonically on the floor and plots the making of a film about Wittgenstein.

Opened November 21, 1977, for a limited engagement Closed December 4, 1977

REVIEWS

"Wendy Wasserstein has satirical instincts and an eye and ear for the absurd, but she shows signs of harnessing these talents to a harder discipline. . . . Her play is exuberant to the point of coltishness. Miss Wasserstein, who is young, uses her very large gift for being funny and acute with a young virtuosity that is often self-indulgent. . . . A terror of choices and the future afflicts all of them, and Miss Wasserstein has made this anguish most movingly real, amid all the jokes and the knowing sophistication. . . . Her gifts for characterization are supported by Steven Robman's supple and inventive direction, and by splendid acting." — Richard Eder, *The New York Times (11-22-77, p. 48)*

"The laughs are there, many of them genuine thigh smackers, but Miss Wasserstein has shown triumphantly that she knows when to stop. . . . The real triumph of *Uncommon Women* is that you leave the theater caring deeply about its characters." — Edmund Newton, *New York Post (11-22-77, p. 22)*

"While the play is laced with affectionately bantering humor and a gamy ration of powder-room candor, the characters are stereotypical." — T. E. Kalem, *Time (12-5-77, p. 111)*

"Funny, ironic, and affectionate. . . . The acting, under Steven Robman's direction, is in every instance as right and satisfying as the script, and it more than makes up for any dramatic lapses." — Edith Oliver, *The New Yorker (12-5-77, p. 115)*

Eulogy for a Small-Time Thief

Socorro Santiago and Shawn Elliott

By Miguel Piñero. Presented by Ensemble Studio Theatre, Curt Dempster, artistic director; directed by Jack Gelber; set design by Christopher Nowak; costumes by Carol Oditz; lighting by Cheryl Thacker; production stage manager, Jennifer Hershey. Ensemble Studio Theatre, 549 West 52nd Street.

Panama Smith, the "small-time thief" of the title, is a sometime pimp, sometime drug pusher, sometime participant in other illegal activities. Like his women and other associates, Piñero suggests, he is caught in a pattern, unable to break out even though he may want to.

Panama lives with Tina, his woman, in a Philadelphia slum. He is attracted to her younger sister, Little Bit, who leads him on. His apartment serves as a part-time brothel; in between, he holds up stores and takes cocaine. Alternately dreamy, violent and loving, he would like a place in the country, a way out of his present life.

Piñero permits no possibility of anyone living happily ever after, however — not the clients, not the purveyors, not even the relative innocents. Panama is destined to die at the hands of a hired hit man from New York; the others must face up to some other fate from which there seems to be no escape.

Opened November 27, 1977, for a limited engagement
Closed December 11, 1977

THE CAST

Panama Smith. . . . . Shawn Elliott
Tina Pauls . . . . Marcia Haufrecht
Little Bit . . . . Socorro Santiago
Rita . . . . Cheryl Galeano
Rose . . . . Ann Spettell
Terry Logan . . . . Christopher Allport
Carlos . . . . Alberto Vazquez
Miles . . . . .Jack Hollander

REVIEWS

"Despite marks of Mr. Piñero's impressive dramatic talent, [it seems likely that *Eulogy*] will turn out to be a weaker play than its predecessor. . . . The part [of Panama] is well-played by Shawn Elliott, whose eyes dart as he speaks and whose hands gesticulate like panicky moths. . . . The acid, perceptive writing of the beginning deteriorates. . . . Mr. Piñero's characters, like puppets, have only a trait or two apiece, and move nowhere but upon the strings of his intention." — Richard Eder, *The New York Times (11-28-77, p. 41)*

"If there's a fault with the play, it's the too-leisurely pace of the first act. One or two of the eight-member cast are not up to the skill of Elliott, Haufrecht and Allport. But there's a kind of passionate courage to Piñero's vision which overwhelms any minor dramaturgical flaws." — Edmund Newton, *New York.Post (11-28-77, p. 27B)*

"At the moment, the play is beset by many of the faults common to early drafts: the characters tell us far too much about themselves . . . and the second act is — or was on the night I saw it — still a mess. . . . Nevertheless, the first act is almost ready, and there *are* characters, almost all of them complete and interesting and supremely playable." — Edith Oliver, *The New Yorker (12-12-77, p. 92)*

"A badly-made play full of coincidence and self-pity, with compassion and individual scenes for all. As workshop writing it isn't terrible: amateurs rarely have a sense of structure, and Piñero does manage to get his words out right." — Terry Curtis Fox, *The Village Voice (12-12-77, p. 96)*

Gibson Glass and members of the Company

A dramatic response to Franz Kafka and his work, devised by the Lion Theatre Company. Presented by the Lion Theatre Company, Gene Nye, producing director; directed by Garland Wright; setting and lighting by John Arnone and Mr. Wright; costumes by David James; production stage manager, Steve Shlansky. Westside Airlines Terminal, 42nd Street and 10th Avenue.

Although based on Kafka's *The Trial, K* is not an actual dramatization of the book. Rather, it introduces other selections from the author's diaries and letters in an effort to produce what the director calls "impressions."

Eventually each of the cast members portrays Joseph K., who initially is seen sitting and pouring coffee and observing. Always seen in a formal black coat, he looks on, is viewed in a room, where he is alone, while a party is taking place next door. He is man in isolation. In time, he and others begin to act out scenes from the novel, including that of his arrest, featuring a very suave investigator, who questions vaguely, refuses to explain the charges but nonetheless insists that he is under arrest. He is, however, free to move about, participant in a surreal world of alienation and terror.

Opened November 28, 1977
Closed

K

With: Kim Ameen, Mary E. Baird, Tony Campisi, Janice Fuller, David Gallagher, Gibson Glass, Greg Grove, John Guerrasio, Jim McLure and Gene Nye

REVIEWS

"An original and totally stunning set of theatrical variations. . . . It displays devotion, imagination and a very high form of theater craftsmanship. . . . The formal movements of the actors, who have achieved a rare fineness and unity of style, recall the stillness of a Seurat, or that sense of being fixed forever in an archaic emotion that comes through in old sepia photographs. . . . This constantly shifting K is a brilliant device; another dramatic means of conveying the sense of things slipping invisibly away that is found in Kafka's book. It has its disadvantages. It tends to dissipate the focus. . . . But the overall mood is rendered most compellingly, and there is a shifting variety in the scenes that compensates for their lesser concentration." — Richard Eder, *The New York Times (12-10-77, p. 17)*

"The most successful rendering that I have ever seen of a dream state on stage. . . . Much of the credit must go to director Garland Wright, whose staging touch is lighter than a butterfly's wing. . . . Unfortunately, what this company gains in delicacy of creation, it loses in dramatic tension. There is a quality of dreams that makes you want to escape from them. Nevertheless, [it] is a brilliant experiment that almost succeeds." — Edmund Newton, *New York Post (11-29-77, p. 55)*

"The handsomeness of the production is an impressive achievement in itself. . . . The piece is beautifully harmonized, full of stunning and disturbing moments involving visual and sound effects. . . . Yet there ought to be more to it. . . . What is done in *K*, handsome and finely executed as it may be, is often imitated from recent experimental productions." — Michael Feingold, *The Village Voice (1-16-78, p. 89)*

"An ensemble impression of *The Trial* which is a strikingly accurate theatrical representation of the original. . . . Every element of the production has been carefully chosen and painstakingly honed to create a seamless effect. . . . *K* is one of those rare evenings of theatre; it is pageant, it is drama, it is intellectually stimulating, and it happens to be located in its ideal theatre." — Debbi Wasserman, *New York Theatre Review (2-78, p. 43)*

Esther

Stephen Keep, Dianne Wiest and Charles Turner

By Carol K. Mack. Presented by Saul Novick and Jomeloin Productions; directed by Joel Zwick; setting by Franco Colavecchia; costumes by David James; music by Bruce Coughlin; lighting by Edward M. Greenberg; production stage manager, Barret Nolan. Promenade Theatre, Broadway and 76th Street.

Ms. Mack draws upon the biblical Book of Esther to dramatize a story both historic and contemporary. A Jewish girl named Hadassah (subsequently to become Esther) becomes Queen to the King of Persia. With the assistance of her uncle, she succeeds in persuading the King that he should liberate the Jews.

Ms. Mack hints that the relationship between Esther and her uncle, Mordecai, is not entirely altruistic and that he is a clever manipulator and she something of a reluctant heroine, one who initially prefers palace life to the possibility of martyrdom and only belatedly becomes a B.C. feminist.

Opened November 29, 1977
Closed

THE CAST

Ahasuerus	Charles Turner
Haman	John Milligan
Dotus, the Scribe	Bruce Kornbluth
Esther/Hadassah	Dianne Wiest
Heghe	Joel Kramer
Mordecai	Stephen Keep

REVIEWS

"The interpretation is moderately interesting, but execution is stale and pretentious. The language is as fraudulent as the set designer's foliage. . . . The actors seem unabashed by their absurd assignments. . . . Dianne Wiest manages to bring a certain Cleopatra-like coquettishness to the role of Esther, which gives a speck of seasoning to an otherwise unpalatable evening. . . . Off Broadway one does not expect a large cast, but the paucity of Joel Zwick's production is alarming. . . . It is as if we are in a movie studio and someone has fired all the extras. . . . In an attempt to avoid writing a Biblical epic, Miss Mack has created an empty-closet drama." — Mel Gussow, *The New York Times (11-30-77, p. C 26)*

"For those whose dramatic discernments are broad enough to embrace Biblical interpretations in two acts, becomingly costumed in period Persian and modestly laced with fashionable feminism, the Promenade Theatre has just the thing. . . . But *Esther* is not just scriptural melodrama, it has relevance. Through one woman's arduous passage from innocence to maturity in the political gardens of Persopolis, it traces the struggle of womankind for identity and survival." — Joseph Mancini, *New York Post (11-30-77, p. 61)*

"Joel Zwick has directed the melodrama without much of the passion that the plot itself implies, and the characters seem neither impelled by their various purposes nor seriously involved with one another in the struggle for survival. . . . *Esther* is not without flaws, but with time the performances will improve and the point of the play reveal itself with more clarity." — P. Gregory Speck, *Show Business (12-1-77, p. 19)*

The Offering

Olivia Williams and Charles Weldon (standing);
Katherine Knowles and Douglas Turner Ward (seated)

By Gus Edwards. Presented by the Negro Ensemble Company; directed by Douglas Turner Ward; setting by Raymond C. Recht; lighting by Paul Gallo; costumes by Arthur McGee; production stage manager, Horacena J. Taylor. St. Mark's Playhouse, 133 Second Avenue.

A successful young murderer-for-hire decides to take his Las Vegas showgirl to meet the older man who taught him all he knows about the criminal business. The young man, Martin, is cordial; his white girlfriend something of a tourist in the lower depths. The initially indifferent Bob Tyrone gradually begins to thaw — at least toward Ginny. Meanwhile, Tyrone's wife, Princess, remains largely apart, looking on, very quiet.

Martin and Ginny decide to spend the night and, the next day, when Tyrone has to go out, Ginny asks whether she may accompany him. By the time they return, all the relationships have altered. After a confrontation with Martin, Tyrone takes Ginny into the bedroom and the others join each other in the sofa bed, with Martin insisting that it has all been his idea. "Like it or not," he tells Princess, "it's me and you."

Opened December 1, 1977
Closed April 2, 1978

THE CAST

Bob Tyrone . . . . Douglas Turner Ward
Princess . . . . Olivia Williams
Martin . . . . Charles Weldon
Ginny . . . . Katherine Knowles

REVIEWS

"It is both polished and crude; keenly heard, beautifully paced and acted, and perhaps with not quite enough blood in it. . . . [Edwards] has a remarkable narrative talent: the drama develops very largely as comedy — and it is often very funny — with violence looming and retreating. In part the outcome is foreseeable, but it is never given away. . . . Mr. Ward has directed with quite as much power and persuasiveness as he performs. . . . *Offering* is dramatically literate, observant and most worthwhile. For a first play it is remarkable." — Richard Eder, *The New York Times (12-2-77, p. C 3)*

"Its characters, who happen to be three blacks and one white, could as easily be three whites and one black or any other color combination. . . . The issue is the interplay or, more precisely (and Pinteresquely), the power plays among four people, and the concerns are more than skin deep. . . . What helps immeasurably, in the first act at least, is the playwright's ability to astonish us. . . . And then there is the acting, which is first-class." — John Simon, *New York (12-26-77–1-2-78, p. 87)*

"Gus Edwards' writing is distinguished for its realistic tone and highly natural humor. . . . A first-rate directing effort is made by Douglas Turner Ward, who also plays the role of Bob Tyrone, the old man. His staging on the extremely appropriate, handsome set is fluent and flexible. . . . Every member of the four-person cast gives a pleasurable performance." — L. M. Evers, *Show Business (12-15-77, p. 26)*

"Each scene (except the penultimate one) is clear enough, well written, provocative, and all of it well acted." — Harold Clurman, *The Nation (12-31-77, p. 732)*

"A promising new playwright who hasn't got his act(s) together." — Marilyn Stasio, *Cue (12-24-77–1-6-78, p. 34)*

"A black imitation of *The Homecoming.* . . . *The Offering* lacks, however, the brilliant obliquity of its original. . . . Mr. Edwards has written some good speeches and some playable confrontations, and the actors make the whole thing seem more substantial than it is. . . . But *The Offering* is really too second-hand to be very interesting." — Julius Novick, *The Village Voice (12-26-77, p. 79)*

The Passing Game

THE CAST

Debbie . . . . Susan MacDonald
Randy. . . . . Paul C. O'Keefe
Richard. . . . . William Atherton
Julie . . . . Margaret Ladd
Andrew. . . . . Pat McNamara
Henry . . . . .Howard E. Rollins, Jr.
Rachel. . . . . .Novella Nelson

Margaret Ladd and Pat McNamara

By Steve Tesich. Presented by the American Place Theatre; directed by Peter Yates; basketball sequences choreographed by Richard D. Morse; set by Kert Lundell; costumes by Ruth Morley; lighting by Neil Peter Jampolis; production stage manager, Nancy Harrington. American Place Theatre, 111 West 46th Street.

Two couples, one white, the other black, have come to a more or less deserted small upstate resort; have come because several mysterious killings have taken place there. Both men are actors and both feel they have in one way or another betrayed or been betrayed by their talents. Now, they mainly make television commercials. Richard, the white actor, looks on Henry, whom he labels "Mr. Residuals," as one who has deprived him of some of the commercials he might otherwise have appeared in.

On the small basketball court between the two cottages they go one-on-one with each other in what becomes a deadly game. They do, however, lower the basket, just as they have been able to lower their aspirations. Here, they "can make [their] own standards." Each hopes that the mysterious killer will strike his wife, the reminder of the might have been, of the ambitions of their early careers. But it does not immediately happen, so they enter into a pact whereby each will kill the other's spouse. "If you have witnesses to your decline," one asks the other, "don't you try to get rid of them?" But they are not strong enough for it, just as they have not been strong enough to pursue their dreams.

Opened December 1, 1977, for a limited engagement
Closed December 11, 1977

REVIEWS

"*Passing Game* has only passing moments of comedy. It is meant to be a drama — and it is far less convincing than his earliest work. . . . Mr. Tesich continues to be a provocative writer, but in common with some other efforts at the American Place, his new play needs more nurturing before exposure on a public stage." — Mel Gussow, *The New York Times* (12-2-77, p. C 3)

"If the melodramatic climax with its ironic twist and the still more ironic denouement are not entirely unpredictable, they are no less powerful for that. Unfortunately, Tesich has not made them as convincing as, for all their absurdity, they might be. It is as if his writing had grown perfunctory here in his haste toward a conclusion in which the demon of geometric neatness takes over once more. But no one should be deterred by this from a provocative play, strongly and clearly directed by Peter Yates. . . . There is solid acting from everyone." — John Simon, *New York* (12-19-77, p. 103)

"The skillful cast saturates the evening with menace, mockery, melodrama and some one-on-one macho on a night-lit basketball court that brings the two men closer to each other than they have ever been to their wives." — T. E. Kalem, *Time* (12-12-77, p. 96)

"*Passing Game* seems to have no bounce left in it." — Christopher Sharp, *Women's Wear Daily* (12-2-77, p. 10)

"Takes the elements of a domestic drama, adds some features of a mystery melodrama, and winds up with a schizzy personality. . . . The heavy atmospheric pressures are okay for inducing thrills and chills, but they can't replace such technical niceties as characterization and plotting." — Marilyn Stasio, *Cue* (12-24-77–1-6-78, p. 33)

John Ferraro, James Lally, Wallace Shawn and
Tom Costello

The Mandrake

By Niccolo Machiavelli; translated by Wallace
Shawn. Presented by the New York Shakespeare Festival, Joseph Papp, producer, Bernard Gersten, associate producer; directed and with setting by Wilford
Leach; music by Richard Weinstock; costumes by Patricia McGourty; lighting by Victor En Yu Tan; production stage manager, Bill McComb. Public Theatre/
Other Stage, 425 Lafayette Street.

A young Florentine nobleman, Callimaco, who is
in love with the beautiful Lucrezia, manages to have
himself introduced to her by her aging husband, Nicia.
He pretends to be a doctor who is capable of curing
her of her supposed sterility. To bring that about, he
proposes the mandrake, which will, however, have a
fatal effect on the first man to sleep with her after-
ward. Since he clearly does not want to be that first
man, Nicia accepts Callimaco's suggestion that he
seize a passerby at night and close him in with his
wife. Callimaco also enlists a friar, who is Lucrezia's
confessor, to help overcome her scruples. It follows
as the night the day that Callimaco will be the assault-
ed passerby. Overcome by his ardor, Lucrezia agrees
to continue with their affair.

Opened December 5, 1977
Closed April 30, 1978

THE CAST

Prologue and Siro . . . . Wallace Shawn
Callimaco. . . . . James Lally
Ligurio . . . . John Ferraro
Professor Nicia . . . . Tom Costello
Madonna Sostrata, her mother . . . . Angela Pietropinto
Brother Timothy. . . . . Larry Pine
Woman at the church . . . . Corinne Fischer
Lucrezia, his wife . . . . Thelma Nevitt
Musicians. . . . . Dan Carrillo, Charley Gerard

REVIEWS

"It has dead moments, and sometimes its talents are ap-
plied too heavily and without let-up. But even as it stands it
provides some of the most stimulating theater in town, and its
further possibilities are very bright. . . . Mr. Leach has brought
a rhythm to the production that makes it a dance of comedy
and passion." — Richard Eder, *The New York Times (11-18-77,
p. C 3)*

"Wilford Leach has done a capital job in both its staging
and design. . . . Shawn . . . has done a charming, dexterous job
with his adaptation. The wheels of the play's clockwork move
tickingly, and the various clowns lurch into view with good-
natured predictability." — Clive Barnes, *New York Post
(12-7-77, p. 59)*

"The production has been directed and designed by Wilford
Leach, and it is in every respect a sensationally attractive one."
— Brendan Gill, *The New Yorker (12-12-77, p. 91)*

"It has the elan and color of Machiavelli's exuberantly
wicked vision. Director-designer Wilford Leach has done a
brilliant job of stylization in which everyone goes wonderfully
ape with cupidity, stupidity, duplicity or lubricity." — Jack
Kroll, *Newsweek (12-19-77, p. 87)*

"Leach is better than this (and so, I suspect, are at least
some of his cast). His set is a marvel — slides are projected upon the backdrop to create the precise modern-period layer
gloss his direction lacks. Wallace Shawn's translation plays
well . . . and Richard Weinstock's music is inoffensive if im-
memorable." — Terry Curtis Fox, *The Village Voice (11-28-77,
p. 83)*

"A vulgarization of Machiavelli's elegantly cynical and
superbly subversive (1520) play. . . . Many people (and some
reviewers) enjoy the exhibition. It fits the ordinary taste of
our time." — Harold Clurman, *The Nation (12-31-77, p. 732)*

Ken Kliban, William Hurt,
Michael Ayr and Sharon Madden

Ulysses in Traction

THE CAST

Bruce Garrick . . . . Michael Ayr
Emma Konichoski . . . . Trish Hawkins
John Morrisey . . . . William Hurt
Doris Reinlos . . . . Sharon Madden
Dr. Steven Klipstader . . . . Ken Kliban
Dr. Stuart Humphreys . . . . Jack Davidson
Mae . . . . Joanna Featherstone
Leonard Kaufman . . . . Jake Dengel

By Albert Innaurato. Presented by the Circle Repertory Company; directed by Marshall W. Mason; setting by John Lee Beatty; costumes by Laura Crow; lighting by Dennis Parichy; sound by Charles S. London and George Hansen; production stage manager, Fred Reinglas. Circle Repertory Theatre, 99 Seventh Avenue South.

Innaurato, author of the Broadway success *Gemini*, has set his new work in a theatre where various teachers and students are rehearsing a parody of a Vietnam War play. Meanwhile, outside there is a real race riot, complete with virtually non-stop machine-gun fire, going on. Against this background, he explores the lives and sexual inclinations of his characters, who include a young actor, an aging flower child, a failed stage director, a gay theatrical dilettante and a black cleaning woman. All are to some extent cowards, individuals who have accepted mediocrity as a way of life.

Opened December 8, 1977, for a limited engagement
Closed January 22, 1978

REVIEWS

"Some of these things are interesting and some are amusing, but the play is a mess. . . . He is using an old melodramatic device and using it badly. . . . The cast, directed by Marshall W. Mason, are all good." – Richard Eder, *The New York Times* (12-9-77, p. C 3)

"The playwright has a sweet satiric touch. The cast is all top quality. . . . The play ends on a pat hopeful note, but its perception is unsentimental and unforgettably true." – Edmund Newton, *New York Post* (12-9-77, p. 40)

"Its principal weakness, I think, is that so much of what we learn about the characters has to be told in monologues. . . . The acting by every member of the cast is excellent." – Edith Oliver, *The New Yorker* (12-19-77, p. 112)

"Mr. Mason's staging is in his characteristic vein of realistic ensemble work, appropriately broader than usual here and there, but as usual beautifully fluid and relaxed." – Julius Novick, *The Village Voice* (12-19-77, p. 101)

"The play is, to say the least, a disappointment." – Gerald Rabkin, *The Soho Weekly News* (12-15-77, p. 46)

"Generally well cast and acted." – Harold Clurman, *The Nation* (12-31-77, p. 732)

Joe Masiell, Not at the Palace

Joe Masiell and Company

A musical in concert, with special material by Jerry Herman, Will Holt, Fred Ebb, John Kander. Presented by Lily Turner; directed by James Coco; choreographed by Tod Jackson; arranged and conducted by Christopher Bankey; lighting by James Nesbit Clark; sets and costumes by C. Tod Jackson; production stage manager, James Nesbit Clark. Astor Place Theatre, 434 Lafayette Street.

Joe Masiell, Not at the Palace supposedly evolved during a nighttime meeting between Masiell and James Coco and Lily Turner, director and producer, respectively, as they sat lamenting the fact that none of them had ever played the legendary Palace Theatre.

What resulted is a two-hour concert, devoted primarily to works of well-known composers that have not themselves been overexposed either on radio or on records.

Masiell is assisted by four Las Vegas-type show girls, and some of the numbers include: "When I'm Playin' the Palace" (an original by Jerry Herman); "Two for the Road," by Bricusse and Mancini; "The Lady is a Tramp," by Rodgers and Hart; "In My Life," by Lennon and McCartney; Masiell's own "We Were Young" and "But the World Goes 'Round," by Kander and Ebb.

Opened December 11, 1977, for a limited engagement
Closed January 8, 1978

Starring: Joe Masiell, with Debra Dickinson, Anita Ehrler, Gena Ramsel, Nancy Salis

REVIEWS

"A big, buoyant and joyful sound. . . . Its source is a handsome fellow who sings and goes by the name of Joe Masiell. . . . After sitting through this genial evening, one is tempted to believe Mr. Masiell might just bypass the Palace and head for one of the big halls; filling it might not be too demanding a chore. . . . The show romps along in easy good humor. . . . His voice is clear and big, but it runs the acoustic range from a no-decibel low recitative to a booming finale. . . . James Coco has staged it with what comes across as refreshing and most effective simplicity. Both he and the star and everyone concerned have a sense of fun, and you should, too." — Richard F. Shepard, *The New York Times (12-13-77, p. 54)*

"A tour-de-force performance. . . . Masiell has an excellent voice. His interpretations are a lesson in bel canto singing at its pop best. . . . Tod Jackson's choreography is appropriate and Christopher Bankey has done a splendid job of arranging and conducting. James Nesbit Clark also deserves mention for his subtle lighting." — *Variety (12-14-77, p. 88)*

"All class. . . . Here is his chance to burst out and strut his stuff. It is a chance fully realized. . . . James Coco's staging of this mini-extravaganza is a revelatory new dimension of his talent, providing a striking theatrical showcase for a charismatic talent and a complete showman." — Alvin Klein, *New York Theatre Review (2-78, p. 44)*

Green Pond

Christine Ebersole, Stephen James,
Stephanie Cotsirilos and Richard Ryder

THE CAST

Liz . . . . . Stephanie Cotsirilos
Dana. . . . . Christine Ebersole
Sam . . . . .Stephen James
Frank . . . . . . .Richard Ryder

Words by Robert Montgomery; music by Mel Marvin.   Presented by the Chelsea Theatre Center, Robert Kalfin, artistic director; directed by David Chambers; vocal arrangements and orchestrations by Mel Marvin; sets and costumes by Marjorie Kellogg; lighting by Arden Fingerhut; production stage manager, Dorothy J. Maffei.   Chelsea Westside Theatre, 407 West 43rd Street.

According to the program, *Green Pond* is "a musical play about relationships."   Those relationships are among four young people who are on an extended vacation on the South Carolina coast.   As the play opens, they are in a good humor, but as it progresses each of them begins to reveal anxieties and failings of a fairly standard and recognizable kind.   As a hurricane impends, their previous good feelings deteriorate.

The play takes place on the front porch of a summer house owned by one of the character's fathers.   Sam, the young man in question, is a song writer; Dana, his companion, is an actress who seems to spend more time worrying about herself than acting.   Frank is a decidedly gloomy writer and his wife, Liz, a photographer.   All four profess to be there in order to answer the question: "Don't we know how to love any better than we do?"   Much of their lamenting, musing and occasional good times occur to music, of which "Woman to Woman" is the song that has been most widely remarked upon.

Opened December 13, 1977
Closed January, 1978

REVIEWS

"The inadequacies and anxieties [of the characters] are a standard middle-priced brand, reliably contemporary and untroubled by insight or originality. . . .   Richard Ryder and Stephen James are pleasant enough as Frank and Sam.   The women are most interesting, perhaps because there is a hint of tartness amid unflagging charm. . . .   David Chamber's direction is as lively as possible.   Whatever their talents, though, they disappear without trace into *Green Pond*." — Richard Eder, *The New York Times (12-15-77, p. C 19)*

"A mild-mannered, light-toned yet rather graceful little musical. . . .   It does have the atmosphere of its time, a certain languid way of thought combined with a surprisingly moralistic manner of behavior.   The playwright, Robert Montgomery, and this is definitely a play with music rather than a musical with a book, has created people in the vacuum of a situation rather than the throes of a story.   The people are real enough, but nothing much happens to them. . . .   The music by Mel Marvin is neither brilliant nor memorable, yet supremely appropriate." — Clive Barnes, *New York Post (12-15-77, p. 51)*

"They just sing Montgomery's trite lyrics and Mel Marvin's repetitive tunes — all heavy beat, relentless percussion or ground. . . .   *Green Pond* is very short on book, very long on grins for part of the time and grumpiness for the rest. . . .   The four singers have nice voices and Christine Ebersole can act. . . .   David Chambers' direction is arbitrary, stilted and awkward.   The only 'relationship' *Green Pond* illuminates is the one between a dull show and a deadened audience." — Tish Dace, *The Soho Weekly News (12-22-77, p. 46)*

"To point out that a green pond is a stagnant pool seems obvious, but it's apparently something that the people concerned with putting this show together never considered. . . .   David Chambers has directed his actors to sit during most of the songs which only enhances the dullness of the script." — Leah D. Frank, *New York Theatre Review (2-78, p. 44)*

Suzanne Costallos

Play
and Other Plays

By Samuel Beckett. Presented by the Manhattan Theatre Club; Lynne Meadow, artistic director; Barry Grove, managing director; directed by Alan Schneider; setting and costumes by Zack Brown; lighting by William Mintzer; associate director, Thomas Bullard; associate artistic director, Stephen Pascal; production stage manager, Jody Boese. Manhattan Theatre Club, 321 East 73rd Street.

Three plays make up the Manhattan Theatre Club's Beckett triple-bill, of which two receive their New York premiere: *That Time* and *Footfalls.* The third, which opens the evening, *Play,* was produced in New York several seasons ago.

In *That Time* the only elements are the head and voice of a man (reminiscent, to some extent, of the more complicated *Not I,* which focused upon the mouth and voice of a woman). The man seems not fully awake. He recalls being out in the rain and cold and taking shelter in such public buildings as the Portrait Gallery and the Post Office, but also remembers when he was much younger and sitting on a bench in the sunlight with a girl he loved. He remembers being a child. By the time the play ends, he is merely about to sink into a void.

Footfalls has certain almost mocking adversions to the mock-Gothic. A woman shuffles back and forth across the stage, dragging her feet and speaking to her aged and unseen mother, who replies over a microphone. Perhaps the daughter is confined to an institution, perhaps she is not; in neither case has she had much of a life.

Opened December 14, 1977, for a limited engagement
Closed January 15, 1978

REVIEWS

"The new works are relatively limited in scope. They have Beckett's vision and voice, and they would be valuable alone. . . . The splendid performance put on at the Manhattan Theatre Club is, in a sense, also more musical than dramatic. Mr. Schneider doing Beckett is like Casals playing Bach: There are the authority, the economy, the grave, clean bite and the total submersion of the performers in the work." – Richard Eder, *The New York Times (12-19-77, p. 44)*

"He gives us moments of truth encapsulated in memory — and oddly enough the memory is our own. . . . All three actors . . . are beautifully adept at presenting this Beckett/Schneider view of love, life and death transfigured in the frozen prism of experience." – Clive Barnes, *New York Post (12-19-77, p. 22)*

"In both cases Beckett's meaning is obscure, and he fails to meet a basic test of drama: the clash of character and idea." – Gerald Clarke, *Time (1-2-78, p. 59)*

"It's a bit hard to know what to do: recommend the plays or condemn the evening for the productions. . . . This is Beckett with tears, Beckett made easy. It's actually Beckett without trust, Beckett made boring." – Terry Curtis Fox, *The Village Voice (1-2-78, p. 74)*

"The production . . . is impeccable, and therein lies its flaw. . . . These pieces glint in the dark like a scalpel-blade. They're a bit cold and ruthless. But this is clearly just Schneider's reflection in Beckett's star for now, the reflection of a brilliant director in harmony with a brilliant cast." – Tom Simpson, *Show Business (1-5-78, p. 18)*

"Both are deliberately minor and remote, and both are written with great beauty and wit. . . . The performance as a whole, under Alan Schneider's direction, is a bit too muffled and precious and remote, and in each instance the audience must supply the Irish lilt. But what a wonderful writer Beckett is, and how funny!" – Edith Oliver, *The New Yorker (1-2-78, p. 49)*

Where the Mississippi Meets the Amazon

Ntozake Shange, Jessica Hagedorn and Thulani Nkabinde

By Jessica Hagedorn, Ntozake Shange and Thulani Nkabinde ("The Satin Sisters"). Presented by the New York Shakespeare Festival, Joseph Papp, producer, Bernard Gersten, associate producer; directed by Oz Scott; costumes by Beverly Parks; lighting by Victor En Yu Tan; the band, Teddy and His Sizzling Romancers; David Murray, musical director; production supervisor, Jason Steven Cohen; stage manager, Peter Glazer. Public Theatre/Cabaret, 425 Lafayette Street.

Ntozake Shange, author of the Broadway hit *For Colored Girls Who Have Considered Suicide/When the Rainbow Is Enuf,* leads a three-woman group known as the Satin Sisters in one of the Public Theatre's first evenings in a new cabaret series. Each of the participants has written her own dramatic poems, which are recited to the music of a jazz band, Teddy and His Sizzling Romancers.

Much of the evening has to do with sexual and racial repression, as the three performers comment: "Warriors and the dreams of girlhood are an addiction." "Women lick their wounds until they heal." "I want to take just a moment to dream my dreams." "Whatever there is to get you should. Just get that and feel good." Prose poem more than play, it has some striking similarities to *Colored Girls.*

Opened December 18, 1977, for a limited engagement
Closed February 5, 1978

With: Ntozake Shange, Jessica Hagedorn and Thulani Nkabinde

REVIEWS

"Ntozake Shange is a forceful performer as well as poet and playwright. In her acting as well as in her writing, she is charged with emotion and self-awareness. . . . Although the authorship is individual, the evening — directed by Oz Scott — is in harmony. . . . Miss Shange is the truest poet and the most dramatic performer. Her images burgeon with sensuality, as in the hyperbole of the title poem. She invests her work with urgency, and her sister performers take the lead from her. . . . The band evokes images of the late 1950's when jazz was cool and occasionally poetry was read to music. . . . Since all the women have musical as well as poetic talent, one could wish that they actually sang a full lyric or that they danced a bit more. . . . But this is an informal, unpretentious act rather than a fully staged show. As such it brings melodious sounds and considerable warmth to Mr. Papp's cabaret." — Mel Gussow, *The New York Times (12-20-77, p. 45)*

"The poems and the music go hand in hand, and the music supports the movements of the three performers in an approximation of dancing. The poems are lyrical, humorous, erotic, witty, dramatic, tender, and, as if Miss Shange had used up most of her rage and spleen . . . frequently lighthearted." — Edith Oliver, *The New Yorker (1-2-78, p. 48)*

"The intimate concert stage is Shange's natural metier. . . . She rejoices in the freedom of 'My Space,' unself-consciously wooing the audience to join her." — Marilyn Stasio, *Cue (1-7—20-78, p. 32)*

"Provided audiences stay away from the treacherous seafood crepe that is being served, they likely will be caught up in the music and the poetry of the evening. . . . It gets bogged down in repetitive lines that sometimes sound like song titles listed together. Shange regains her sharpness when she writes with purpose; specifically, when dealing with oppression in either sexual or racial terms." — Christopher Sharp, *Women's Wear Daily (12-22-77, p. 7)*

A Photograph
A Study of Cruelty

Avery Brooks and Michele Shay

THE CAST

Michael . . . . .Michele Shay
Sean David. . . . . Avery Brooks
Nevada . . . . Petronia Paley
Earl . . . . Count Stovall
Claire . . . . .Hattie Winston

By Ntozake Shange. Presented by the New York Shakespeare Festival, Joseph Papp, producer, Bernard Gersten, associate producer; directed by Oz Scott; setting by David Mitchell; costumes by Beverly Parks; lighting by Victor En Yu Tan; music composed by David Murray; choreography by Marsha Blanc; visuals by Collis Davis and David Mitchell; production stage manager, Richard S. Vioa. Lu Esther Hall/Public Theatre, 425 Lafayette Street.

A young black photographer named Sean David is trying to launch his career and thinks himself just on the brink of real success. Three women more or less love him. The first, Michael, is unsubmissive, a dancer and an artist; the second, Nevada, is a successful businesswoman who owns a Porsche and deals with the white world largely through repressing her own instincts. Then there is Claire, an entertaining whore. He also has a male friend, a lawyer named Earl, who was formerly a classmate.

Sean behaves savagely to his women. A prisoner of his ambition, he needs women to follow him. He is, as one critic has noted, a misogynist under the guise of a lover, a weak man who pretends to be strong. Eventually his facade must collapse, and it does when he is turned down for a fellowship, a gallery exhibition and other of the things that would have given him status. It remains for Michael to ask him: "Can you love your photographs even though they are rejected?"

Opened December 21, 1977
Closed January 22, 1978

REVIEWS

"Miss Shange is something besides a poet but she is not — at least not at this stage — a dramatist. . . . The work is forced, and finally broken by its form. The perceptions are made to do the donkey-work of holding up what attempts to be a whole dramatic structure, and they fail. . . . Everything, and every character, is really set up as a prop against which Michael can be wonderful. And she is quite wonderful, both as written and acted." — Richard Eder, *The New York Times (12-22-77, p. C 11)*

"She writes beautifully, and her earlier director, Oz Scott, is still on hand to give that beauty its gesture. The play itself is a cliché about a nonentity who imagines himself otherwise. . . . Most of the time the sheer ordinariness of the play — its soap-opera obviousness — dramaturgically insists on it not working. The play, to me, was silly." — Clive Barnes, *New York Post (12-22-77, p. 39)*

"Her own poetic talent and passion carry the show, and her characters are given flesh and blood by the actors." — Edith Oliver, *The New Yorker (1-2-78, p. 48)*

"An obvious departure for Shange. . . . Avery Brooks' version of the photographer offers an impressive range of frustration, humor, desperation and charm. He is supported by an able cast." — Christopher Sharp, *Women's Wear Daily (12-22-77, p. 7)*

"Shange hasn't got a grip on the dramatic form. She doesn't make it work for her. . . . Shange's poetic dialogue is often arresting, but more often it just tints the play with distracting, overly lush colors, as if to protect it from the rigors of real dramaturgy." — Marilyn Stasio, *Cue (1-7–20-78, p. 31)*

The Dybbuk

Bruce Myers and Marcia Jean Kurtz

THE CAST

Rabbi Azriel. . . . . .Richard Bauer
Osher (Servant of Sender). . Robert Blumenfeld
Chana-Esther,
    Mother of the Bridegroom. . Shami Chaikin
Woman in Town,
    Musician . . . . Alice Eve Cohen
Wedding Guest, Judge . . . . . . Joseph Davidson
Henoch, Beggar. . . . . Bernard Duffy
Maggid,
    Wandering Storyteller. . . . . .Corey Fischer
Pregnant Woman, Beggar. . . . . . Jenn Hamburg
Leah. . . . . Marcia Jean Kurtz
Student, Beggar. . . . . .Hal Lehrman, Jr.
Woman in Town,
    Basia, Musician . . . . .Ellen Maddow
Chanon . . . . Bruce Myers
Student, Bridegroom . . . . .Mark Nelson
Woman in Town,
    Rich Woman. . . . . Marcell Rosenblatt
Man in Synagogue,
    Father of the Bridegroom . . .Mark Samuels
Rabbi's Wife, Beggar . . . . .Margo Lee Sherman
Michol (The Shames),
    Musician . . . . Arthur Strimling
Sender. . . . . Jamil Zakkai
Shimshon, Musician . . . . .Paul Zimet
Freyda . . . . Sonia Zomina

By S. Ansky. Presented by the New York Shakespeare Festival; directed by Joseph Chaikin; translated by Mira Rafalowicz; new version developed by Mira Rafalowicz and Joseph Chaikin; setting by Woods Mackintosh; costumes by Mary Brecht; lighting by Beverly Emmons; production stage manager, Louis Rackoff; produced by Joseph Papp; associate producer, Bernard Gersten; Public/Newman Theatre, 425 Lafayette Street.

Chaikin, who is best known for his experimental work with the now defunct Open Theatre, which he founded, evokes the atmosphere of the Eastern European shtetl, with its men praying in the synagogue, chanting and studying the Torah, and its women gossiping outside.

After a time, the play proper starts. Chanon, a poor student, enters and reveals his love for Leah. But her father has other ideas in mind, specifically a rich bridegroom. Chanon admits to another young man that he has explored the kabala, with its mystical and occult beliefs. A servant enters to announce that Leah's father has found a bridegroom for the girl. Only Chanon does not share in the rejoicing. Instead, he has a seizure and dies. Later, Leah goes to the cemetery to visit her mother's grave and invite the dead Chanon to her wedding. As he sits offstage during the ceremony, Leah begins to speak with his voice and sometimes in unison with him, for Chanon has become a dybbuk, one of the wandering souls of Jewish tradition, and has entered her body.

The remainder of *The Dybbuk* is devoted to various, and finally successful attempts at exorcism. It is absorbing, in its way innovative, yet true to the tradition of Ansky.

Opened December 22, 1977
Closed January 29, 1978

REVIEWS

"Joseph Chaikin achieves a splendid balance. . . . He gets this play, with its interweaving of commonplace and otherworldly, just right. Using a new and limpid translation by Mira Rafalowicz and going on with her to make a number of adaptations, he constructs a *Dybbuk* of high intelligence; dreamlike, even cool, but haunting. . . . It is a passionately thoughtful production, exciting, and winged." — Richard Eder, *The New York Times* (12-23-77, p. C 3)

"Technically Chaikin gets to the heart of the play, and emotionally he makes that heart its soul. . . . Here we have a group of beautifully dedicated actors walking, running and jumping through the specific images of Ansky's unfulfilled yet significant play. . . . You feel for these people making their oddly ritual gestures in an oddly ritualized world." — Clive Barnes, *New York Post* (12-23-77, p. 37)

"This revival is a good one, not rigid and literal, but sensitive and faithful. . . . He has staged *The Dybbuk* with a fine Open Theatre simplicity. . . . [It] is not by any means a definitive production, but it does show how experimental techniques growing out of the '60s can be used to create the classical theatre of the '70s." — Julius Novick, *The Village Voice* (1-2-78, p. 73)

"The company of actors is perfect. While portraying a community of people who have known each other for years and whose lives are inextricably connected by Judaism, each of the actors retains individuality. Even the smallest parts hold one's interest." — William Harris, *The Soho Weekly News* (1-5-78, p. 39)

The Elusive Angel

Brad Davis and Martha Gaylord

By Jack Gilhooley. Presented by the Phoenix Theatre, T. Edward Hambleton, managing director; Daniel Freudenberger, artistic director; Marilyn S. Miller, executive director; directed by Steven Robman; songs by Arthur Miller and Mr. Gilhooley; setting and lighting by James Tilton; costumes by Jennifer von Mayrhauser; production stage manager, Tom Aberger. Manhattan Marymount Theatre, 221 East 71st Street.

In *The Elusive Angel* a shy and poor couple who cannot have a child are trying desperately to adopt one. Mary welcomes her husband home from work, where he is a car-waxer, though he has a considerably fancier name for it. Mary, who has a convent-school background, has been traumatized by their failure to have a child. She prays to St. Jude, the patron saint of apparently hopeless causes, and has a doll that she treats as if it is an actual child.

Through the manager of a dance hall of distinctly disreputable tone, they become entangled with an operation where people who are unable to adopt children from legitimate agencies can buy one, with no questions asked, for $10,000. Mary and Carlton do not, however, have that kind of money, so she turns prostitute in order to acquire it.

Opened December 26, 1977, for a limited engagement
Closed January, 1978

REVIEWS

"Basically it has the dimensions of a newspaper clipping. The incident portrayed is commonplace without the thought and reflection that would make it significant, and mildly grotesque without a spark of dramatic life." — Richard Eder, *The New York Times (12-27-77, p. 51)*

"Skilful, direct but a shade unsurprising. In fact, it's about as unsurprising as a rabbit jumping from a magician's hat. Yet it's not a bad-looking rabbit. . . . The superficials of story-line and texture are made more significant than any true dramatic revelation or observation. . . . The production is full of a care-worn, poignant shabbiness, an atmosphere carefully and lovingly conveyed by director, cast and designers alike." — Clive Barnes, *New York Post (12-27-77, p. 55)*

"Mr. Gilhooley has a genuine talent for small realistic touches and moderately poignant moments. The real limitation of *The Elusive Angel,* more fundamental even than its divided focus, is that the realistic play about pathetic innocents bewildered in a hard world is very familiar. Mr. Gilhooley writes it well, but he has nothing sufficiently special to bring to it." — Julius Novick, *The Village Voice (1-9-78, p. 67)*

"Jack Gilhooley has a fine ear but fails abysmally in both investigation and interpretation, producing an exercise in 'so what?'" — Joe Enright, *Show Business (1-5-78, p. 18)*

"It has some good ingredients, but the' ingredients have not mixed together. . . . All the actors are better prepared for the production than the play itself is." — Christopher Sharp, *Women's Wear Daily (1-3-78, p. 23)*

Cabin 12

Edward Seamon and Jonathan Hogan

THE CAST

Bob McCullough . . . . .Jonathan Hogan
Harold McCullough . . . . .Edward Seamon
The Girl. . . . . Nancy Snyder
The Man . . . . Michael Ayr

By John Bishop. Presented by the Circle Repertory Company; directed by Marshall Oglesby; setting by Gary S. Seltzer; costumes by Irene Nolan; lights by Ruth Roberts; stage manager, Joanne Seltzer. Circle Repertory Theatre, 99 Seventh Avenue South.

A father and his son arrive at a shoddy motel somewhere in Virginia, brought to the area by the death of a second and younger son who has died in a highway crash. They talk, drink and telephone to other members of the family and it soon becomes evident that something more than the obvious is afoot. Meanwhile, bits and pieces of their lives emerge, lives of disappointment and mutual failure. The dead son epitomizes their frustration. Though he in his way craved other things, he had limited himself to driving a truck. Perhaps merely as a way of passing the time between birth and death. Eventually, his father must come to terms with his death, recognize that he has not given direction to either of his sons, and the other son must recognize that he was unable really to show love for his brother while that brother remained alive. It seems clear the brother's death was not an accident, very possibly a suicide.

Opened January 5, 1978, for a limited engagement
Reopened March 4, 1978 (as part of a double-bill
    with *Brontosaurus*)
Closed April 9, 1978

REVIEWS

"The play is austere. This is a work that offers intimations rather than revelations. . . . *Cabin 12* could be more expansive in revealing character. . . . The play is immeasurably aided in performance. . . . Both actors, as directed by Marshall Oglesby, are subtle in their evocation of character. They communicate the closeness and the intimacy of kinship; we believe that they are father and son. In common with Mr. Bishop's play, they are quietly and gently affecting." — Mel Gussow, *The New York Times (1-6-78, p. C 3)*

"When it is good, and more importantly where it is good, it is as natural as an Olympic diver. . . . It is handsomely done, and in Marshall Oglesby's staging, exquisitely acted. . . . Bishop evokes the common poetry of people." — Clive Barnes, *New York Post (1-7-78, p. 12)*

"A flawed but interesting one-act play, graced by the meticulous direction and the outstanding, naturalistic acting for which the Circle is noted. . . . The terse, idiomatic dialogue suits the emotionally inarticulate characters. And while the subject matter is grim, the tone remains brave. . . . Bishop is lucky in having Edward Seamon and Jonathan Hogan as his principal actors. Detailed but not fussy, their performances fill in many of the holes in the text." — C. Lee Jenner, *The Villager (1-12-78, p. 13)*

"There are moments of contrivance in the way the play is structured, but what impresses one about Bishop's writing is how skillful he is at putting the most basic, awkward things . . . on stage. . . . You feel you are seeing a playwright grappling with something that matters, which doesn't seem to happen often in our theater." — Howard Kissel, *Women's Wear Daily (1-10-78, p. 32)*

Fefu and Her Friends

Margaret Harrington and Rebecca Schull

By Maria Irene Fornes. Presented by the American Place Theatre, Wynn Handman, director, Julia Miles, associate director; directed by Ms. Fornes; settings by Kert Lundell and Nancy Tobias; costumes by Theo Barnes; lighting by Edward M. Greenberg; production stage manager, Nancy Harrington. American Place Theatre, 111 West 46th Street.

Fefu and seven of her women friends come together in her New England living room in the spring of 1935. There is to be some sort of reunion, but before it can actually begin Fefu casually picks up a shotgun and shoots out the window at her husband, a shot that will be repeated at the end of the play. In between, the playwright explores the lives, mainly the sorrows, of her eight characters, showing them as they eat, play, suffer and work on a fund-raising show.

But the essence of *Fefu*'s interest lies less in plot or even character than in technique. For, after the initial scene in the living room, the audience is moved about, in groups and in no selected order, to the lawn, the kitchen, the study and a bedroom, to view various simultaneously occuring events, before eventually returning to the central living room set. In one, it sees a love affair renewed; in another looks on a paralyzed woman in her bed, a woman as paralyzed in mind as in body, who hallucinates: "Women are evil. Woman is not a human being. . . . Unpredictable. . . ." In this as in other images, Ms. Fornes demonstrates her view of men and women as loving enemies, of a sisterhood that shares at least some dreams.

Opened January 13, 1978, for a limited engagement
Closed February 5, 1978

THE CAST

Fefu . . . . Rebecca Schull
Cindy . . . . .Dorothy Lyman
Christina . . . . Elizabeth Perry
Julia . . . . Margaret Harrington
Emma . . . . .Gordana Rashovich
Paula. . . . . .Connie LoCurto
Sue. . . . . Arleigh Richards
Cecilia . . . . .Judith Roberts

REVIEWS

"Uneven but fascinating. . . . *Fefu* is the dramatic equivalent of a collection of poems. . . . There are many . . . fine things in *Fefu*, which Miss Fornes directs, generally well. There are also incidents and encounters that do not convey very much. Some of the characters have little expressive function. . . . Furthermore, some of the action — particularly a horseplay scene involving a water fight — is awkwardly directed and performed. It is an imperfect evening but a stimulating one; and with moments of genuine splendor in it." — Richard Eder, *The New York Times* (1-14-78, p. 10)

"The form . . . proved engrossing. The content seemed more of a mystique than a mystery, more of a message than a statement. The form was mildly exhilarating. . . . The writing is stupidly self-indulgent, lounging from sentence to sentence, hoping to be admired. . . . One plus for the play is the warmness it has for women together. . . . It is better than going backstage to a TV soap-opera — but probably not that much better." — Clive Barnes, *New York Post* (1-14-78, p. 12)

"If the author has any point to make, which I doubt, it is to show the presumed subservence of women of that day. But one can't be sure, because so much of the talk consists of blurry aphorisms and stilted poetics. . . . You can't really judge the acting in a piece like this. . . . But I did find Gordana Rashovich a young actress of mettle." — Douglas Watt, *Daily News* (1-14-78, p. 12)

"The play's compassion and tender strength override weaknesses of structure and narrative, and *Fefu* becomes a vision of woman in the contradictions of her power and plight." — Jack Kroll, *Newsweek* (1-23-78, p. 87)

"There is today a cult of the imprecise. It flirts with the so-called unconscious. Adicts will find *Fefu* especially beguiling. To others I say, 'Beware!'" — Harold Clurman, *The Nation* (2-11-78, p. 154)

"Not to mince words, Maria Irene Fornes's rich, astonishing play . . . seems to me the only essential thing the New York theatre has added to our cultural life in the past year." — Michael Feingold, *The Village Voice* (1-23-78, p. 75)

One Crack Out

James Greene and Kenneth Welsh

THE CAST

Al . . . . .Jerry Zaks
Jack the Hat. . . . . Norman Snow
Earl . . . . Ed Cambridge
Bulldog . . . . Al Freeman, Jr.
Wanda. . . . . Christine Baranski
Charlie Evans . . . . .Kenneth Welsh
Suitcase Sam . . . . James Greene
Helen . . . . Teri Garr
McKee. . . . . .John Aquino

By David French. Presented by the Phoenix Theatre, T. Edward Hambleton, managing director; directed by David Freudenberger; scenic design by James Tilton; lighting design by Paul H. Everett; costume design by Julie Weiss; billiard consultant, Steve Mizerak. Marymount Manhattan Theatre, 221 East 71st Street.

Canadian playwright David French sets *One Crack Out* in a Toronto pool hall. Charlie, who is a pool hustler on the skids, has been making his money playing pool, with occasional cons on the side. He and his partner, Suitcase Sam, who poses as an eccentric who carries his money around in a suitcase, have successfully been setting up suckers for years. Now, however, they find that their game is no longer working. Charlie has lost his touch and has just been taken for three thousand dollars by a drug-dealing pimp named Jack the Hat. Another pimp, Bulldog, is now a "collector" of delinquent debts. His weapon is an iron pipe. Between the opening prologue, a game played in complete silence, and the conclusion, which finds another game beginning, Charlie regains his confidence as he is about to start playing for the highest stakes of his life. A win will wipe out his debt; a loss will result in the collector breaking his hands.

Opened January 16, 1978, for a limited engagement
Closed January 29, 1978

REVIEWS

"Taut, entertaining, well paced and well performed. It is also lightweight, and there would be nothing wrong with that if its author did not seem to think that there was. . . . David French has not given his characters much originality or depth, but he has given them a measure of style, buoyancy and vitality; enough so that we care about them and take an interest in Charlie and what will happen to him. . . . On James Tilton's useful set, laying out the poolroom and bar and with one wall lifting at times to show Charlie's apartment, the director, Daniel Freudenberger, has achieved a pace and a whole range of performances that keep us generally engrossed." — Richard Eder, *The New York Times* (1-17-78, p. 39)

"The plot is detailed and contrived — in fact, overcontrived. This, together with the play's inconclusive ending, is a weakness. But the atmosphere clings to the piece with authenticity. . . . Daniel Freudenberger has staged the play with caring attention, and the acting is fierce and clear." — Clive Barnes, *New York Post* (1-17-78, p. 21)

"For all its credibility of style and place . . . the play fails to generate much excitement, beyond the excitement of watching the actors at work." — Edith Oliver, *The New Yorker* (1-30-78, p. 72)

"The performances are adequate, and in the case of Kenneth Welsh as Charlie, and especially the much underrated James Greene as his sidekick, much better than that." — John Simon, *New York* (1-30-78, p. 60)

"David French . . . can build a play (or at least part of a play) like it's made of mortar and bricks. . . . Where the production succeeds is in its pungent sense of atmosphere and in its taut build-up of events leading to the duel." — Marilyn Stasio, *Cue* (2-4—17-78, p. 19)

Lulu

Trish Hawkins and Jack Davidson

THE CAST

Animal Tamer	Ken Kliban
August	Michael Ayr
Lulu	Trish Hawkins
Dr. Schön	Jack Davidson
Schwarz	Jeff Daniels
Dr. Goll	Gerard Russak
Alwa Schön	William Hurt
Schigolch	William Robertson
Escherich	Michael Ayr
Prince Escerny	Burke Pearson
Countess Geschwitz	Jacqueline Bertrand
Roderigo Quast	Ken Kliban
Alfred Hugenberg	Danton Stone
Ferdinand	Michael Ayr
Marquis Casti-Piani	Mark Soper

and: Sharon Madden, Mariellen Rokosny, Nancy Snyder, Joyce Reehling, Robert E. Barnes, Jr.

By Frank Wedekind. Presented by the Circle Repertory Company, Marshall W. Mason, artistic director; directed by Rob Thirkield; setting by John Lee Beatty; costumes by David Murin; lighting by Ruth Roberts; music by Norman L. Berman; sound by Charles S. London; production stage manager, Amy Schecter. Circle Repertory Theatre, 99 Seventh Avenue South.

Lulu fuses two Wedekind plays, *Earth Spirit* (1899) and *Pandora's Box* (1903), which also provide the basis for Alban Berg's celebrated contemporary opera *Lulu*.

Rob Thirkield's production is set in a circus ring and views Lulu as a whore, an archetypal if partially innocent destroyer of men, but nonetheless a figure of lust who corrupts every man she encounters. Finally, she confronts Jack the Ripper, and he is too much for her. Her path, in the meantime, has included a lover who dies of a stroke, another who commits suicide, one she shoots, an acrobat who does the one thing an acrobat cannot — grows fat — and a schoolboy who is expelled. They are seen in various stages of destruction, but always through the eye of the imagination rather than reality.

Opened January 17, 1978, for a limited engagement
Closed February 28, 1978

REVIEWS

"It is a disaster. This is true despite a gallant and interesting performance by Trish Hawkins. . . . It is the only major thing that comes out right, and it is not nearly enough to counteract the growing sense of entrapment in a production that is a fratricide of talents. . . . Aside from Miss Hawkins, the performances tend to be mannered blurs. . . . There is no style or rhythm in the delivery, and so there is little sense." – Richard Eder, *The New York Times (2-18-78, p. 16)*

"The evening never quite works out. Thirkield very properly tries to set his production in a circus ring . . . but he almost instantly loses the image. And that frankly is that. . . . Thirkield has missed no chance at misunderstanding the essential nature of Wedekind. . . . This, let us face it, is a travesty of the play." – Clive Barnes, *New York Post (2-18-78, p. 17)*

"An unredeemed disaster. . . . The continuity is often sabotaged by the cuts, but when everything about Rob Thirkield's mounting is sheer desolation — visually, verbally, histrionically — what matter a little added incomprehensibility? I have neither the space nor the heart to itemize the horrors." – John Simon, *New York (3-6-78, p. 91)*

"The actors go about their evil business with an air of embarrassment. . . . To her credit, Trish Hawkins's Lulu hawks her wares with conviction." – Marilyn Stasio, *Cue (3-4–17-78, p. 20)*

A Prayer for My Daughter

Laurence Luckinbill and George Dzundza

By Thomas Babe. Presented by the New York Shakespeare Festival; Joseph Papp, producer; Bernard Gersten, associate producer; directed by Robert Allan Ackerman; setting by Bil Mikulewicz; costumes by Bob Wojewodski; lighting by Arden Fingerhut; production stage manager, Kitzi Becker. Public/Anspacher Theatre, 425 Lafayette Street.

Two men have been arrested by the New York City police in a homicide case. An elderly woman has been murdered for a small amount of money and the suspects are a neurotic middle-aged homosexual and a young junkie. One of the policemen is a large, almost caricatured tough guy; the other smaller, seemingly more sympathetic. It emerges that the first is a drunk, the second himself on drugs. In other words, no one is the soul of stability.

The first of the suspects regards his younger associate as his "daughter," yet finds no difficulty in blaming him for the killing. He, however, is not the only "daughter" of the play. The blustering Irish cop's daughter commits suicide offstage and he makes little effort to prevent it. The homosexual suspect has an actual daughter, whose birth he describes in considerable detail. In one way or another, each daughter is betrayed. Hence, "a prayer for my daughter."

Opened January 17, 1978
Closed April 16, 1978

THE CAST

Kelly. . . . . .George Dzundza
Jack . . . . Jeffrey De Munn
Jimmy. . . . . Alan Rosenberg
Simon . . . . Laurence Luckinbill

REVIEWS

"A strange and compelling play. . . . Though Mr. Babe's sharp dialogue is grounded in gritty reality and Robert Allan Ackerman's staging is carefully naturalistic, there is a feeling of heightened reality. It is as if the characters are in limbo, where, injected with truth serum, they will tell one another more than they would otherwise reveal. The result is a play that sneaks up on us, makes us overlook questionable details, and unsuspectingly, delivers swift body punches. . . . The acting is impeccable, and the play . . . confirms Mr. Babe's position as one of our most challenging young dramatists." — Mel Gussow, *The New York Times (1-18-78, p. C 16)*

"Fascinating, because while it clings tenaciously like a grimy, battered terrier to the trappings of realism, the play also possesses strands of apparent symbolism that are never made completely evident. It is a play with a sub-text, that contrives to make much of its naturalistic workings seem dangerously ludicrous. . . . Robert Allan Ackerman's direction, which focuses on the person-to-person confrontations by which the drama progresses, proves crisp in its action and imaginative in its detail. And the acting has a most natural energy to it." — Clive Barnes, *New York Post (1-18-78, p. 53)*

"Was there a compelling reason for writing this? . . . George Dzundza is supremely right to the least detail of shading. . . . Robert Allan Ackerman has directed appropriately amid suitably shabby surroundings." — John Simon, *New York (1-30-78, p. 60)*

"It is weakened, I think, as so many plays by young dramatists are weakened, by monologues, which, whatever their value, tend to impede progress. Nevertheless, the accomplishment is impressive. . . . The acting, under Robert Allan Ackerman's direction, couldn't be better." — Edith Oliver, *The New Yorker (1-23-78, p.46)*

"Ackerman and his cast hardly miss a beat." — Terry Curtis Fox, *The Village Voice (1-23-78, p. 75)*

Donal Donnelly

My Astonishing Self

An entertainment devised by Michael Voysey from the writings of George Bernard Shaw. Presented by Arthur Cantor. Astor Place Theatre, 434 Lafayette Street.

My Astonishing Self, which has been assembled and edited from the letters, essays and other writing — though apparently not from the plays — of George Bernard Shaw, is partly a showcase for the writer's views on such subjects as religion, sex, war and vegetarianism and partly a showcase for the actor Donal Donnelly, who is the only member of the cast. It does, however, also show Shaw in some of his more personal moments, as he reflects on his parents, his relations with his wife and with other women and his attitude toward old age.

In the first act, Mr. Donnelly comes on in the garb so familiar from numerous portraits of Shaw: a striped suit with a Norfolk jacket, complete with red beard. By the second act, the beard and hair have turned white and the suit is tweed. The audience sees Shaw at forty, reflecting on his first job (in a Dublin real-estate office), his coming to London, his beginning as a speaker for socialism and as an unsuccessful novelist. Later, there are scenes involving his career and Mrs. Patrick Campbell, to be followed by a concluding one depicting him doddering about in his garden shortly before his death. It is a composite portrait and, of necessity, only a partial one, but replete with clues to a complex man.

Opened January 18, 1978
Closed March 5, 1978

With: Donal Donnelly

REVIEWS

"An engaging if not totally satisfying evening. . . . The material is selected widely and contains many marvelous things. . . . In his effort to cover a great deal of ground, Mr. Voysey produces a rather scattered effect. In the earlier portions, particularly, he goes too quickly from one theme to the next to give Mr. Donnelly a chance to seize the character solidly. . . . Mr. Donnelly has achieved full possession of the character, and if we never think we are seeing Shaw, we begin to feel that we are hearing him." — Richard Eder, *The New York Times (1-19-78, p. C 15)*

"The impish clownishness of Shaw travels well — one might have a few initial doubts about Donnelly, particularly at the very beginning, but he ends strongly with decrepitude. . . . What Voysey achieves here is a portrait of Shaw — his compassion, his wonderful sense of the ridiculous and his ability to laugh at himself before laughing at anyone else, his nervous vanity, and total decency." — Clive Barnes, *New York Post (1-19-78, p. 30)*

"By and large, Mr. Voysey has chosen and edited well, and because Mr. Donnelly talks directly to us, and never at us, the effect is of G.B.S. in intimate conversation with the audience." — Edith Oliver, *The New Yorker (1-30-78, p. 72)*

"The main problem lies with Donal Donnelly, whom I have always liked as an actor, but whom I deplore as Shaw. There is something sluggish, flabby, and unctuous about his impersonation. . . . Even his looks and makeup are an awful softening and prettification of Shaw." — John Simon, *New York (2-6-78, p. 76)*

"Short of going to a good séance, the best bet for meeting the indefatigable soul of George Bernard Shaw is at the Astor Place Theatre, where Irish actor Donal Donnelly is presenting a remarkable one-man show on Shaw." — Christopher Sharp, *Women's Wear Daily (1-19-78, p. 12)*

Black Body Blues

Samm-Art Williams and Catherine Slade

By Gus Edwards. Presented by the Negro Ensemble Company; directed by Douglas Turner Ward; setting by Raymond C. Recht; lighting by Paul Gallo; costumes by Arthur McGee; production stage manager, Horacena J. Taylor. St. Mark's Playhouse, 133 Second Avenue.

A gentle and innocent former boxer who works as a butler for a white man is living with a prostitute and drug addict. Into their drab apartment comes his brother, a bank robber who is on the run from the police. Not surprisingly the former boxer, Arthur, is cuckolded by his brother, who makes a pass at his mistress, then accepts a job working for the same white businessman, who has always treated Arthur with both fairness and food for thought, including an introduction to Beethoven's *Ninth Symphony.* He seems to be the only person who has taken him seriously. Joyce is not really in love with him, but continues to turn tricks to pay off her pusher and ex-pimp whenever she needs a fix. Upstairs lives Fletcher, a fanatical blind man, who professes appreciation for Arthur's attentions, but is perfectly willing to enjoy sex with Joyce. Perhaps inevitably, Arthur is exploited by all, particularly by his brother and the pimp, who return to the house where he has gotten employment for them and burglarize it. Arthur's employer kills the pusher; his brother kills his employer. Presumably, it will take only a moment for his brother to shoot down Arthur as well.

Opened January 24, 1978
Closed March 5, 1978

REVIEWS

"Until its melodramatic ending, this play is the soul of terseness. It is almost all atmosphere. . . . The performances are, for the most part, realistic, particularly Mr. Williams and Mr. Faison as the two unlike brothers. . . . *Black Body Blues* is merely a mood piece with little substance." — Mel Gussow, *The New York Times (1-25-78, p. C 13)*

"It is a play with the casually accidental quality of life to it. There is little narrative — only incident. And the incidents would win no prizes in the tidy world of playwrighting [sic], and perhaps are too high-tensioned for reality. Yet it works. . . . It is a good play, and what is impressive about it is simply its spareness and simplicity. Edwards doesn't waste words, but even more significantly he doesn't waste scenes. Douglas Turner Ward is a marvelous director. He never misses a beat, or lets his actors miss one... : . This man is a writer, and Ward has seen it, and proved it." — Clive Barnes, *New York Post (1-25-78, p. 53)*

"For all the violence of the action, there is little tension . . . and little depth of character. . . . This show just doesn't work." — Edith Oliver, *The New Yorker (2-6-78, p. 68)*

"Edwards has made his hero too simple — both mentally and as a dramatic character. The latter impoverishment he shares, moreover, with the other dramatis personae, all of whom are too one-sidedly eager to use him. . . . The conflicts, then, lack plasticity and complexity; *Black Body Blues* is hardly more than an outline for a play. . . . The acting is most accomplished." — John Simon, *New York (2-13-78, p. 74)*

"Shrouded in veils of mood and mystery. Strip them away and you'll see that, behind all that murk there's nobody home. One half-interesting character lurks in the gloom, and maybe the germ of a theme. But flushing them out is barely worth the effort." — Marilyn Stasio, *Cue (2-18–3-3-78, p. 28)*

Othello

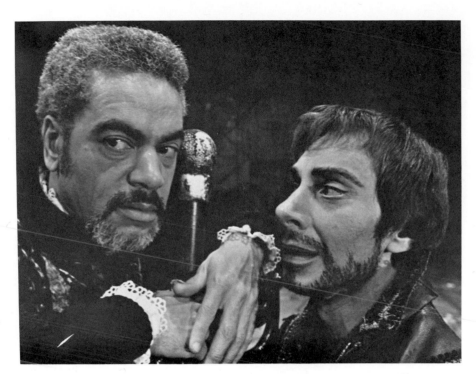

Earle Hyman and Nicholas Kepros

THE CAST

Othello. . . . . Earle Hyman
Iago . . . . Nicholas Kepros
Desdemona . . . . Mary Carney
Emilia . . . . .Carmen de Lavallade
Cassio. . . . . Edmund Davys
Roderigo. . . . . .Powers Boothe
Brabantio, Gratiano . . . Wyman Pendleton
Bianca . . . . Elizabeth Owens
Duke, Lodovico . . . . John Straub
Montano, a Senator . . . . . . .Craig Dudley
Officer and Gentleman . . . . . .Kale Brown
Gentleman and Officer . . . .Wesley Stevens
Senator and Officer. . . . . Thomas Brooks
Attendants . . . . Michael Arabian,
James Scott Bell, Jane Milne,
Mary Grace Pizzullo, Thomas M. Ries

By William Shakespeare. Presented by the Roundabout Theatre; directed by Gene Feist; setting by Jeff Fiala; costumes by Christina Giannini; lighting by John McKernon; score by Philip Campanella; production stage manager, Holley Jack Horner. Roundabout/Stage One, 333 West 23rd Street.

Iago has been bypassed for promotion in favor of the younger Cassio and decides to take vengeance on his commander, Othello, the Moor of Venice. To do so, he plays upon Othello's jealousy concerning his wife Desdemona, employing as pawns Cassio and Roderigo, one of Desdemona's former suitors, in order to destroy her reputation. Othello falls into the trap and soon is ready to believe all he is told about his wife's behavior. Iago adroitly sets his pawns against each other, bringing about the death of all but Cassio. But it is too late for either Desdemona or Othello. He smothers her, then takes his own life. His machinations revealed, Iago is put to death.

Opened January 30, 1978, for a limited engagement
Closed April 8, 1978

REVIEWS

"The Roundabout has given us a well-paced and lucid *Othello*. This is not enough. What *Othello* has to offer is not lucidity, but the properties of classical tragedy: pity and terror. . . . The quality of this play rests with the actors who play Othello, Iago and Desdemona and, to a lesser extent, Cassio and Emilia. It is in these performances that the production becomes useful and absorbing, but something less than overwhelming. . . . We never fully enter into Mr. Hyman's emotions, his passion or his despair. . . . Miss Carney is sometimes affecting as Desdemona, but she plays the part too slightly, too wispily." — Richard Eder, *The New York Times (1-31-78, p. 15)*

"Earle Hyman . . . acts without rhetoric or recitation, so even the great speeches are never allowed to become set pieces; they seem fresh and spontaneous. . . . Mr. Hyman aside, the performance as a whole is, as I say, lacklustre, without poetry or depth or wonder." — Edith Oliver, *The New Yorker (2-13-78, p. 88)*

"In your standard *Othello*, one of the characters is unjustly strangled; in this one, all of them deserve to be. . . . By way of further originality, this *Othello* reduces tragedy to farce." — John Simon, *New York (2-13-78, p. 74)*

"Although Gene Feist's production is not bent out of traditional shape in any destructive way, it is neither explored nor stretched to give a new perspective on a familiar classic." — Marilyn Stasio, *Cue (2-18–3-3-78, p. 28)*

"A respectable way to introduce *Othello* 'to students, though I would gladly be spared Earle Hyman's Moor." — Michael Feingold, *The Village Voice (2-27-78, p. 71)*

By Strouse

Donna Marshall, Gary Beach, Gail Nelson and
Maureen Moore

Music by Charles Strouse; lyrics by Strouse, Lee Adams and Martin Charnin. Presented by Norman Kean; directed by Charles Strouse; designed by Connie and Peter Wexler; choreography by Mary Kyte; musical director, Randy Barnett; production manager, David Rubinstein. The Ballroom, 458 West Broadway.

By Strouse, originally presented by the off-Off Broadway Manhattan Theatre Club, is a one-hour collection of songs by Broadway composer Charles Strouse, who has also directed the production.

Some numbers, most of which have lyrics by Strouse's frequent partner Lee Adams, are drawn from such musicals as *Bye, Bye, Birdie; All American; Golden Boy; It's a Bird, It's a Plane, It's Superman; Applause* and *Annie,* but others come from several unproduced musical comedies in which Strouse had a part.

Opened January 31, 1978
Closed

With: Gary Beach, Donna Marshall, Maureen Moore, Gail Nelson

REVIEWS

"You don't go out humming the tunes so much as you go out humming the idiom — this entire sheaf of musical reminders has a style and sweetness of its own, and a certain wit and acerbity, that you might have given less credit than was due in the first heat of the original show.

"*By Strouse* . . . has a lovely cast of four. In this kind of show the chemistry of the cast and its material is so vital, and here every equation works out. . . . In that misty land — mildly rose-colored — between Broadway and cabaret, *By Strouse* does very nicely." — Clive Barnes, *New York Post (2-3-78, p. 41)*

"A thoroughly entertaining musical revue. . . . Besides Strouse's melodic ingenuity, the songs bristle with literate, clever lyrics. . . . Individually [the cast] are first-rate singers, and together they are dynamic. . . . The show has been meticulously staged by the composer, who has left nothing to chance. . . . Connie and Peter Wexler have designed an attractive new stage for the Ballroom. Mary Kyte has done a nice job with the choreography, and fine support at the keyboard is provided by Randy Barnett." — *Variety (2-15-78, p. 84)*

Old Man Joseph and His Family

By Romulus Linney. Presented by the Chelsea Theatre Center, in collaboration with the Colonnades Theatre Lab; directed by Robert Kalfin; scenery and costumes designed by Carrie F. Robbins; lighting designed by Mark DiQuinzio; music composed by Ken Guilmartin. Chelsea Theatre Center at the Brooklyn Academy of Music, 30 Lafayette Avenue, Brooklyn, New York; Chelsea Westside Theatre, 407 West 43rd Street.

Drawing upon the gospels and folk tales about biblical figures, Romulus Linney portrays Joseph as an aged carpenter, Mary as a teenage bride and their son Jesus. The playwright is primarily concerned with two questions: How did Joseph feel to be the father of the son of God and what was that son like as a boy.

Most of the major events in all their lives are kept offstage, among them the birth of Jesus and the coming of the three Wise Men. Instead, Linney attempts to humanize the Holy Family, finding Joseph suspicious about the idea of the Immaculate Conception and reluctant to believe that Jesus is different from anyone else. Mary is presented as a total believer and Jesus as something of a troublemaker, at least during the years when he is growing up.

Members of the cast often double in the numerous roles, change the scenery and play on various instruments.

Opened January 18, 1978 (in Brooklyn), for a limited engagement
Opened January 24, 1978 (in Manhattan), for a limited engagement
Closed February 5, 1978

With: Lou Gilbert (as Joseph), Nesbitt Blaisdell, Jacqueline Cassel, Louis Giambalvo, Donna Haley, Marica Hyde, Peter Kingsley, Berit Lagerwall, Peter Scolari and Charles Stavola

REVIEWS

"The work has a childlike innocence, and cut to one hour it might have an appeal as a holiday entertainment for children. But as a full-length evening of theater, it is of limited interest. . . . Lou Gilbert is convincing as the patriarchal Joseph. . . . Jacqueline Cassel is properly saintly as Mary." — Mel Gussow, *The New York Times (1-20-78, p. C 3)*

"The idea is super. Only the play went wrong. . . . The tone is too folksy, too contrived and patronizing. . . . Kalfin's direction, stylized to within an inch of its death, with trickily cutesy scenery . . . is all too much. . . . It is a children's tale for adults that not even children could relate to." — Clive Barnes, *New York Post (1-21-78, p. 13)*

"Banal in the extreme. . . . Robert Kalfin's staging is proficient and even clever at points, but his actors . . . are a clumsy and amateurish bunch." — Michael Feingold, *The Village Voice (2-6-78, p. 77)*

Molly

By Simon Gray. Presented by the Hudson Guild Theatre; directed by Stephen Hollis; costumes by Patricia Adshead; setting by Philipp Jung; lighting by John H. Paull; original music by Andy Bloor. Hudson Guild Theatre, 441 West 26th Street.

A retired businessman who is married to a considerably younger woman is rapidly losing his self-respect as not only his age but also deafness set in. The wife, Molly, finds herself increasingly frustrated, though solicitous, and seduces a young gardener, who is a half-wit.

When the husband becomes aware of the relationship between the boy and his wife he dismisses Oliver, only to be stabbed to death with the garden shears.

Molly, by the author of such critically acclaimed plays as *Butley* and *Otherwise Engaged,* reportedly is based on an actual British murder case which the playwright came upon while browsing through a paperback he found in a railroad compartment.

Opened January 22, 1978, for a limited engagement
Closed February 12, 1978

THE CAST

Molly . . . . Tammy Grimes
Teddie. . . . . Michael Higgins
Eve. . . . . Margaret Hilton
Oliver . . . . Josh Clark
Greaves . . . . Kenneth T. Scott
P. C. . . . . William A. Serow

REVIEWS

"A curious, stormy melodrama. . . . Mr. Gray has created a powerful dramatic image out of the story but he has not created a play. . . . None of it is much more than a civilized embroidery on the rather ordinary melodrama that Mr. Gray discovered." — Richard Eder, *The New York Times (1-23-78, p. C 16)*

"There is nothing much to the story. . . . Yet Gray has made it into an extremely interesting study of character. . . . Miss Grimes has never been better. . . . Hollis has directed the play with deft accuracy. Yet, like the play itself, the production seems only part finished." — Clive Barnes, *New York Post (1-23-78, p. 17)*

"All the parts are good . . . and, under Stephen Hollis's direction, they are most ably performed." — Edith Oliver, *The New Yorker (2-6-78, p. 68)*

"A curiously floundering effort from one of England's most fastidiously eloquent playwrights." — David Ansen, *Newsweek (2-6-78, p. 91)*

Statements after an Arrest under the Immorality Act
and
Scenes from Soweto

Veronica Castang and Robert Christian

By Athol Fugard (*Statements*) and Steve Wilmer (*Scenes*). Presented by the Manhattan Theatre Club, Lynne Meadow, artistic director; directed by Thomas Bullard; setting by David Potts; costumes by Judy Dearing; lighting by Dennis Parichy; dialect coach, Gordon Jacoby; production stage manager, Jody Boese. Manhattan Theatre Club, 321 East 73rd Street.

In *Statements After an Arrest Under the Immorality Act,* a colored principal of a slum area school and a white librarian meet and make love in a library in Noupoort, Cape Province. They are thus in violation of South Africa's 1957 Immorality Act which prohibits intercourse between white and colored people. The man has a wife and child, whom he does not want to leave, and the woman, a relative newcomer of the town, was a virgin before she met him. As they speak softly to each other and make love, there is a commotion outside. The lights go up and a white policeman is seen at the left holding a dossier. The police have been alerted by a neighbor and what follows is, in effect, a physical nudity that becomes a metaphor for the psychological baring of souls that takes place.

Scenes from Soweto portrays a young black man who has returned home to Johannesburg from Oxford. He gets a job with an Anglo-American company which he hopes will enable him to help both his family and his fellow blacks peaceably to improve their lots. But when the Soweto riots erupt, he inevitably is politicized and, almost against his will, becomes a hero and martyr.

Opened February 5, 1978, for a limited engagement
Closed March 3, 1978

THE CASTS

Statements

Frieda Joubert . . . . Veronica Castang
Errol Philander . . . . Robert Christian
Detective Sergeant J. DuPreez . . . . .John C. Vennema

Scenes

Black Actor . . . . Robert Christian
White Actor . . . . .John C. Vennema

REVIEWS

"The relationship between Errol, restless and intellectually curious but fragile, and the librarian who loves him is touching and beautifully portrayed. . . . The Manhattan Theatre Club production, finely directed by Thomas Bullard, is built on the lovely performances of the two principal actors. . . . Despite its static moments and sometimes excessive contrivance, [it] has force, authority and a broad and compassionate vision. . . . *Scenes from Soweto* is a far thinner and more strident work. . . . It turns into the shallowest kind of polemic documentary." — Richard Eder, *The New York Times (2-6-78, p. C 18)*

"A political statement about South Africa that must not be ignored. . . . This is political dynamite. . . . The potency of these words you are afraid to hear is immeasurably powerful. . . . Fugard's play is a beautiful piece of work — full of echoes and resonances. . . . Thomas Bullard has directed both of these plays most movingly. . . . And the acting has the dignity of grief. Robert Christian . . . is memorable in both plays." — Clive Barnes, *New York Post (2-6-78, p. 20)*

"Fugard creates an atmosphere of relentless intimacy, of anguish reduced — or, rather, enlarged — to essentials. . . . But the play has its weaknesses, too. Fugard, commendably wishing to surpass mere documentary realism, reaches for poetic heightening. . . . Lyricism . . . tends to escape him in the best circumstances; here, the fast shifts into and away from it make it clumsier yet. . . . The acting by all three performers is very fine." — John Simon, *New York (2-20-78, p. 76)*

"*Statements* is an eloquent, poetic tragedy, as eloquent at times in its silences as in its words. . . . The characters he explores and presents so artfully and the situations they are in are persuasion enough. The performance, under Thomas Bullard's direction, is entirely worthy of the play. . . . In *Scenes from Soweto* . . . the hero starts out to be quite interesting — or, at least, Mr. Christian makes him so — and Mr. Vennema is persuasive enough, but the play soon dwindles into just another polemic." — Edith Oliver, *The New Yorker (2-20-78, p. 104)*

"Though neither is an outstanding achievement, each possesses a special importance." — Harold Clurman, *The Nation (2-25-78, p. 221)*

The Devil's Disciple

George Rose and Chris Sarandon

With: Margaret Hamilton, Luise Heath, Randy Pelish, Barnard Hughes, Carole Shelley, Fred Stuthman, Allan Lurie, Robert Cornthwaite, Betty Ramey, Peggy Rae, Chris Sarandon, John Orchard, Earl Boen, George Rose, Ken Letner, Norman Abrams, Timothy Askew, Jason Buzas, Paul Diaz, George McDaniel, Robert Rhys, Holly Villaire, Ron Perkins, Rudolph Ranier, Rex Stallings

By George Bernard Shaw. Presented by the BAM Theatre Company, in association with the Center Theatre Group—Ahmanson Theatre (Los Angeles); directed by Frank Dunlop; settings and costumes by Carl Toms; lighting by F. Mitchell Dana; stage managers, Barbara-Mae Phillips, Norman Abrams, Paul Diaz. Brooklyn Academy of Music, 30 Lafayette Avenue, Brooklyn, New York.

The Devil's Disciple (1897) is Shaw's spoof of, among numerous other targets, the military mentality. It features Parson Anderson, the saintly and sage local preacher, with a touch of deviltry to add a fillip; Dick Dudgeon, the social rebel, whose swaggering begins to turn toward religion, and "Gentleman Johnny" Burgoyne, the sophisticated general fighting a losing war, in which he is betrayed by indifference and ineptitude back home in London.
The scene is New Hampshire during the American Revolution and, against this background, Shaw shows his young hero, Dudgeon, "starved of religion, which is the most clamorous need of his nature. . . . With Pity instead of Hatred as his master passion, he pities the devil; takes his side; and champions him . . . against the world. He thus becomes, like all genuinely religious men, a reprobate and an outcast."

Opened February 8, 1978, for a limited engagement
Closed February 19, 1978

REVIEWS

"Mr. Dunlop has chosen to respond to the problems of the play's first part by making a strenuous and stylized farce out of its slow comedy. . . . The pace is frenetic and leads us quite a ways from Shaw. The actors are encouraged to speak with the comical over-emphasis of a radio broadcast designed to bring culture to the backlands, and make sure the listeners don't miss a thing. The stylistic over-emphasis totters somewhat, as well, because some of the actors are not quite up to its demands. . . . The set, designed by Carl Toms, is a revolving wooden scaffolding that represents various rooms and, finally, the gibbet. Sometimes it revolves to little purpose but it is handsome, and allows Mr. Dunlop to move and position his actors with unfailing stylishness." — Richard Eder, *The New York Times (2-9-78, p. C 16)*

"What is important is not really the individual playing, or even this particular play. More, infinitely more, it is Frank Dunlop's ability to make the play move as an ensemble operation." — Clive Barnes, *New York Post (2-9-78, p. 43)*

"George Rose's choleric and ironic General Burgoyne is the best and most interesting Gentleman Johnny I've ever seen. . . . For the rest, this is a broad and merry *Devil's Disciple,* but not a particularly pointed one. Shaw must be taken seriously even when he is at his funniest — something that Mr. Rose and Miss Shelley never forget but that Mr. Dunlop occasionally seems to." — Edith Oliver, *The New Yorker (2-20-78, p. 104)*

"Done so wretchedly that one is forced to wonder whether the Brooklyn idea is viable. . . . Dunlop has cast all but one or two parts so badly, or elicited such poor performances in them, that excuses based on his Englishness or his actors' Americanness simply won't wash." — John Simon, *New York (2-27-78, p. 66)*

Museum

By Tina Howe. Presented by the New York Shakespeare Festival, Joseph Papp, producer, Bernard Gersten, associate producer; directed by Max Stafford-Clark; scenery by Robert Yodice; costumes by Patricia McGourty; lighting by Jennifer Tipton; production stage manager, Alan Fox. Public Theatre/LuEsther Hall, 425 Lafayette Street.

Not surprisingly, *Museum* is set in a museum. It is the final day of the current exhibit and playwright Tina Howe brings on a series of visitors to the white-on-white gallery. Some are alone, some are couples; all, apparently, are expected to depict some aspect in humanity that concerns the playwright.

Ms. Howe shows her characters reacting to the various works of art and occasionally to each other. The works themselves engage the characters in differing ways, in particular a series of three totally white canvases by a French painter who is termed a "reductionist." He, the audience is informed, was born of parents who were deaf and mute and this is the form of expression he discovered for himself. His parents appear at the end to view mutely his work. Other visitors include three photographers, a woman who wanders into the wrong exhibit and a curator who experiences some form of ecstasy over the works she portentously describes.

Opened February 26, 1978
Closed April 2, 1978

REVIEWS

"It is serious but it is also extremely diffuse. Whiffs of message seem to emerge but they are ambiguous. Essentially the play is as abstract as the three exhibits onstage.... *Museum* is well-performed and it is lucidly directed by Max Stafford-Clark. Robert Yodice has designed a fine antiseptic gallery. The play is sometimes interesting and sometimes funny and sometimes expressive. But it never commits itself clearly to what it is expressing, and it never really makes much of an impression." — Richard Eder, *The New York Times (2-28-78, p. 28)*

"*Museum* is really an extended revue sketch — sometimes bitchily funny, but overextended, shapeless, revelling in cheap laughs at easy targets. . . . Her caricatures are certainly campily exaggerated, but many of them are rooted either in truth or the popular truisms of prejudice.... The physical production is beautiful. . . . The acting is glossily impeccable." — Clive Barnes, *New York Post (2-28-78, p. 17)*

"An enchanting show. . . . It has plenty of wit and humor, and no idea appears to be emphasized over any other. Each successive incident builds and then dissipates, yet the play takes shape and holds firm." — Edith Oliver, *The New Yorker (3-6-78, p. 67)*

"There is so much openly and demonstrably wrong with Tina Howe's *Museum* . . . that it is hard to believe the play is as moving and beautiful as it happens to be.... Max Stafford-Clark . . . has welded the 18 actors who perform the various roles into a superbly efficient unit." — Terry Curtis Fox, *The Village Voice (3-6-78, p. 75)*

Robyn Goodman and Larry Bryggman

THE CAST

The Guard	Larry Bryggman
Michael Wall, 1st photographer	Bruce McGill
Jean-Claude	Jean-Pierre Stewart
Françoise	Frederikke Meister
Annette Froebel, lost woman	Kaiulani Lee
Liz	Robyn Goodman
Carol	Kathryn Grody
Blakey	Kathleen Tolan
Mr. Hollingsford, lost man	Gerry Bamman
Elizabeth Sorrow, silent woman	Dianne Wiest
Peter Ziff, silent man	Dan Hedaya
Mr. Salt, man with recorded tour	Steven Gilborn
Mrs. Salt	Jane Hallaren
Maggie Snow, lost woman	Lynn Milgrim
Bob Lamb	Jeffrey David Pomerantz
Will Willard	Joel Brooks
Fred Izumi, 2nd photographer	Calvin Jung
Mira Zadal, inquiring woman	Robyn Goodman
First man in passing	Gerry Bamman
Second man in passing	Jean-Pierre Stewart
Barbara Castle	Lynn Milgrim
Barbara Zimmer	Karen Ludwig
Mr. Gregory, man with loud recorded tour	Jean-Pierre Stewart
Chloe Trapp, curator	Kaiulani Lee
Ada Bilditsky, curator's 1st guest	Frederikke Meister
Gilda Norris, sketcher	Kathryn Grody
Tink Solheim	Dianne Wiest
Kate Siv, Tink's friend	Robyn Goodman
Bill Plaid, curator's 2nd guest	Jeffrey David Pomerantz
Lillian, 1st laughing lady	Frederikke Meister
Harriet, 2nd laughing lady	Lynn Milgrim
May, 3rd laughing lady	Karen Ludwig
Giorgio	Gerry Bamman
Zoe, his wife	Jane Hallaren
Julie Jenkins, 3rd photographer	Kathleen Tolan
First Guard	Steven Gilborn
Second Guard	Dan Hedaya
Steve Williams	Joel Brooks
An Elderly Couple	Steven Gilborn, Karen Ludwig

The Play's the Thing

Carole Shelley and Rene Auberjonois

By Ferenc Molnar; adapted by P. G. Wodehouse. Presented by the BAM Theatre Company; directed by Frank Dunlop; lighting by F. Mitchell Dana; setting by Santo Loquasto; costumes by Nancy Potts; production stage manager, Frank Bayer. Helen Carey Playhouse/Brooklyn Academy of Music, 30 Lafayette Street, Brooklyn, New York.

Molnar's 1925 play revolves about a celebrated playwright, Sandor Turai, and his collaborator, Mansky, who arrive unannounced at a Riviera castle with their composer protege. The first two men overhear a love scene between the composer's fiance and an aging actor. In an effort to restore the composer's faith in his fiance, Turai writes a play which includes the overheard dialogue.

Molnar relies primarily on some rather obvious double entendres and plays upon dramatic technique for his humor and has characters provide background details directly, thus avoiding more conventional forms of exposition. The rehearsal of Turai's play within the play, in addition, toys with other dramatic conventions.

Opened February 26, 1978, for a limited engagement
Closed March 19, 1978

THE CAST

Mansky	Kurt Kasznar
Sandor Turai	Rene Auberjonois
Albert Adam	Austin Pendleton
Johann Dwornitschek	Rex Robbins
Ilona Szabo	Carole Shelley
Almady	George Rose
Mell	Stephen Collins
Two Lackeys	Norman Abrams, Paul Diaz

REVIEWS

"A lively and playable artifact of a time when there was a thriving popular theater in Hungary as well as in America, this comedy makes an art out of artifice and tips its hat to the dramatist as *deus ex machina*. . . . As director, Mr. Dunlop never misses a chance for a laugh — although not usually at the play's expense. The pinnacle of the production is Mr. Auberjonois, who has a grandness of manner without resorting to mannerisms. . . . Santo Loquasto's set . . . is its own exercise in elegance." — Mel Gussow, *The New York Times (2-28-78, p. 28)*

"It was a pure, sugar-spun delight, and demonstrated, perhaps more clearly than ever, that the company's artistic director, Frank Dunlop, has the capability of building a major classic repertory company at the Brooklyn Academy of Music. The play practically giggled with expertise." — Clive Barnes, *New York Post (2-27-78, p. 23)*

"A splendid revival. . . . Rene Auberjonois is charming as the quick-thinking playwright. . . . Frank Dunlop has pumped new life into this 52-year-old valentine to playwrights and actors." — *Variety (3-8-78, p. 107)*

"The thing is played not impeccably but very well by a cast that includes some of the finest high comedians extant anywhere. Mr. Dunlop's staging shows signs here and there of his persistent tendency toward overkill, but the central scenes come through beautifully." — Julius Novick, *The Village Voice (3-13-78, p. 77)*

"P. G. Wodehouse's adaptation from the Hungarian is witty and apt. . . . I enjoyed the performance as a whole." — Edith Oliver, *The New Yorker (3-13-78, p. 58)*

"It is hard to understand why Frank Dunlop thought the play was worth reviving except as a vehicle for his actors." — Howard Kissel, *Women's Wear Daily (2-28-78, p. 22)*

Red Fox/Second Hanging

Frankie Taylor, Gary Slemp and Don Baker

Story-theatre by Don Baker and Dudley Cocke. Produced by the Roadside Theatre; presented by the Manhattan Theatre Club; directed by Michael Posnick; setting by David Potts; lighting by Curt Ostermann. Manhattan Theatre Club, 321 East 73rd Street.

A group of "story-tellers" relates the apparently true story of the murder conviction of a compassionate former sheriff named Ole Doc Taylor in Wise County, Virginia, in the 1890s, and his subsequent hanging.

Blending his saga with other tales of the mountain people of the period, it recounts how the wealthy Devil John Wright, who had never forgiven Taylor for arresting his crony and hit man, engineered a frame-up. Everything is set against a backdrop of rural mountain society, left feud-ridden by the Civil War, subsequently exploited by the rich city folks, who realize the enormous potential wealth waiting to be taken from the region's mineral deposits.

The three "story-tellers" use neither costumes, props nor scenery (apart from a few chairs). Instead, they narrate and demonstrate, in Story Theatre style, the events and personages, moving from one character to another, including that of narrator.

Opened March 1, 1978, for a limited engagement
Closed

With: Don Baker, Gary Slemp, Frankie Taylor

REVIEWS

"A charming little show, shaped and directed by Michael Posnick. . . . The tellers unassumingly but precisely take on all the characters, male and female, in the stories, which are illustrated by projections of old snapshots and accompanied, to delightful effect, by recordings of country fiddling." — Edith Oliver, *The New Yorker (3-20-78, p. 90)*

"A kind of documentary storytelling which not only is wonderfully engaging but also provides the audience with a rich sense of the history of the Appalachian mountain culture in which the theatre is rooted. . . . The actors present their tale with impressive skill, charm, wit, and love." — Eileen Blumenthal, *The Soho Weekly News (3-16-78, p. 44)*

"Weaves fact, fun, and a dash of fantasy into a vigorous presentation. . . . Three personable young men . . . narrate the tale and act out various characters, conveying the flavor of a whole community, the individuals within it, and a bit of social history in the bargain. The performance is greatly enhanced by projected period photographs of the region and its inhabitants." — Holly Hill, *New York Theatre Review (5-78, p. 43)*

Curse of the Starving Class

James Gammon and Ebbe Roe Smith

THE CAST

Wesley......................Ebbe Roe Smith
Ella.......................Olympia Dukakis
Emma...........................Pamela Reed
Taylor.......................Kenneth Welsh
Weston......................James Gammon
Ellis..........................Eddie Jones
Malcolm.......................John Aquino
Emerson.....................Michael J. Pollard
Slater......................Raymond J. Barry

By Sam Shepard. Presented by the New York Shakespeare Festival, Joseph Papp, producer, Bernard Gersten, associate producer; directed by Robert Woodruff; scenery and costumes by Santo Loquasto; lighting by Martin Tudor; music by Bob Feldman; production stage manager, Zane Weiner. Public/Newman Theatre, 425 Lafayette Street.

Early in the first act of his *Curse of the Starving Class*, Sam Shepard has a character observe: "No one's starving in this place. There's a starving class, and we're not part of it." But they are, figuratively — metaphorically — if not otherwise. What they are starving for is not so much food — though they periodically open a refrigerator only to find it empty — but for life itself, for communication, for acceptance, for success, for a few moments of joy.

As produced by the New York Shakespeare Festival, the stage is bare, furnished only with a table and chairs, a stove and a refrigerator. The father, Weston, is an alcoholic, currently off on a binge. The daughter, Emma, has been preparing a 4-H Club project involving a chicken she is going to dissect. Her mother kills the chicken for food. The son, apparently in his late teens, is attempting to construct a door to replace the one his father has demolished. Ella, the mother, in the meantime, has been involved with a con man who is attempting to take over the house and land for a pittance. She has agreed. Almost simultaneously, Weston has agreed to sell it to someone else. Only young Wesley seems really to care about the land on which, and in which, the family lives.

Shepard is not, however, writing a family drama; he is writing an allegory about an America consumed by its dreams of consumption, its greed and its misplaced values. He does it in ways that are at times gory, but also in ways that are poetic and almost mythical, ways that possess the originality that Shepard himself has always possessed.

Opened March 2, 1978
Closed April 9, 1978

REVIEWS

"Mr. Shepard has worked out the message in images of considerable power, and in a style that oscillates between realism and savage fantasy. A violent humor predominates, slipping into plain violence. Unfortunately, much of the force hangs in the air. It plays like a play that reads well, as if Mr. Shepard had failed to consider what would happen when his parable took physical form on the stage, and his images were played out by real actors performing in real time. . . . The director, Robert Woodruff, has allowed the action to drag excessively, accentuating the play's tendency to self-indulgence."
— Richard Eder, *The New York Times (3-3-78, p. C 3)*

"The play was ornate, opaque, at time almost tauntingly ineluctable, gory, explicit, but it had the quality of statement to it, that hoarse cry for an artist trying to be heard which always reverberates through the slightest fragment of Shepard's highly profiled work. . . . Robert Woodruff's staging caught the nervy ambivalence of the piece very well, and Santo Loquasto's stripped-down setting, a white box on a high raked stage, proved the perfect space. I admired all the actors."
— Clive Barnes, *New York Post (3-3-78, p. 29)*

"Shepard has fashioned a play of eloquent intensity, whirlwind farce and resonantly poignant insight. The cast all get A's. The ensemble work they do cannot be matched off-Broadway." — T. E. Kalem, *Time (3-20-78, p. 85)*

"At one time or another, Weston and his children speak their thoughts or memories in soliloquies so imaginative and right that they become truly hypnotic. . . . Under Robert Woodruff's direction, every shift in mood and all the complexities of character and plot are realized." — Edith Oliver, *The New Yorker (3-13-78, p. 57)*

"His most important play since *The Tooth of Crime*. . . . For the first act and a half, *Curse* rolls along as if this were Shepard's first all-out comedy hit. Woodruff's actors know exactly how to seize the material." — Terry Curtis Fox, *The Village Voice (3-13-78, p. 77)*

"Shepard stokes a simmering heat under the whole play, even under the punchy comic sections, a ruthlessness, a kind of anger that makes the essential drama seem to be not in the story but between the writer himself and the world. Once again a Shepard play testifies to the fact that he is a true man of the theater: he doesn't see life as material for drama, he sees life *as* drama." — Stanley Kauffmann, *The New Republic (4-8-78, p. 24)*

The Promise

Christopher Goutman and Marilyn McIntyre

THE CAST

Marat .... Christopher Goutman
Lika .... Marilyn McIntyre
Leonidik .... Davis Hall

By Aleksei Arbuzov; translated by Ariadne Nicolaeff. Presented by the Roundabout Theatre Company, Gene Feist/Michael Fried; directed by Michael Fried; setting by Ron Antone; costumes by Nancy L. Johnson; lighting by Robert Strohmeier; sound sequences by Philip Campanella; production stage manager, Paul Moser. Roundabout/Stage Two, 307 West 26th Street.

Aleksei Arbuzov, one of the Soviet Union's most popular postwar playwrights, sets his play in Leningrad during the great siege that occurred in World War II and in the years that followed.

Two teenagers, Lika and Marat, are found in a bleak, barren room in the bombed-out city. They have only the meagerest of amenities to sustain themselves. Into their midst comes Leonidik, who is ill with the flu and whom they bring back to health. He becomes one of their trio. There is a great difference between the two boys: Marat is outgoing, even flamboyant; Leonidik, on the other hand, is a poet, bitter and sarcastic. Though deeply loyal to each other, both also love Lika, who loves Marat. Over the course of the 17 years encompassed by the play, both young men succeed in their promise: one becomes a bridge-builder, the other a poet; the girl becomes a physician. But little else really works out for them.

Opened March 8, 1978
Closed April 9, 1978

REVIEWS

"The trouble with the play is that Arbuzov never shows us that the suffering and the hardship are organically connected to the domestic relationships. . . . The heroic and the romantic, usually so compatible together, are uneasily, though wordily, joined in this effort. . . . Marilyn McIntyre as Lika . . . is most convincing. The early scenes with Christopher Goutman as Marat have a wistfulness, a tenderness that one is reluctant to see end. Davis Hall as Leonidik, the poet, is formal in a wooden way. . . . Michael Fried's direction cunningly exploits the small stage, keeping the action fluid and adding expressive touches that add enormously to the play. Ron Antone has used his ingenuity to transform what starts out as the barest of rooms into a livable habitation." — Thomas Lask, *The New York Times (3-9-78, p. C 19)*

"It came together in a way it never quite had in the Broadway version. . . . Michael Fried . . . has staged this revival with a pellucid brilliance [and] been extremely well served by his cast." — Clive Barnes, *New York Post (3-9-78, p. 31)*

"Though it is long, it never loses its emotional drive, thanks principally to the performances." — William Harris, *The Soho Weekly News (3-30-78, p. 70)*

"Though weak in parts, [it] provides an excellent opportunity to see a seldom-done production by this first-rate playwright. *The Promise*, a strange and touching love story, is an example of Arbuzov at his best." — Steven Hager, *Show Business (3-16-78, p. 25)*

Molière in Spite of Himself

THE CAST

The Pont Neuf

Scaramouche . . . . Bill E. Noone
The Young Molière . . . . Berit Lagerwall
Grandfather . . . . Nesbitt Blaisdell
Street People . . . . The Company

The Troupe

Jean-Baptiste Poquelin de Molière . . . . . Tom V. V. Tammi
Madeleine Béjart . . . . Donna Haley
Armande Béjart de Molière . . . . Marcia Hyde
Mariette Rivale . . . . Jacqueline Cassel
Charles Varlet de La Grange . . . . Peter Scolari
Zacharie Moirron . . . . Peter Kingsley
Jean-Jacques Bouton . . . . Charlie Stavola
Genevieve Du Croisy . . . . Katherine Parks
Jodelet . . . . Louis Giambalvo
Charlatan . . . . J. Allen Suddeth
Mazatan . . . . Michael O'Keefe
Fefee . . . . Rebecca Kreinen

The Court

Louis XIV, King of France . . . . Bill E. Noone
D'Orsini (One-Eye) a Black Musketeer . . . . Nesbitt Blaisdell
Philippe, Duc d'Orleans . . . . Edward Edwards
Archbishop de Charron . . . . Louis Giambalvo
Honest Cobbler . . . . Berit Lagerwall
Brother Fidelity . . . . Michael O'Keefe
Marquis de Lessac . . . . David Morgan
Father Barthelmy . . . . J. Allen Suddeth

Peter Kingsley (above), Marcia Hyde
and Tom V. V. Tammi

By Mikhail Bulgakov; adapted and directed by Michael Lessac; music and sound design by Michael Jay; set designed by Robert U. Taylor; costumes designed by Hilary A. Sherred; light by Randy Becker; special props by Bill E. Noone; company stage manager, Arthur J. Schwartz. Colonnades Theatre Lab, 428 Lafayette Street.

The late Soviet playwright Mikhail Bulgakov fell into disfavor with Stalin and saw his fate as analogous with that of Molière, who experienced a similar situation with Louis XIV in France.

Adaptor-director Michael Lessac draws upon Bulgakov's 1929 "A Cabal of Hypocrites" to show a Molière who goes from very favorite protegé of the French court to beaten old man, primarily at the instigation of the French clergy. Many of the scenes occur backstage, as the company struggles for survival and experiences triumphs; assorted affairs and would-be affairs occur, one of them involving Molière, which leads to his fall from grace.

Opened March 9, 1978, for a limited engagement

REVIEWS

"A brilliantly theatrical study of power. In its American premiere at the Colonnades Theatre Lab, it has been given a superb, magical production. . . . [There are] beautifully schooled and styled performances. They are put together in a production whose every element — pace, music, Randy Becker's lighting — is a stroke of shining craftsmanship. Mr. Lessac has given us one of the most powerful and engrossing theatrical experiences of the season." — Richard Eder, *The New York Times (3-13-78, p. C 20)*

"It is a major theatrical event. . . . A marvelous play. . . . Where the play is perfectly magnificent is in its concept of a great artist destroyed by venomous despotism. . . . Lessac is much helped by the cohesive dedication of his emergent ensemble." — Clive Barnes, *New York Post (3-11-78, p. 18)*

"Elaborate, foolish, and interminable. Nevertheless, it is certainly actable, and the troupe at the Colonnades, under Mr. Lessac's direction, does it justice. . . . Most of all I admired Robert U. Taylor and Hilary A. Sherred, who designed the lovely set and costumes." — Edith Oliver, *The New Yorker (3-20-78, p. 90)*

Conjuring an Event

Michael Cristofer

THE CAST

Charlie . . . . Michael Cristofer
Annabella . . . . .Sigourney Weaver
Waiter. . . . . .John Jellison
Man . . . . MacIntyre Dixon
Smitty. . . . . Dan Hedaya
Sleeves . . . . .Frank Hamilton

By Richard Nelson. Presented by the American Place Theatre; Wynn Handman, director; Julia Miles, artistic director; directed by Douglas C. Wager; set by David Lloyd Gropman; costumes by William Ivey Long; lighting by Paul Gallo; sound design by Carol Waaser; production stage manager, Peggy Peterson. American Place Theatre, 111 West 46th Street.

Reporters have, in many recent instances, themselves become news*makers*, not solely reporters on the event. Nelson's central character, a newsman named Charlie who is obviously a bit off the mental track, seeks to conjure himself an event.

At first, the audience sees him in the library of the Pen and Pencil Club. He is blindfolded and sniffs at various substances that have been brought to him by Annabella. But he has something far more portentous in mind: he intends to bring about events, not merely report on them. It is obviously going to be a dangerous game and he is egged on by another man, a Mephisthophelean figure, as he seeks his myth. "Give me your passions, your events and your history, and I will express them for you," he asserts, only to meet his gory apocalypse.

Opened March 19, 1978, for a limited engagement
Closed April 2, 1978

REVIEWS

"[A] windy and extraordinarily bad play. . . . There is a complete lack of any theatrical effort to get the author's symbols to move. What we see is as arbitrary as it is unpleasant. Mr. Cristofer plays his part as one continual shudder, interrupted by retching." — Richard Eder, *The New York Times (3-21-78, p. 30)*

"Nelson's play is a symbolic picture of ironic failure. Yet one never quite comprehends Nelson's own commitment to the practice of journalism itself. . . . As Charlie, a journalist trying to make something happen so close to himself that even his trouser-buttons will get singed, Michael Cristofer is remarkable." — Clive Barnes, *New York Post (3-21-78, p. 21)*

"The thick layers of boredom cannot be shattered even by frequent onstage explosions. . . . Michael Cristofer plays Charlie with manic gusto and a certain shallow but undeniable expertise." — John Simon, *New York (4-3-78, p. 80)*

"The temptation to walk out during the intermission of *Conjuring an Event* was almost overpowering for this writer, but there was one thing that held me to my seat: I had no idea of what the play was supposed to be about, and I thought the second act would enable me to describe it a little better. Unfortunately, at the end of the play I was even more confused than at the end of the first act." — Christopher Sharp, *Women's Wear Daily (3-20-78, p. 10)*

"The kind of play that is often damned by being called interesting, which it happens not to be." — Edith Oliver, *The New Yorker (3-27-78, p. 96)*

P.S. Your Cat Is Dead!

Peter Simon and Vasili Bogazianos

By James Kirkwood. Presented by Haskell/Spiegel Productions; directed by Robert Nigro; set by Judie Juracek; lighting by Michael Orris Watson; production stage manager, H. Todd Iveson. Promenade Theatre, Broadway and 76th Street.

It is New Year's Eve, the apartment of an actor named Jimmy Zoole. Jimmy, unfortunately, has little to celebrate. His girl has deserted him for a university professor, he has been fired from a Broadway play he was rehearsing and written out of the TV soap opera he has counted on for sustenance. And, P.S., he finds in a note, his cat has died in an animal hospital. Not exactly the ideal way to start the New Year.

But Jimmy has other problems as well, as he soon finds out; specifically a burglar by the name of Vito who is hiding under his bed and, on a previous visit, took and destroyed the manuscript of his novel. Jimmy captures him and ties him half-naked on top of his kitchen sink. What follows is a variation on black and gallows humor, as the two men goad each other, with Vito trying to convince Jimmy he is gay, then promising to go straight and work while he completes his novel, if only he will release him. Jimmy mainly teases, feeding Vito with Kontented Kitty cat food. By play's end, Jimmy and Vito have struck a certain kind of bargain. Whether they will go to bed together remains to be seen.

Opened March 22, 1978

THE CAST

Vito . . . . Vasili Bogazianos
Kate . . . . Claire Malis
Jimmy . . . . Peter Simon
Fred . . . . John Shearin

REVIEWS

"Admittedly, some of this is amusing — though funnier on first than on second hearing. Mr. Kirkwood's pen can be a waspish needle. But most of the jokes are simply setups — slaps at obvious and easy targets. The play itself is as contrived as a pretzel. . . . In the showiest role, Mr. Bogazianos is shifty, eager to please and eventually as cozy as a kitten — a thief to warm a hearth. As the once and former mistress, Claire Malis is attractive and actressy. Peter Simon is forthright as handsome Jimmy. . . . Evidently in an attempt to enliven the evening, Robert Nigro as director oversauces the stew." — Mel Gussow, *The New York Times (3-23-78, p. C 19)*

"This is a zany comedy of total desperation. Kirkwood's writing is hip and funny and the play has a special sparkle to it. . . . As Jimmy and Vito both Peter Simon and Vasili Bogazianos showed charm. . . . *P.S. Your Cat Is Dead!* is unquestionably not one of the world-shattering comedies of our time. Yet it has a friendly giggle, and a special open sense of humanity to it. It is a play that questions attitudes and a play that makes some stealthily clever jokes. That must be a winning combination." — Clive Barnes, *New York Post (3-23-78, p. 34)*

"Another absurd and unnecessary act was the reviving of *P.S. Your Cat Is Dead.*" — John Simon, *New York (4-17-78, p. 101)*

"The show shapes up as even more amusing than before. Judging by audience reaction . . . it should, mainly by word of mouth, catch on and enjoy a much longer stay in New York this time. . . . Peter Simon is excellent as the 38-year-old actor/writer. Claire Malis is fine as the girlfriend, and John Shearin gives good support in the newly written part of the other man. Vasili Bogazianos is superb as the burglar." — *Variety (3-29-78, p. 90)*

Marcia McClain

A Bistro Car on the CNR

With: Marcia McClain, Patrick Rose, Henrietta Valor, Tom Wopat

A musical, with music by Patrick Rose, lyrics by Merv Campone and Richard Ouzounian and dialogue by D. R. Anderson. Presented by Jeff Britton and Bob Bisaccia; directed by Richard Ouzounian; choreography by Lynne Gannaway; scenery and costumes by John Falabella; lighting by Ned Hallick; musical direction by John Clifton; associate producer, Jimmy Merrill; stage manager, Craig Saeger. Playhouse Theatre, 359 West 48th Street.

For a time, the baggage car of the Rapido, a Canadian National Railways train running between Toronto and Montreal, was turned into a cabaret, complete with bar and performances. *Bistro Car* is based on experiences that may or may not have occurred during what is offered as its final run.

The show's highpoint comes after a recorded announcement that the train has just crossed the border from Ontario into Quebec, at which point the company of four breaks into a serenade to "La Belle Province." There is singing, banjo-playing and a general air of informality, and the most effective numbers include "Four Part Invention," a round about assignations, in which each of the singers has a telephone; "Ready or Not," a lyrical duet; a torch ballad called "Other People's Houses" and "Genuine Grade-A Canadian Superstar."

Opened March 23, 1978
Closed

REVIEWS

"The show might just get by on the BMT in a blizzard. . . . Of 23 numbers, some with rudimentary skits attached, all but one or two are trite, dull and sometimes embarrassing. Haziness has set in. . . . The score, by Patrick Rose, is to music as typewriting is to writing. Of the performers, only Marcia McClain and Tom Wopat show some heavily beaten-down appeal. . . . Otherwise, the whole thing, with lyrics by Merv Campone and Richard Ouzounian, and direction by Mr. Ouzounian, should be towed away. It cannot possibly move under its own power." — Richard Eder, *The New York Times (3-24-78, p. C 3)*

"Has a special ingenuous charm all of its own. It is a strangely awkward, yet strangely lovable show. . . . Ten minutes, or so, after the disaster of the show's first ghastly proposition, you find yourself interested, and finally, very soon you find yourself loving it. It has a bewitching simplicity to it. . . . It has an ease and a style to it. Rose's music is derivative but from the best sources . . . and the lyrics possess a decent grace and sensibility. The performances are great." — Clive Barnes, *New York Post (3-24-78, p. 30)*

"A stylish and agreeable little import from Canada, with a melodic and varied score by Patrick Rose, lyrics (some very good and some so-so) by Merv Campone and Richard Ouzounian, and dialogue (minimal and apt) by D. R. Anderson. . . . I hope that their stay is long and pleasant." — Edith Oliver, *The New Yorker (4-3-78, p. 112)*

"Devotees of musical revue type entertainment will definitely discover a winner in *A Bistro Car.* . . . This delightful and unpretentious musical romp . . . should, by word of mouth alone, be insured a healthy run. . . . The music by Patrick Rose is refreshingly melodious, though in several instances, reminiscent in style to impressive tunes from other classy shows of this type. . . . There are also literate and often clever lyrics. . . . Richard Ouzounian has succeeded with the expertise of a director who knew exactly what he was reaching for." — *Variety (3-29-78, p. 89)*

Julius Caesar

By William Shakespeare. Presented by the BAM Theatre Company; directed by Frank Dunlop; costumes by Dona Granata; lighting by F. Mitchell Dana; scenic disposition, Carole Lee Carroll; music by Frank Bennett; speech consultant, Edith Skinner; production stage manager, Barbara-Mae Phillips. Brooklyn Academy of Music/Lepercq Space, 30 Lafayette Avenue, Brooklyn, New York.

Julius Caesar is, of course, one of Shakespeare's best-known and most widely-played tragedies, having had its earliest recorded performance on September 21, 1599.

Fearing that Caesar desires to become King of Rome, which would change the state from republic to monarchy, Brutus, an idealist and Stoic, convinces himself he should join a conspiracy to assassinate him, little realizing the jealousy and other motives of his fellow conspirators, in particular Cassius. After the success of the plot, Caesar's loyal lieutenant, Antony, asks permission to address the crowd at the funeral. He turns the crowd against the conspirators, then joins with Caesar's great-nephew, Octavius, and Lepidus in a triumvirate to rule Rome and avenge Caesar. The two sides meet at Philippi, where much bloodshed ensues and Antony and Octavius pay homage to the noble Brutus.

Opened April 9, 1978, for a limited engagement
Closed April 23, 1978

REVIEWS

"His *Julius Caesar* works upon quirks, sharpens upon points of individual psychology, and quite loses the play's moral and tragic sweep. Mr. Dunlop is never wishy-washy. He always comes up with a defined manner, but in this case it is a manner that works against the play and is executed, furthermore, with only middling success. . . . Even with superb actors, superbly directed, such an abstract conception seems unsuitable for a play whose theme is so public. But with all the weight thrown upon it, it is the acting that fails in this production." — Richard Eder, *The New York Times (4-10-78, p. C 17)*

"A deeply political, cunningly intelligent and ritualistically tragic staging. . . . The performances are largely at the service of the directorial concept, as was, initially, the often seemingly perverse casting. . . . You should find it one of the three or four most stimulating performances of native Shakespeare to be seen in America in the past decade." — Clive Barnes, *New York Post (4-10-78, p. 15)*

"Director Frank Dunlop's conception of the play is so aberrant, so devoid of all sense and meaning, that when it does not border on the ludicrous it achieves the inane." — T. E. Kalem, *Time (4-24-78, p. 81)*

"Regrettably, the funniest show around town. . . . The production promptly settles for the obvious, occasionally relieved by the clumsy or strained." — John Simon, *New York (4-24-78, p. 73)*

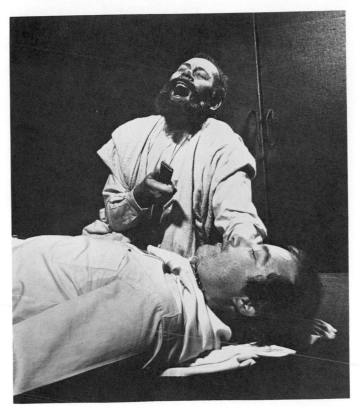

Ken Letner and Richard Dreyfuss

THE CAST

Julius Caesar	George Rose
Octavius Caesar	Thomas Hulce
Marcus Antonius	Austin Pendleton
M. Aemilius Lepidus	Sheldon Epps
Cicero	Ken Letner
Popilius Lena	George McDaniel
Marcus Brutus	Rene Auberjonois
Cassius	Richard Dreyfuss
Casca	Rex Robbins
Trebonius	Stephen Davies
Decius Brutus	Justin Deas
Metellus Cimber	Philip Kraus
Cinna	Terry Alexander
Flavius	Paul Perri
Marullus	George McDaniel
Artemidorus	Paul Perri
A Soothsayer	Sheldon Epps
Cinna, A Poet	Paul Perri
Lucilius	Stephen Davies
Titinius	Ken Letner
Messala	George McDaniel
Young Cato	Rex Stallings
Volumnius	Paul Perri
Strato	Philip Kraus
Lucius, Servant to Brutus	Michael Gennaro
Pindarus, Bondman to Cassius	Justin Deas
Servant to Antony	Rex Stallings
Servant to Caesar	Paul Diaz
First Soldier	Terry Alexander
Second Soldier	Paul Diaz
Third Soldier	Norman Abrams
Calpurnia, Wife to Caesar	Sloane Shelton
Portia, Wife to Brutus	Holly Villaire
Plebians, Workpeople of Rome	The Company

Mother Courage and Her Children

David Schramm and Mary Lou Rosato

By Bertolt Brecht; translated by Ralph Manheim; music and lyrics by Paul Dessau. Presented by the Acting Company; John Houseman, producing artistic director; directed by Alan Schneider; musical direction by Albert Hague; costumes by Jeanne Button; settings by Ming Cho Lee; lighting by David F. Segal; production stage manager, Daniel Morris. American Place Theatre, 111 West 46th Street.

Brecht's 1941 play is a chronicle of the Thirty Years' War. It is in 12 scenes and includes nine songs.

Anna Fierling (Mother Courage) is the mother of three illegitimate children by three different fathers. With her traveling canteen and her children in tow, she follows the Swedish and Imperial armies selling goods to the soldiers. She lives off the war, but the war also lives off her, never more than as it begins to take her children.

The first to go is her son Eilif, who is recruited as a soldier. Decorated in battle, he soon loses his life. Next comes her "honest son," Swiss Cheese, who becomes a paymaster in the Swedish army. He, in fact, is the first to die, when his mother haggles over the amount of a bribe that would save him from death at the hands of the Catholic army. When Kattrin overhears a plan to surprise the city of Halle and awakens the townspeople by beating a drum, she, too, dies at the hands of the Imperial forces.

Brecht does not view Mother Courage as a martyr, but rather as a woman who has sacrificed her humanity. She embodies many of the most familiar themes in Brecht, not least the avaricious contest in which he, as a Communist, felt the modern world was engaged.

Opened April 5, 1978, for a limited engagement
Closed April 23, 1978

(Played in repertory with *King Lear*)

THE CAST

PROLOGUE
Mother Courage . . . . Mary Lou Rosato
Kattrin, her mute daughter . . . . Frances Conroy
Eilif, her eldest son . . . . Kevin Conroy
Swiss Cheese, her younger son . . . . .Jeffrey Hayenga

SCENE 1
A highway near the city
Recruiting Officer . . . . Tom Donaldson
Protestant Sergeant . . . . Tom Robbins

SCENE 2
The general's tent
Cook. . . . . David Schramm
Swedish General . . . . .James Harper
Chaplain . . . . Anderson Matthews

SCENE 3
An army camp
Ordnance Officer. John Greenleaf
Yvette. . . . . Patricia Hodges
Soldier with Cannon . . . . Henry Stram
One Eye . . . . Brooks Baldwin
Catholic Sergeant . . . . Tom Robbins
Yvette's Colonel . . . . Tom Donaldson
Stretcher Bearers. . . . . Henry Stram, Daniel Corcoran

SCENE 4
Outside an officer's tent
Regimental Clerk. . . . . .Dennis Bacigalupi
Young Soldier. . . . . Ron Jacobson
Old Soldier. . . . . Gregg Almquist

SCENE 5
Near a devastated village
Soldier with Fur Coat. . . . . Brooks Baldwin
Second Soldier . . . . Tom Robbins
Peasant Woman. . . . . Leslie Geraci
Peasant Man. . . . . John Greenleaf

SCENE 6
Inside Mother Courage's tent
Soldiers . . . . . Daniel Corcoran, Gregg Almquist, Henry Stram

SCENE 7
On the highway

SCENE 8
A summer morning
Young Man . . . . .Daniel Corcoran
Old Woman . . . . Harriet Harris
Yvette's Servant . . . . .Dennis Bacigalupi
Soldiers with Eilif . . . . . . Tom Donaldson, Gregg Almquist,
Henry Stram, Ron Jacobson

SCENE 9
Outside a half demolished presbytery — winter

SCENE 10
On the highway
Peasant Woman. . . . . Leslie Geraci

SCENE 11
Outside the town
Lieutenant. . . . . Brooks Baldwin
Soldiers . . . . . Henry Stram, Tom Donaldson, Ron Jacobson
Peasant Man. . . . . Gregg Almquist
Young Peasant . . . . .Dennis Bacigalupi
Peasant Woman. . . . . Harriet Harris

Frances Conroy and Mary Lou Rosato

REVIEWS

"This is not a titanic performance, but it is mordant and resolute. To her credit, Miss Rosato does not overwhelm the play. . . . In the subordinate role of the cook, Mr. Schramm combines charm with an incorrigible selfishness. . . . The rest of the actors are young and in some cases less poised." — Mel Gussow, *The New York Times (4-6-78, p. C 17)*

"Alan Schneider, who is directing this version, has sensibly decided to eschew precedent. He, and his marvelous designer Ming Cho Lee, maintain the proprieties of the Brechtian theatrical world. . . . The messages were muted, the connections seemed oddly disjointed." — Clive Barnes, *New York Post (4-6-78, p. 44)*

"An accomplished and creditable production. . . . The play is there, the points are made, and the style and the momentum are always maintained." — Edith Oliver, *The New Yorker (4-17-78, p. 104)*

"Courage, Mary Lou Rosato surely embodies, but the heartrending passion of a mother is somehow lacking." — T. E. Kalem, *Time (4-17-78, p. 50)*

Mary Lou Rosato

By William Shakespeare. Presented by the Acting Company; John Houseman, producing artistic director; directed by Mr. Houseman; music by Marc Blitzstein; costumes by Nancy Potts; settings by Ming Cho Lee; lighting by David F. Segal; production stage manager, Daniel Morris. American Place Theatre, 111 West 46th Street.

King Lear (c. 1605) is generally regarded as one of Shakespeare's greatest tragedies, but also as one that poses numerous problems in staging. In this Acting Company production, director John Houseman eschews both gimmicks and any attempt at a modern reinterpretation in favor of a straightforward presentation.

Thus, his main focus is on the central plot: what happens to the aged King Lear as he goes about his decision to divide his kingdom among his three daughters. Goneril and Regan, the two eldest, married to the dukes of Albany and Cornwall respectively, flatter him. The young Cordelia, his favorite, relies simply on her love for him. He is enraged and disinherits her, banishing her from the kingdom. In the ensuing scenes, Goneril and Regan reveal their base motives and mistreat the old man, before finally turning him out to wander on a stormy night. On the heath, he goes mad. Cordelia and a French army land and right the wrongs done to Lear, who is restored to sanity. But a secret execution order has been issued against her and, before it can be countermanded, she is hanged.

Opened April 9, 1978, for a limited engagement
Closed April 22, 1978

(Played in repertory with *Mother Courage and Her Children*)

King Lear

David Schramm as Lear, Dennis Bacigalupi as
the Fool and Kevin Conroy as Edgar

THE CAST

Earl of Kent	James Harper
Earl of Gloucester	Gregg Almquist
Edmund	Tom Donaldson
Lear	David Schramm
Goneril	Mary Lou Rosato
Cordelia	Frances Conroy
Regan	Patricia Hodges
Duke of Burgundy	Ron Jacobson
King of France	Daniel Corcoran
Duke of Albany	Anderson Matthews
Duke of Cornwall	Tom Robbins
Edgar	Kevin Conroy
Oswald	Brooks Baldwin
Fool	Dennis Bacigalupi
Lear's Knight	Daniel Corcoran
First Servant	Jeffrey Hayenga
Second Servant	Henry Stram
Doctor	Henry Stram
Captain	Jeffrey Hayenga
Herald	Tom Robbins
Gentleman	Ron Jacobson

Attendants, Servants,
Soldiers, Knights . . . . Brooks Baldwin, Leslie Geraci,
John Greenleaf, Harriet Harris,
Jeffrey Hayenga, Diane Kamp, Henry Stram

REVIEWS

"The Acting Company makes a brave effort but is miscast for *Lear*. . . . The first act seems to dawdle with exposition. . . . The Acting Company production is eager but misguided." — Mel Gussow, *The New York Times (4-10-78, p. C 17)*

"Ming Cho Lee has provided a marvelously adaptable setting. . . . The costumes . . . by Nancy Potts go handsomely against all this simplicity, and the lighting by David F. Segal is consistently helpful. . . . Houseman believes so far as possible, in letting the text speak for itself — no 'conceptual Shakespeare' for him, merely clear-speaking, rapid movement, as few cuts as humanly possible. . . . The performers react to such treatment with clarity." — Clive Barnes, *New York Post (4-10-78, p. 14)*

"The production is an extremely good one. Schramm plays a Lear whose anger coats his passion. . . . The acting ranges from excellent to adequate, with only Mary Lou Rosato's version of Goneril being obviously wrong. . . . All in all, this Lear is a moving experience. As in all good productions of this play, we come out feeling that we've heard a comprehensive statement on the human condition." — Christopher Sharp, *Women's Wear Daily (4-11-78, p. 22)*

Harold Gary, Joel Polis and David Garfield

Family Business

THE CAST

Isaiah Stein	Harold Gary
Jerry Stein, his son	Joel Polis
Norman Stein, another son	David Garfield
Bobby Stein, another son	Richard Greene
Phil Stein, another son	David Rosenbaum
Young Man	Richard Levine

By Dick Goldberg. Presented by Honey Waldman; directed by John Stix; scenic design by Don Jensen; stage manager, Richard Delahanty. Astor Place Theatre, 434 Lafayette Street.

Goldberg's play takes place in the late autumn of 1974, in the main room of Isaiah Stein's home in Beverly, Massachusetts.

Isaiah, the patriarch of the family, is a wealthy merchant who is about to die. One of his last acts has been to arrange an interlocking will designed to take what he thinks of as the best care of his four sons. The shares are not to be equal.

The four brothers, who are less than enthusiastic about his plan, include: Bobby, 35, a disgruntled psychologist who is deep in debt; Phil, 32, who runs the store and resents the money that is being handed out; Norman, 28, who is mother obsessed and wants to retain the family's large house and do things just the way his mother did; and 20-year-old Jerry, a closet homosexual.

Isaiah dies of a heart attack at the end of the first act and the remainder of the play is a working out of the relationships of the four brothers, who, surprisingly, do seem to love one another. It is the revelation of Jerry's homosexuality that provides the catalyst.

Opened April 12, 1978

REVIEWS

"No cosmic truths are uttered, no great revelations made, but in the lives of four brothers who at long last come to know one another, every spectator will discover something of himself. . . . The acting is on a high level throughout." — Thomas Lask, *The New York Times (4-13-78, p. 17)*

"Family Business gives the impression of something just removed from a time capsule. . . . Still, despite the pat ending, there's a seamless, polished quality to both the play and the production. Goldberg constructs skillfully. The actors are skillfully directed and uniformly convincing." — Edmund Newton, *New York Post (4-13-78, p. 38)*

"Engrossing. . . . John Stix's directing has a convincingly realistic quality, a quality matched by the actors' performances, which make it seem as if we might have stumbled on a domestic crisis of the people who live down the block or the hall." — Ernest Leogrande, *Daily News (4-13-78, p. 75)*

"What a lugubrious lot these men are! . . . The current production [is] a drab affair with almost no acting to speak of. . . . Don Jensen's setting of the father's living room seems entirely appropriate." — Edith Oliver, *The New Yorker (4-24-78, p. 96)*

"The actors bring so much intelligence and understanding to their roles one wishes the playwright had developed them more fully. Director John Stix has done a marvelous job of building the human plausibility of the play, even when the playwright strains for histrionic effect." — Howard Kissel, *Women's Wear Daily (4-13-78, p. 14)*

Patio/Porch

Fannie Flagg and Ronnie Claire Edwards

THE CAST

Patio
Jewel . . . . Ronnie Claire Edwards
Pearl. . . . . Fannie Flagg

Porch
Dot. . . . . Fannie Flagg
Lucille. . . . . Ronnie Claire Edwards

By Jack Heifner. Presented by Milton Justice, in association with Ken Cohen; directed by Garland Wright; scenery by John Arnone; costumes by David James; lighting by Marc B. Weiss; production stage manager, Lani Ball. Century Theatre, 235 West 46th Street.

Patio/Porch takes place in a small town in Texas. The scene for *Patio,* the first of the two one-act plays, is a suburban bungalow's picnic area where Pearl is readying for a farewell party for her sister Jewel. Pearl regrets her obviously empty life and Jewel, whose future is long since past, is about to depart for the big city. Both are leading futile lives.

In *Porch,* Dot, an old woman, sits talking interminably to her daughter Lucille. She is something of a tyrant and Lucille obviously will not escape.

There is an aura of Tennessee Williams to Heifner's plays, especially in terms of the Southern locale and its "belles," but the play never comes alive to the extent that the author's continuing success *Vanities* did.

Opened April 13, 1978
Closed April 30, 1978

REVIEWS

"The two plays are unrelated in subject, but both give the effect of burial by landslide. . . . Ronnie Claire Edwards plays with some humor and a wiry bitterness as Jewel in the first play, and Lucille in the second. Fannie Flagg is reasonably accurate as the tidy Pearl, but her effort to play an old woman is a clumsy impersonation." — Richard Eder, *The New York Times (4-14-78, p. C 3)*

"The plays are sometimes not unamusing, but they are also slight, trivial and essentially unconvincing. . . . There is no development. . . . I would not recommend going on either the 'Patio' or the 'Porch.'" — Clive Barnes, *New York Post (4-14-78, p. 35)*

"Humor is derived from Texas twangs, carefully if not compatibly executed by the two actresses, but content is nil, and pathos is as artistically wrung as those plastic flowers on the patio bed." — Alvin Klein, *New York Theatre Review (6-78, p. 58)*

The Neon Woman

A burlesque by Tom Eyen. Presented by Bruce Mailman and Ina Melbach Minkin; directed by Ron Link; setting and graphics by Herbert Naglè; lighting by Jack Ranson; costumes and makeup by Van Smith; production stage manager, Jack Kalman. Hurrah, 36 West 62nd Street.

Eyen goes backstage at a tacky strip joint where the characters, including the Neon Woman, are undressing for the evening's work. Among them are a lesbian, who is played by a man, and someone billed as "the world's first totally deaf and dumb stripper." Their convoluted plot includes a series of murders in which no one stays dead.

The Neon Woman is, however, primarily a showcase for Divine, the celebrated "underground theatre" transvestite, who plays a character known as Flash Storm, "the last of the pink hot strippers," and is to some extent a sequel to Eyen's *Women Behind Bars,* which was a satire on the all-women prison films of a few decades ago.

Opened April 16, 1978
Closed

THE CAST

Joni	Maria Duval
Kitty LaRue	Sweet William Edgar
Speed Gonzalez	George Peterson
Willy	William Duff-Griffin
Rita	Debra Greenfield
Connie	Helen Hanft
Kim	Brenda Bergman
District Attorney	Lee Corbet
Flash Storm	Divine
Laura	Hope Stansbury
Senator	William Duff-Griffin

REVIEWS

"Lacks the author's usual spontaneous tomfoolery. This one seems to have been typed with a sledgehammer. It is raucous, aggressively insistent and as subtle as a television laugh track. . . . As directed by Ron Link, the other members of the company necessarily trail in Divine's wake — and, for the most part, they are submerged." — Mel Gussow, *The New York Times (4-17-78, p. C 19)*

"Ron Link directs with the conviction that the louder the funnier. He has his cast screaming at such a pitch you can't always hear the words for the sound. . . . *Neon Woman* is not for sensitive ears or morals. But there are plenty of others who'll think it a bash." — Frances Herridge, *New York Post (4-17-78, p. 55)*

"Divine is a consummate clown, the ultimate loving parody of female flamboyance, encased in a succession of outrageous costumes. . . . This is a personality and performance of enormous theatrical energy. . . . Ron Link has kept the momentum sustained throughout, and a good time is had by all." — Gerald Rabkin, *The Soho Weekly News (4-27-78, p. 52)*

Helen Burns

Catsplay

THE CAST

Mrs. Bela Orban, nee Ersike Skalla . . . . Helen Burns
Giza, her sister . . . . Katherine Squire
Paula Krausz. . . . . .Jane Cronin
Yanos, a waiter. Charles Mayer
Mrs. Mihaly Almasi, called Mousie . . . . .Bette Henritze
Ilona, Mrs. Orban's daughter . . . . .Susan Sharkey
Yoshka, Mrs. Orban's son-in-law. . . . . .Peter Phillips
Victor Vivelli . . . . Robert Gerringer
Madame Adelaida Vivelli, Victor's mother . . . .Eleanor Phelps

By Istvan Orkeny; translated by Clara Gyorgyey. Originally presented by the Manhattan Theatre Club and the New York Shakespeare Festival; directed by Lynne Meadow; setting by John Lee Beatty; costumes by Jennifer von Mayrhauser; lighting by Dennis Parichy; music by Robert Dennis; sound by Chuck London; production stage manager, David S. Rosenak. Manhattan Theatre Club, 321 East 73rd Street; Promenade Theatre, 2162 Broadway.

Ersike Orban is a widow in her sixties. She lives in Budapest and can look back upon her life with little if any regret. Her husband was faithful, her life fulfilling. Now, however, she is entering upon a new romance and hardly acting her age as she argues with her daughter, talks the butcher into giving her choice cuts of meat and generally goes about being idiosyncratic.
Catsplay employs an exchange of letters between Ersike and her sister in Germany as a framework for a play that takes place partly in the past, partly in the present. As Ersike goes about her meetings with a woman friend over brandy alexanders in a cafe, her liaisons with the opera singer Victor and her games with her mousie nextdoor neighbor, her sister, Giza, sits off to one side in a wheelchair. By the time the play ends, Ersike's heart has been broken, she has attempted suicide and emerged with a show of bravado.

Opened April 16, 1978

Robert Gerringer

Helen Burns and Jane Cronin

REVIEWS

"An affectionate and wistful character sketch . . . and the actress, Helen Burns, elevates the woman with her own buoyancy and comic imagination. . . . Such is the imprint left by the actress on the role that it is difficult to envision the play without her. . . . One of the difficulties with the play is that too much is recounted. . . . The parallel lives are awkwardly correlated. . . . The ending, with the sisters meeting for the first time in years, and Ersike archly descending into infantilism, severely damages the evening. . . . As directed by Miss Meadow, the rest of the cast is Miss Burns's buffer. . . . John Lee Beatty's utilitarian set is a definite asset." — Mel Gussow, *The New York Times (4-18-78, p. 47)*

"It is a work of much charm and a certain depth. . . . It is a quaint, amusing and rather touching play. It is almost a farce, but its heart-beat is too strong for the merciless mechanism of farce, its people too warm, and its sentiments too natural. . . . Miss Meadow has been fortunate in getting Helen Burns as Ersike. . . . She is as forceful as a pressure cooker, and as pathetic as an ebullient sparrow. . . . An affectionate little play — warm, cuddly and touching." — Clive Barnes, *New York Post (4-18-78, p. 48)*

"Much of it is funny and appealing, and some of it has a kind of Middle European playfulness that becomes a bit trying. Yet that playfulness is one of many details that give the show its invaluable atmosphere . . . which is maintained throughout in Lynne Meadow's capable directorial hands." — Edith Oliver, *The New Yorker (4-24-78, p. 93)*

"Imported sentimentality, posed against the past. . . . The play's extravagant reception here proves yet again that if glop manages to slop across the Atlantic, it has a much better chance to be treasured than the same stuff exuded domestically." — Stanley Kauffmann, *The New Republic (5-28-78, p. 23)*

"It is artistically accomplished and meltingly humane. . . . This is the best new play of the season . . . full of aching laughter and mocking heartbreak, both equally exhilarating. . . . Lynne Meadow has directed with economy and purposefulness in John Lee Beatty's modest but apt set." — John Simon, *New York (5-1-78, p. 72)*

The Best Little Whorehouse in Texas

Joan Ellis and Pamela Blair

A musical comedy, with book by Larry L. King and Peter Masterson; music and lyrics by Carol Hall. Presented by Universal Pictures; directed by Peter Masterson and Tommy Tune; musical numbers staged by Tommy Tune; costumes by Ann Roth; settings by Marjorie Kellogg; lighting by Dennis Parichy; musical direction and vocal arrangements by Robert Billig; hair styles by Michael Gottfried; sound by John Venable; production stage manager, Paul Phillips. Entermedia Theatre, 12th Street and Second Avenue.

The Best Little Whorehouse is an outgrowth of an article written by Larry L. King several years ago concerning an old-fashioned whorehouse, the Chicken Ranch, which, despite the indulgent outlook of the local residents, finally was closed thanks to the efforts of a crusading TV moralist, who looked less kindly on its 150 years of hanky-panky.

As a sheriff and a state senator look benignly on, the audience looks in on the adventures of the current madame, Mona, who seems to be running it as a form of community service. There are group rates on Blue Cross, the girls wear long dresses in the evening and, among the principal clients are the local college football team (courtesy of an alumni gift).

But good things can't go on forever and the TV personality, one Melvin Thorpe, who wears an American flag necktie, eventually brings about its demise.

Opened April 17, 1978

With: Clint Allmon, Cameron Burke, Tom Cashin, Joan Ellis, Becky Gelke, Bradley Clayton King, Susan Mansur, Louise Quick-Bowen, Michael Scott, Pamela Blair, Gerry Burkhardt, Carol Chambers, Henderson Forsythe, Carlin Glynn, Donna King, Jan Merchant, James Rich, Paul Ukena, Jr., Lisa Brown, Jay Bursky, Don Crabtree, Jay Garner, Delores Hall, J. Frank Lucas, Edna Milton, Marta Sanders, Debra Zalkind

REVIEWS

"A musical on a milk diet. It takes a small, bright, wry idea and expands and dilutes it at the same time. . . . It is all put together too loosely and blandly though; it has good humor but not the manic ferocity that makes good humor infectious. . . . The book is not really strong enough to carry a full musical, and there is some odd padding. . . . The small adjectives that come to mind are 'pleasant,' 'agreeable' — like school gold stars given for things that have turned out well." — Richard Eder, *The New York Times (4-18-78, p. 44)*

"A fun new musical. . . . What we have here is rambustious genre musical, full of flavor, charmingly accurate in its tonality of place and time, and, best of all, consistently amusing. . . . The performances are delightful." — Clive Barnes, *New York Post (4-18-78, p. 46)*

"A font of fun and friendliness. The evening has the flavor of a tall tale recounted by an accomplished barroom raconteur." — T. E. Kalem, *Time (5-1-78, p. 95)*

"The production, directed by Masterson and Tommy Tune, has an eager desire to be Broadway good without being Broadway slick. Perhaps inevitably, it falls with a certain charm between those poles. Carol Hall's songs embody this impasse — they are fresh, but saucy rather than meaty." — Jack Kroll, *Newsweek (5-1-78, p. 74)*

"[It] has all the satiric bite of a playful puppy, and, like a playful puppy, it tends to climb uninvited into one's lap; it is literally too ingratiating. Yet the relish as well as the proficiency of all concerned make the show appealing. Admirable, handsome costumes, sets, and lighting. . . . Expert direction by Mr. Masterson and Mr. Tune." — Edith Oliver, *The New Yorker (5-1-78, p. 67)*

The Twilight Dinner

Karen Bernhard, Leon Morenzie and Reuben Green

By Lennox Brown. Presented by the Negro Ensemble Company; directed by Douglas Turner Ward; setting by Samuel Gonzalez; lighting by James Fauvell. St. Mark's Playhouse, 133 Second Avenue.

Not for the first time, a playwright is asking: What happened to the bright hopes and promise of the 1960s?

Jimmy is a successful black who has abandoned the civil-rights movement to take a job in the city bureaucracy. As the play opens, he sits in a restaurant back room. The week has been tiring and he craves the sympathy and ministrations of the white proprietress, whom he seems to have known for some time. As a rule, she serves him dinner in private, but on this particular night an unwelcome old friend is to join him. It is, he explains, "a racial thing."

Ray is a West Indian and they have not seen each other since both were undergraduates at Columbia, 17 years before. Then, they were active members of S.N.C.C. Since, Jimmy has taken several degrees, been divorced and given up the revolutionary ship. Ray, on the other hand, returned to the Caribbean and entered politics. Before long he was as corrupt as the politicians he had gone to fight.

Eventually, a bond of sorts is established between them. Jimmy decides to call his former wife, and is told not to call again; Ray reaches the mother of a girl he once loved and should have married, only to be told that the girl committed suicide several years earlier. The play ends with the sound of music from the nearby Riverside Church in the background and everyone wondering what has gone wrong.

Opened April 18, 1978, for a limited engagement
Closed May 14, 1978

THE CAST

Jimmy. . . . . .Leon Morenzie
Elissa . . . . Karen Bernhard
Ray . . . . Reuben Green

REVIEWS

"It is a clumsily constructed, badly written work that drags out every available cliche, and goes on to invent a few more. . . . Just about everything has [gone wrong]; although Reuben Green and Leon Morenzie are competent as Jimmy and Ray, and Karen Bernhard is stiff and affected as Elissa, it is probably because the part is unplayable. *Twilight Dinner* serves obviousness as its main course and obscurity as dessert."
— Richard Eder, *The New York Times* (4-19-78, p. C 19)

"The three actors move together and against each other with an impressive understanding for subtleties. . . . It's a difficult play, maybe too self-consciously theatrical at times, but full of short bursts of vibrant dialogue. Faced with all the talk and little action, Douglas Turner Ward has directed it faultlessly, never missing a shade of meaning." — Edmund Newton, *New York Post* (4-18-78, p. 43)

"The performance, under the impeccable direction of Douglas Turner Ward, the artistic director and co-founder of the N.E.C., goes very well." — Edith Oliver, *The New Yorker* (5-1-78, p.67)

"Little of interest is said about anything at all. This happens within script and production frameworks that have not been professionally enough achieved to be called frameworks."
— Mr. First Nighter, *Cue* (4-29-78, p. 17)

The 5th of July

Danton Stone, Nancy Snyder and William Hurt

THE CAST

Kenneth Talley, Jr. . . . . .William Hurt
John . . . . Jonathan Hogan
Gwen . . . . Nancy Snyder
Jed. . . . . Jeff Daniels
June Talley, Ken's sister . . . . .Joyce Reehling
Shirley, her daughter . . . . .Amy Wright
Aunt Sally . . . . .Helen Stenborg
Weston Hurley . . . . .Danton Stone

By Lanford Wilson. Presented by the Circle Repertory Company; directed by Marshall W. Mason; setting by John Lee Beatty; costumes by Laura Crow; lighting by Marc B. Weiss; original song by Jonathan Hogan; sound by Chuck London; production stage manager, Fred Reinglas. Circle Repertory Theatre, 99 Seventh Avenue South.

The 5th of July takes place in and around a Missouri farmhouse on Independence Day, 1977, and on the following morning. Kenneth Talley, Jr., is a Vietnam veteran who has lost both legs in the war and now uses two wooden ones. He owns the farm, where he has been living with his male lover, and wants to sell it.

Also on the scene are Kenneth's sister and his thirteen-year-old niece; a copper heiress and pop singer named Gwen; her lover and manager, John; her guitarist; and Kenneth's Aunt Sally. The house once belonged to her, but she now lives in retirement in California and has returned to inter the ashes of her late husband.

Gwen is as much a prospective purchaser as a guest, but she is a self-described "burnt-out" case from drugs and alcohol, though only thirty-three. There are spats and serious disagreements and a great deal of random activity, before the play finally concludes with a revelation and something that approaches a resolution.

Opened April 27, 1978

REVIEWS

"The talk is extravagant, funny and often piercing, but its function is to build up the extremities represented by each of the characters rather than to take them in any particular direction. . . . Under Marshall W. Mason's direction, the actors make play out of the frenetic grotesquerie of their characters in a style that is often effective but always exaggerated. None has the repose or even the silence that might make them believably human. . . . John Lee Beatty has provided some conventional Deep-South decay for this sporadically appealing but unworkable play." – Richard Eder, *The New York Times (4-28-78, p. C 3)*

"Wilson's characters talk and talk. . . . It is a play in which absolutely nothing happens except the display of character. . . . Marshall W. Mason directs Wilson with a natural skill . . . and the present result has the ease and grace of an overheard conversation. . . . This is not one of Wilson's best plays. . . . All the actors glided through the play with an understated elegance." – Clive Barnes, *New York Post (4-28-78, p. 33)*

"Like getting no further than the cover blurb of a big, sprawling novel teeming with incident. For all its racy, fluent and sometimes uproarious talk, it leaves us with the feeling of having joined a whirlwind house party only to find ourselves suddenly deposited on the back stoop. The play is entertaining and full of suggestion, yet hollow. . . . The whole cast, briskly directed by Marshall W. Mason, is excellent." – Douglas Watt, *Daily News (4-28-78, p. 5)*

"Mr. Wilson's most ambitious play so far, and, regrettably, it is his most verbose." – Edith Oliver, *The New Yorker (5-8-78, p.90)*

"The actors are first-rate, particularly William Hurt, Helen Stenborg, and Joyce Reehling." – Erika Munk, *The Village Voice (5-15-78, p. 99)*

Life of Galileo

By Bertolt Brecht; translated by Ralph Manheim and Wolfgang Sauerlander. Presented by Columbia University and the New York Actors' Theatre, in association with Penney and Ron Dante, Ilse and Henry Wolf; directed by Rudy Caringi; settings and lighting by James Tilton; costumes by Ursula Belden and Elizabeth P. Palmer; music composed and performed by Howard Harris; stage manager, Frederic H. Orner; production coordinated by John P. Fleming. Havermeyer Hall of Columbia University, 116th Street and Broadway.

Galileo is an underpaid lecturer at the University of Padua when he hears from a student about the invention of the telescope. He abandons his scruples and copies it and presents it as his own to the senators of the Republic of Venice. To find more time for research, he becomes court mathematician of the grand duke of Florence. He soon realizes that reason cannot, as he previously believed, overcome religious dogma. He proves that the earth is not the center of the universe, and the Papal College has to admit his accuracy. The Inquisition forbids him to publish the fact, and he remains silent for eight years. He takes up his studies again, is arrested and brought to Rome, where he is shown the instruments of torture and abjures his teachings, to live until his death in a country house, a prisoner of the Inquisition.

Opened April 5, 1978, for a limited engagement
Closed April, 1978

With: Laurence Luckinbill, Jack Magee, Mary Carver, Michael O'Hare, Joseph Davidson, Richard Zavaglia, Francesca James, Laurence Attlle, Alexander Wells, Henry Grossman, Joel Charap, Robert Mont, Bernie McInerney, Samantha Laine, Lillian Jenkins, Rudy Caringi, Gil Rogers, Peter White

REVIEWS

"A well-paced, lively and cogent version of one of Brecht's stronger and more appealing plays. . . . Rudy Caringi, who directs and also acts in the production, emphasizes intellectual movement over dramatic density. . . . Laurence Luckinbill gives a fine complexity to Galileo." — Richard Eder, *The New York Times (4-6-78, p. C 17)*

"Laurence Luckinbill's Galileo is too explosive, too passionately angry and irascible for a man of reason. . . . Director Rudy Caringi tries to use the classroom setting imaginatively." — Frances Herridge, *New York Post (4-6-78, p. 41)*

"The cast is able, and Luckinbill is imposing as the skeptic son of rationalism. This is an auspicious debut for the New York Actors' Theater." — T. E. Kalem, *Time (4-17-78, p. 50)*

The Proposition

An improvisational revue, conceived and directed by Allan Albert. Presented by the Proposition Workshop, Inc.; musical direction by Donald Sosin; lighting by Dick Williams; stage manager, Matthew Cohen. Actors' Playhouse, 100 Seventh Avenue South.

The Proposition follows the by now more or less time-honored tradition of being what one reviewer has called "semi-improvisational," in that, although suggestions are invited from the audience (and received), there is a basically set pattern. In the case of the current production, the list involves such things as "Historical Characters," "Book and Movie Titles," "Neighborhoods" and "Astrological Signs."

A cast member will, for instance, invite the audience to provide some book titles and then work into a pickup scene in a bar where the Great Gatsby, Moby Dick, Fanny Hill and others are to be found.

The Proposition is a latter-day version, but not quite a second coming of the celebrated Second City, which, although it did not originate the form, gave it much of its American popularity.

Opened May 8, 1978, for a limited engagement
Closed May 21, 1978

With: Raymond Baker, Anne Cohen, Timothy Hall and Shelly Barre

REVIEWS

"At the moment, the most embarrassing situation that I can think of would be to be on stage at the Proposition. . . . It is sad to watch them floundering. Among other things, they lack specificity, which is one of the keystones of improvisation. . . . At the performance that I attended, the audience stayed sharp. It was the Proposition that fell flat." — Mel Gussow, *The New York Times (5-9-78, p. 50)*

"There is no lack of spontaneity or of ingenuity; Mr. Baker, Miss Cohen, Mr. Hall, and Miss Barre are so clever, so knowledgeable, and so appealing that their show, whisking from one kind of parody to the next, is all but irresistible. At least, that was clearly the view of the young opening-night audience. . . . One of the attractions of the show is the echo one receives of other performers in other shows; for some odd reason, this actually enriches the evening. . . . The tradition of improvisation holds, and it could go on forever, for all of me. — Edith Oliver, *The New Yorker (5-15-78, p. 116)*

"The essence of improvisation is spontaneity, and this troupe sometimes seems labored and desperate for original ideas. Their batting average confines them to the minor leagues, but their game has its moments of fun." — Holly Hill, *New York Theatre Review (6-78, p. 51)*

My Mother Was a Fortune Teller

Phyllis Newman

Presented by the Hudson Guild Theatre; directed by Arthur Laurents; musical staging by Elizabeth Keen; musical direction by Herbert Kaplan; setting by Philipp Jung; costumes by Bill Kellard; production under the supervision of Craig Anderson; production stage manager, Edward R. Fitzgerald. Hudson Guild Theatre, 441 West 26th Street.

My Mother Was a Fortune-Teller is, in effect, an autobiography in words and music. The score, however, does not come from the major moments in Miss Newman's career, but from songs that illustrate her life and thoughts.

She depicts herself as a woman undergoing a "mid-life crisis" and attempting to justify her existence to her teenage daughter. She is indecisive. She keeps making lists and has, as she admits in one lyric, "a very solid base on which my house of guilt is built."

But she goes beyond this, in particular into a medley of songs about women, hinting at the male chauvinism underlying a song such as "I Enjoy Being a Girl" (emphasis on the word "girl"). Always, there is the conflict between home and career.

Miss Newman's mother, incidentally, apparently was a fortune-teller.

Opened May 5, 1978, for a limited engagement
Closed May 21, 1978

With: Phyllis Newman

REVIEWS

"With her crystalline singing voice, her wholesome good looks, her self-mocking humor and her forthright, effusive manner, Phyllis Newman is a natural musical comedy leading lady. . . . The musical half of the evening is sharply in focus and in tune with the solo performer, but the text is rambling and discursive. . . . The show does not take advantage of her ability as a dancer. . . . [It] is entertaining, but someone with Miss Newman's versatility — as actress, singer and writer — should have a more stylish showcase for her talent." — Mel Gussow, *The New York Times (5-8-78, p. C 13)*

"The show is very adventurous and very daring. . . . It is a statement about New York, and also, and this is the brave part, about a woman who is admitting that she has not really fulfilled herself. . . . It is a good evening. . . . It shows her brilliance, her openness, and her ability to be totally herself." — Clive Barnes, *New York Post (5-8-78, p. 20)*

"It is a skillful performance of songs, with some connective words, by an entertaining, refreshing singer and actress. . . . The show was impeccably directed by Arthur Laurents." — Edith Oliver, *The New Yorker (5-22-78, p. 93)*

"Newman's satire is misspent . . . and her attempts to be current and sing Streisand Manilow merely show the gap between soft rock and musical comedy songs." — Terry Curtis Fox, *The Village Voice (5-22-78, p. 85)*

The Biko Inquest

Written and directed by Norman Fenton and John Blair; prologue by Donald and Wendy Woods. Presented by Arthur Cantor, by arrangement with Paddington Press, Ltd., Mr. Fenton and Mr. Blair; settings by Eric Head; costumes by Patricia McGourty; lighting by Clyde Kuemmerle; production stage manager, Christopher Kelly. Theatre Four, 424 West 55th Street.

According to the program, *The Biko Inquest* is "based on transcripts of the inquest into the death of Stephen Bantu Biko held in Pretoria, South Africa, from November 14 to December 2, 1977." Biko was a rebellious young black leader who died because of injuries sustained during interrogation by the Security Police of South Africa. He was transported, semi-comatose and in chains, in a Land Rover from Port Elizabeth to Pretoria and, at the instigation of his family, an inquest that aroused international attention was held, presided over by Pretoria's chief magistrate. Despite the effective and affecting efforts of the Bikos' attorney, Sidney Kentridge, the magistrate ruled that there was no evidence of impropriety in the prisoner's handling.

Fenton and Blair draw upon secretly obtained transcripts of the trial to present a no-holds-barred documentary that reveals the events that led up to Biko's death and how the doctors who examined him minimized or ignored what had taken place. Faced with what has happened, everyone concerned prevaricates, justifies himself and convinces himself that what he is doing is in the best interests of the State. Necessity is the mother of invention, but also of injustice in the land of apartheid.

Opened May 17, 1978
Closed June 10, 1978

THE CAST

Sidney Kentridge	Fritz Weaver
Martinus Prins	David Gale
Jan van Rensburg	Bill Moor
Col. Pieter Goosen	Philip Bosco
Maj. Harold Snyman	Jess Osuna
Lieut. Eric Wilken	John Vennema
Prof. Johann David Loubser	James Cook
Prof. Proctor	William Myers
Dr. Ivor Lang	Martin Shakar
Dr. Benjamin Tucker	Carl Low
Dr. Colin Hersch	Jonathan Moore

Philip Bosco and Fritz Weaver

REVIEWS

"Taut, powerful and revealing. . . . Their editing of the court transcripts achieve[s] authentic and skillful dramatic life. . . . The authors — who have also done a superb job of directing — have found the only possible means to make this testimony into a living courtroom drama. . . . It is a drama that Mr. Fenton and Mr. Blair have entrusted to an extraordinary group of actors. . . . *The Biko Inquest,* though always engrossing, often drags, taken over by the details of argument. It is not, by its nature, a great play; but it is honest and skillful under its hybrid burdens, and most worthwhile." — Richard Eder, *The New York Times (5-18-78, p. C 17)*

"It is terrifying. . . . The play almost itself suffers from its feelings. It is a marvelous human statement, an opportunity to show this case to an apparently uncaring world. . . . The staging is, happily, superlative. The big virtuoso role comes to Fritz Weaver. . . . Weaver has a great cast around him — some of our best actors. . . . It is a play that has the interest of the courtroom, the fascination of fact, and the special truth of a documentary." — Clive Barnes, *New York Post (5-18-78, p. 34)*

"By far the dullest courtroom drama I have ever sat before. . . . All we are left with, then, is a bunch of earnest actors, headed by a repeatedly frustrated Weaver, bringing their personal skills and individuality to bear on cooked-up testimony. . . . *The Biko Inquest* is horror reduced to boredom." — Douglas Watt, *Daily News (5-18-78, p. 103)*

"I have no opinion to offer, except that outrage is not quite enough to sustain an audience for an entire evening." — Edith Oliver, *The New Yorker (5-29-78, p. 84)*

"It is courtroom drama at its most engrossing, except for a very few lax moments." — John Simon, *New York (6-5-78, p. 84)*

The Show-Off

Polly Rowles, Ellen Tovatt, Paul Rudd
and Terence Marinan

THE CAST

Clara Hyland	Ellen Tovatt
Mrs. Fisher	Polly Rowles
Amy Fisher	Kit LeFever
Frank Hyland	Joseph Costa
Mr. Fisher	Harry Ellerbe
Joe Fisher	Terence Marinan
Aubrey Piper	Paul Rudd
Mr. Gill	Joseph Warren
Mr. Rogers	Ken Costigan

By George Kelly. Presented by the Roundabout Theatre Company, Gene Feist/Michael Fried; directed by John Ulmer; setting by Ron Antone; lighting by Robert Strohmeier; costumes by Nancy L. Johnson; sound sequences by Philip Campanella; production stage manager, Paul Moser. Roundabout/Stage Two Theatre, 307 West 26th Street.

First produced in 1924, George Kelly's *The Show-Off* experienced a period of decline and non-production, but has had a resurgence of popularity during the past decade.

Its nominal hero, the "show-off" of the title, is a young man named Aubrey Piper, who manages to couple the traits of liar, braggart and fool with those of the innocent, lovable and aspiring. He is a dangerous combination of the ruthless and the charming, even endearing.

Pitted against Aubrey is his mother-in-law, a formidable foe indeed. Mrs. Fisher sees through Aubrey's facade, while at the same time remaining enchanted by him.

All of this points to the "villain" getting his comeuppance by play's end; Kelly, however, elects to go otherwise, with Aubrey turning instead into the protagonist.

Opened May 18, 1978
Closed July 16, 1978

REVIEWS

"It would take a skillful director and some very polished acting to get its machinery, rusty with old talk, moving again. Neither is to be found in the listless production. . . . It moves slowly, like the automobiles of the time, and the Roundabout cast, geared for higher speeds, chokes and dies on it." — Richard Eder, *The New York Times (5-19-78, p. C 3)*

"It is a simple comedy, well made, written with an elegant spareness, and most amusing in its concept of comedy as an insight into the human condition. . . . Ulmer's staging is calm and gentle. . . . [Rudd's] cocky brilliance, his air of self-satisfied satisfaction, his alert stupidity, is absolutely beautiful. What an actor he is. . . . Polly Rowles as his antagonist mother-in-law, low-keyed yet effective, makes her own square points amusingly, and the entire play bustles along with an ease and certain authority." — Clive Barnes, *New York Post (5-18-78, p. 27)*

"Although the play provides frequent laughs, it seems dated in some respects. . . . All small criticisms aside, it's a fun, old-fashioned play." — Steven Hager, *Show Business (5-25-78, p. 23)*

"Though Ron Antone's scenery and Philip Campanella's music are endearing, this revival is hardly in the APA's class because of John Ulmer's heavy-handed direction and his company's uneven performances." — Mr. First Nighter, *Cue (6-10-78, p. 15)*

International Stud

Harvey Fierstein and Richard Dow

By Harvey Fierstein. Presented by the Players Theatre; directed by Eric Concklin; costumes by Mardi Philips; lighting by Joanna Schielke; musical direction by Ned Levy; production stage manager, Lee Evans. Players Theatre, 115 MacDougal Street.

International Stud, which appeared earlier at the La Mama E.T.C., is the story of "drag queen" named Arnold. A female impersonator, he has at one time or another gone under such names as Virginia Ham, Kitty Litter and Bertha Venation. He never actually performs his act for the audience, which instead views him as he preens before a dressing-room mirror, worries about his looks and otherwise indulges his anxieties amid a torrent of jokes and epigrams. They run along the lines of "A thing of beauty is a joy . . . till sunrise."

Fierstein's only other major character is a bisexual whom he idealizes as the "international stud" of his dreams and fantasies. They are clearly mismatched: the stud unintentionally injuring, Arnold constantly vulnerable.

Between the play's monologues and occasional confrontations, Diane Tarleton sings torch songs from her perch on a piano, among them "Body and Soul" and "That Old Feeling."

Opened May 22, 1978
Closed July 16, 1978

THE CAST

Piano Man . . . . Ned Levy
Lady Blues. . . . . .Diane Tarleton
Arnold . . . . .Harvey Fierstein
Ed . . . . .Richard Dow

REVIEWS

"Despite the homosexual context, this is familiar theatrical territory. . . . Pathos descends to bathos. Richard Dow seems somewhat ill at ease as the bisexual; perhaps it is his dialogue more than his character that is burdensome. However, Mr. Fierstein seems to have no hesitation about his role, leaping into it with enthusiasm." — Mel Gussow, *The New York Times (5-23-78, p. C 6)*

"The writing is sharp and often clever. Fierstein specializes in sizzling, off-beat one-liners. . . . The play has been well-directed by Eric Concklin, and the two actors are Richard Dow as Ed, handsome, confident and hollow, yet hollow with feeling, and Fierstein himself as the drag queen. Perhaps he was less well-cast. . . . Funny, raunchy, might offend, could become a gay cult play, and might also become a straight tourist trip." — Clive Barnes, *New York Post (5-23-78, p. 49)*

"Its dialogue is droll, direct, distressing and, in spite of the pertinent and impertinent one-liners, genuine. . . . Richard Dow as Ed and Fierstein as Arnold, impeccably directed by Eric Concklin, give two of the best performances in town." — Tish Dace, *The Soho Weekly News (6-1-78, p. 68)*

"Written sincerely but uncertainly, and badly performed, its point is that an intense homosexual relationship is better than a faked and unrewarding one. Go argue." — Mr. First Nighter, *Cue (6-10-78, p. 106)*

"In total effect, however, the play suffers from a certain sketchiness. . . . It goes on a little too long. With a firmer commitment to writing a play and filling out his characters, Fierstein's *International Stud* could have been a gay-life *Two for the Seesaw.*" — Ron Cohen, *Women's Wear Daily (5-24-78, p. 30)*

Waiting for Godot

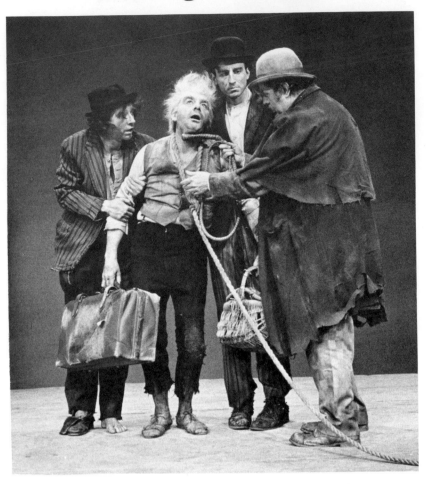

Austin Pendleton, Milo O'Shea, Sam Waterston and Michael Egan

By Samuel Beckett. Presented by the BAM Theatre Company, with the association of the Goethe House, New York; directed by Walter D. Asmus; scenery supervised by Carole Lee Carroll; costumes supervised by Dona Granata; lighting by Shirley Prendergast; production stage manager, Frank Bayer. Brooklyn Academy of Music, 30 Lafayette Avenue, Brooklyn, New York.

Waiting for Godot has been almost universally acknowledged as one of the great plays of the second half of the twentieth century, a work that transcends the moment, a work that impels the audience to examine its own perception of itself and its own perception of the world.

Beyond that, it is many things, not the least of them an exploration of what men are and what they seek to become; of where they are going. Estragon and Vladimir, those who wait for "Godot," and Lucky and Pozzo, who come upon the scene, but suggest far more, seem, in Beckett's terms, to be part of a world that expects, but is always frustrated. A world that always waits.

Opened May 25, 1978
Closed June 18, 1978

THE CAST

Estragon . . . . Austin Pendleton
Vladimir . . . . .Sam Waterston
Lucky . . . . Milo O'Shea
Pozzo . . . . .Michael Egan
A Boy . . . . .R. J. Murray, Jr.

REVIEWS

"The central weakness of the production . . . is that Godot is missing." — Richard Eder, *The New York Times (6-1-78, p. C 18)*

"One of the few masterpieces of the 20th-century theatre." — Clive Barnes, *New York Post (6-1-78, p. 37)*

"The production . . . is unfortunately almost lifeless in itself." — Douglas Watt, *Daily News (6-1-78, p. 73)*

"A production so lucid and, at times so beautiful that it makes every other *Godot* I've seen seem turgid and literal." — Edith Oliver, *The New Yorker (6-12-78, p. 69)*

"There is probably no set of actors in the Western world less suited to such a production than the BAM actors." — Terry Curtis Fox, *The Village Voice (6-12-78, p. 79)*

Off and
Off-Off Broadway

*Plays from Previous Seasons That Continued
to Run During the 1977-78 Season*

Ashes

Roberta Maxwell

By David Rudkin. Presented by the New York Shakespeare Festival, in association with the Manhattan Theatre Club; produced by Joseph Papp, associate producer, Bernard Gersten; directed by Lynne Meadow; setting by John Lee Beatty; costumes by Jennifer von Mayrhauser; lighting by Dennis Parichy; sound design by George Hansen and Charles London; production stage manager, Zane Weiner. Public/Anspacher Theatre, 425 Lafayette Street.

Originally presented at the off-Off Broadway Manhattan Theatre Club on December 8 (where it closed on January 2, 1977), the British playwright David Rudkin's play deals with a man and his wife who are trying urgently, even desperately, to conceive a child. Colin has failed as a playwright and Anne as an actress. He is now a teacher, with a homosexual past and inclinations, but nonetheless deeply in love with his wife. There is nothing wrong with their sexual relationship; it is simply that they have failed to have a child.

Colin and Anne go to doctors, who test his sperm count and her ovulation and offer them endless advice on sexual positions, together with fertility charts. "The things a silly sod will do for fatherhood," says Colin. Or is it fatherhood? Might it not be, instead, "the myth of manliness"?

Finally, Anne does become pregnant, then miscarries and has to have her womb removed. As it turns out, they are also rejected in their attempt to adopt, undoubtedly partly due to Colin's homosexual past. What sort of future lies ahead?

Ashes is a tragi-comedy in terms of their relationship on one level but also in those of a long monologue introduced on the situation in Northern Ireland in the play's later stages, in which Rudkin seems to equate the couple's infertility with that of a country whose relationships have been so permeated by violence and dissatisfaction.

Opened February 8, 1977
Closed June 26, 1977

Cast: Brian Murray, Roberta Maxwell, John Tillinger, Penelope Allen

The Club

A musical diversion by Eve Merriam. Presented by Circle in the Square, Theodore Mann, artistic director, Paul Libin, managing director; directed by T. Tune; musical direction and arrangements by Alexandra Ivanoff; costumes and set decor by Kate Carmel; lighting by Cheryl Thacker; stage manager, Gene Traylor. Circle in the Square, 159 Bleecker Street.

The Club of the title is a men's club in the year 1903. The men, all of them male chauvinists, are, however, played by women, five of them in top hats, white ties and tails, who sing and dance in various songs of the period 1894-1905. Abetted by the club's page and waiter (also played by women), they render such numbers as "Pinky Panky Poo" and such lyrics as "Oh what blissy when we kissy" and "If you talk of the fabulous leg, you needn't go further than Peg." There is even a song that compares a woman with a cigar and finds the woman wanting.

Women are viewed almost entirely as playthings, gold diggers and sex objects, an attitude reflected in such exchanges as: "Do any of you chaps believe in clubs for women?" "If every other form of persuasion fails."

Ms. Merriam, who wrote the connecting material, is a devoted feminist and her intent is clearly satirical, especially in such scenes as the club's annual Spring Frolic and an abundance of familiar anti-wife, anti-marriage observations and asides.

Opened October 14, 1976
Closed May 21, 1978

Cast: M. Dell, G. Hodes, J. Beretta, C. Monferdini, J. J. Hafner, M. Innerarity, T. White

Terri White and Gloria Hodes

Creditors/The Stronger

Rip Torn and Geraldine Page

By August Strindberg. Presented by the New York Shakespeare Festival, in association with Sanctuary Theatre Workshop, Inc.; originally produced by Hudson Guild Theatre; produced by Joseph Papp, associate producer, Bernard Gersten; directed by Rip Torn; translated by Palaemona Morner and R. Spacek; scenery by John Wright Stevens; costume coordination by Carrie F. Robbins; lighting by Ian Calderon; production stage manager, James Pentecost. Newman/Public Theatre, 425 Lafayette Street.

Creditors, which follows the brief curtain raiser *The Stronger,* which has to do with two women who meet in a coffee house on Christmas Eve to vie over the love of one's husband, is one of Strindberg's most clearly autobiographical plays.

A painter by the name of Adolf has recently met a new friend, Gustav, who lectures him on the mistakes he has been making with his currently absent wife. The weak Adolf agrees to conceal himself in the next room while Gustav deals with his wife, then to change roles. Gustav tells him that this will permit him to discover what Tekla, his wife, is actually like. As the game is played out, it becomes obvious that Gustav is in fact Tekla's first and scorned husband, providing the "tragic comedy" that Strindberg labeled it.

Opened May 17, 1977
Closed June 5, 1977

Cast: *(The Stronger)* Geraldine Page, Amy Wright, Judith L'Heureux; *(Creditors)* John Heard, Rip Torn, Geraldine Page, Amy Wright, Judith L'Heureux, Tom Hurt

Dear Liar

By Jerome Kilty, adapted from the correspondence of George Bernard Shaw and Mrs. Patrick Campbell. Presented by Roundabout Theatre; directed by Mr. Kilty; setting by Robin Sherman; costumes by Nancy L. Johnson; lighting by R. J. Turick; musical supervision by Philip Campanella; production stage manager, Errol Selsby. Roundabout Theatre, 333 West 23rd Street.

First presented in 1960, when it starred Katharine Cornell, *Dear Liar* draws upon the correspondence of George Bernard Shaw and Mrs. Patrick Campbell to recreate their celebrated relationship. Shaw is heard remarking that he will send his ankle-bones to her for glove-stretchers, describing his mother's funeral as "wildly funny" but at the same time revealing genuine pain. Mrs. Campbell, however, is not to be bested. She reminds the playwright: "When you were quite a little boy someone should have said 'Hush' just once." In the latter part of the play, when both are old, they write to each other of their frailty, ill health and failing abilities in a tone of plaintiveness foreign to their earlier verbal posturing and acerbity.

Opened May 27, 1977
Closed June 12, 1977

Cast: Jerome Kilty, Deann Mears

Dressed Like an Egg

Taken from the writings of Colette. The Mabou Mines production, presented by Joseph Papp; directed and designed by JoAnne Akalaitis; lighting by Robin Thomas; dance movement by Mary Overlie; costumes by Dru-ann Chukram, Ann Farrington and Sally Rosen; music by Philip Glass. Public Theatre/Old Prop Shop, 425 Lafayette Street.

Derived from the writings of Colette, this experimental work by Mabou Mines is primarily silent in its first half, with minimal dialogue that is distorted. The idea is to present a living tableau, a visual counterpoint to the writer's words.

In the second half, the stage is dimmed and a long story is related.

Mabou Mines are not attempting to present a dramatized biography of the author, though there are some recognizable figures, such as her bulldog, and a boudoir that will seem familiar to those who have either read her works or seen Eleanor Jones's play *Colette.*

Members of the cast alternate as Colette and her characters.

Opened May, 1977
Closed

Cast: JoAnne Akalaitis, Ellen McElduff, Ruth Maleczech, William Raymond and David Warrilow

Exiles

By James Joyce. Presented by the Circle Repertory Company; directed by Rob Thirkield; settings by David Potts; costumes by Jennifer von Mayrhauser; lighting by Dennis Parichy; music by Norman L. Berman; sound by Charles London; production stage manager, Bob Lampel. Circle Repertory Theatre, 99 Seventh Avenue South.

Richard Rowan, a writer obviously patterned on Joyce himself, returns to Ireland after nine years abroad. He is visited by a former rival, a journalist named Robert Hand, who desires the beautiful Bertha who has been living with Rowan. Bertha, however, does not reciprocate, though she is almost encouraged to do so by Rowan. Indeed, he urges her to agree to Hand's request to join him in his quarters so that she will feel as free as he is. When Hand and Bertha do meet, only conversation occurs, but, in an about-face, Rowan is wracked by jealousy, insisting, "I have a deep, deep wound of doubt in my soul." What really troubles Rowan, more than any possible disloyalty by Bertha, however, is his own sense of guilt, the product of his Irish-Catholic heritage, and it is something he clearly never will overcome.

Opened May 19, 1977, for a limited engagement
Closed June 5, 1977

Cast: Alan Jordan, Stephanie Gordon, Anthony Austin, Neil Flanagan, Nancy Killmer, Eleanor Logan

Stephanie Gordon and Alan Jordan

The Fantasticks

A musical with book and lyrics by Tom Jones; music by Harvey Schmidt. Produced by Lore Noto; directed by Word Baker; associate producers Sheldon Baron, Dorothy Olim; musical direction and orchestrations by Julian Stein; designed by Ed Wittstein. Sullivan Street Playhouse, 181 Sullivan Street.

The Fantasticks, which opened on May 3, 1960, is one of the longest running musicals in the history of the theatre. Its best-known numbers include "Try to Remember," in which the Narrator invites the audience to "follow" its characters, primarily a boy and a girl and their fathers — and a wall, which serves to separate the two lovers. The fathers feud, but only in order to make certain their children fall in love, then decide to hire El Gallo to undertake an abduction to wind things up. When the lovers meet, they are interrupted by "The Rape Ballet," complete with swordfights, Indians and a victory for the boy. In Act 2, the fathers actually do quarrel, thus permitting a somewhat more dramatic triumph for love.

Opened May 3, 1960

Cast: Kenneth Nelson, Jerry Orbach, Rita Gardner, William Larsen, Hugh Thomas, Richard Stauffer, Thomas Bruce, George Curley, Jay Hampton

Ellen McElduff and JoAnne Akalaitis

On-the Lock-In

Leon Thomas and the Cast

Book, music and lyrics by David Langston Smyrl. Presented by the New York Shakespeare Festival; Joseph Papp, producer; Bernard Gersten, associate producer; conceived and directed by Robert Macbeth; scenery by Karl Eigsti; lighting by Victor En Yu Tan; costumes by Grace Williams; musical direction by George Stubbs; musical arrangements by Paul Griffin; production stage manager, Toby Scott Macbeth. Public Theatre/LuEsther Hall, 425 Lafayette Street.

On-the Lock-in is an essentially plotless musical in which the audience sits in as a group of prisoners talk, sing, joke and occasionally quarrel with one another. By play's end, however, a pretty good idea of who and what they are has emerged. None of them has been committed for any particularly terrible reason, but for petty crimes, frame-ups or as a result of being victimized by parole officers. They are strictly small-time.

The show occurs during the period between the "lock-in," when they have been placed in their cells for the night, and the "quiet bell." As they talk and sing and a prisoner named "Houndog," played by the author, acts as liaison between them and the audience, certain themes do emerge, perhaps primary among them that, "It is not what you did but the way you did it: you did the wrong thing in the wrong way."

Opened April 27, 1977
Closed June 5, 1977

Cast: David Langston Smyrl, Manuel Santiago, Harold Cromer, Billy Barnes, Henry Baker, Thomas M. Brimm II, Ezra Jack Maret, Leon Thomas, Alan Weeks, Henry Bradley, Don Jay

Peg o' My Heart

By J. Hartley Manners. Presented by Saul Novick, Marion Brasch and Leonard Finger; directed by Gene Nye; setting by Miguel Romero; costumes by David James; lighting by Joseph Spencer; production stage manager, Andrea Naier. Theatre Four, 424 West 55th Street.

J. Hartley Manners wrote this durable comedy about 65 years ago for his bride-to-be, Laurette Taylor. It follows the adventures of a young Irish-American girl who comes to visit her upper-class, but recently bankrupt relatives in England. She and the audience find them overly smug and supercilious, but since Peg herself is thoroughly sassy and vivacious it's obvious who will triumph — and become Lady Peg in the bargain.

Manners's play is a social satire of manners, in which the irrepressible Peg obviously has to win out in the end, finding it is she who is wealthy and they who are not, due to a series of convoluted bankruptcies and legacies.

Opened May 4, 1977
Closed

Cast: Gibson Glass, Mary E. Baird, Kathleen Tremaine, Sandra Halperin, Jim Ricketts, Donovan Sylvest, Sofia Landon, Ken Costigan, Allen Carlsen

Sofia Landon

Scribes

By Barrie Keeffe. Produced by the Phoenix Theatre; directed by Keith Hack; scenery and lighting by James Tilton; costumes by Fran Rosenthal. Marymount Manhattan Theatre, 221 East 71st Street.

Barrie Keeffe's play is an afternoon in the life of a fictional newspaper called *The Ilford Recorder*. Its principal characters are a journalist whose talents are fading but who, despite his envy of another man, lacks the ambition to challenge him, and an editor who is prepared to compromise on any question in order to keep his job and guarantee the paper's continuance. There seems a possibility he will be thwarted when the printers go on a wildcat strike, which threatens the paper with suspension. There is, however, no real confrontation, as Keeffe concentrates more on evoking the office atmosphere than on the potential clash of personalities and values.

Opened May 31, 1977, for a limited engagement
Closed June 5, 1977

Cast: Ann McDonough, Leonardo Cimino, Jeffrey Jones, Stephen Joyce, Russell Horton, Don Scardino, Donald Madden, Alan North, Kristoffer Tabori, Fran Brill, George Taylor

Starting Here, Starting Now

Margery Cohen (front), George Lee Adams and
Loni Ackerman

A revue, with lyrics by Richard Maltby, Jr., and music by David Shire. Presented by Steve Abrams, Mary Jo Slater and Scott Mansfield in association with Morton Schwartz; musical director, Robert W. Preston; costumes by Stanley Simmons; choreography by Ethel Martin; directed by Mr. Maltby; production stage manager, Joan Lipeman. Barbarann Theatre, 349 West 46th Street.

This cafe revue includes approximately two dozen songs by Maltby and Shire, which have been drawn from musicals that never made it to New York.
The numbers include "Crossword Puzzle," "I Don't Believe It," "I'm Going to Make You Beautiful" and "Watching the Big Parade Go By." The reputation of the composers has been established primarily as providers of songs for such popular singers as Roberta Flack and Robert Goulet.

Opened March 7, 1977
Closed June 19, 1977

Cast: Loni Ackerman, Margery Cohen and George Lee Andrews

Vanities

Jane Galloway, Sally Sockwell and Susan Merson

By Jack Heifner. Presented by the Chelsea Theatre Center, the Lion Theatre Company and Playwrights Horizons; directed by Garland Wright; settings by John Arnone; costumes by David James; production stage manager, Ginny Freedman. Chelsea Westside Theatre, 407 West 43rd Street.

Vanities opens in 1963, on the day of John F. Kennedy's assassination, and follows the journeys of three high school cheerleaders through their days as sorority queens, until they are on the brink of their thirties. The aspirations of youth and the realities of maturity emerge, especially when they meet for a tea-time reunion in 1974. By now, one has three children, the second has a garden apartment in Manhattan and the third is operating an expensive gallery devoted to erotic art.

Opened March 22, 1976

Cast: Jane Galloway, Susan Merson, Kathy Bates

New York
Theatre Awards

Antoinette Perry ("Tony") Awards

Brian Murray, Richard Seer, Barnard Hughes and Sylvia O'Brien

BEST PLAY

"Da," by Hugh Leonard

BEST MUSICAL

Ain't Misbehavin'

BEST MUSICAL BOOK

On the Twentieth Century, with book by Betty Comden and Adolph Green

BEST MUSICAL SCORE

On the Twentieth Century, with music by Cy Coleman

John Cullum and Madeline Kahn

BEST ACTOR IN A PLAY

Barnard Hughes, in *"Da"*

BEST ACTRESS IN A PLAY

Jessica Tandy, in *The Gin Game*

BEST ACTOR IN A MUSICAL

John Cullum, in *On the Twentieth Century*

Liza Minnelli and Roger Minami

BEST ACTRESS IN A MUSICAL

Liza Minnelli, in *The Act*

BEST FEATURED ACTOR IN A PLAY

Lester Rawlins, in *"Da"*

BEST FEATURED ACTRESS IN A PLAY

Ann Wedgeworth, in *Chapter Two*

Ann Wedgeworth

BEST FEATURED ACTOR IN A MUSICAL

Kevin Kline, in *On the Twentieth Century*

BEST FEATURED ACTRESS IN A MUSICAL

Nell Carter, in *Ain't Misbehavin'*

Nell Carter and Ken Page

BEST DIRECTOR OF A PLAY

Melvin Bernhardt, for *"Da"*

BEST DIRECTOR OF A MUSICAL

Richard Maltby, Jr., for *Ain't Misbehavin'*

BEST CHOREOGRAPHER

Bob Fosse, for *Dancin'*

BEST SCENIC DESIGNER

Robin Wagner, for *On the Twentieth Century*

BEST COSTUME DESIGNER

Edward Gorey, for *Dracula*

Ann Sachs and Frank Langella

BEST LIGHTING DESIGNER

Jules Fisher, for *Dancin'*

MOST INNOVATIVE PRODUCTION OF A REVIVAL

Dracula

The "Percussion" number

160

SPECIAL AWARD

Long Wharf Theatre, New Haven, Connecticut

LAWRENCE LANGER AWARD

Irving Berlin

New York Drama Critics' Circle Awards

BEST PLAY

"Da," by Hugh Leonard

BEST MUSICAL

Ain't Misbehavin'

Pulitzer Prize for Drama

Jessica Tandy and Hume Cronyn

The Gin Game, by D. L. Coburn

Pulitzer Prize
(for reviews and body of work)

Walter Kerr, *The New York Times*

Drama Desk Awards

OUTSTANDING DIRECTOR OF A PLAY

Melvin Bernhardt, *"Da"*

OUTSTANDING NEW PLAY

"Da," by Hugh Leonard

OUTSTANDING DIRECTOR OF A MUSICAL

Stephen Schwartz, *Working*
Peter Masterson/Tommy Tune, *The Best Little Whorehouse in Texas*

The Cast of *Working*

OUTSTANDING CHOREOGRAPHY

Bob Fosse, *Dancin'*

OUTSTANDING NEW MUSICAL LYRICS

Carol Hall, *The Best Little Whorehouse in Texas*

OUTSTANDING NEW MUSICAL SCORE

Cy Coleman, *On the Twentieth Century*
Carol Hall, *The Best Little Whorehouse in Texas*

Joan Ellis and Pamela Blair

OUTSTANDING ACTRESS IN A PLAY

Jessica Tandy, *The Gin Game*

OUTSTANDING ACTOR IN A PLAY

Barnard Hughes, *"Da"*

OUTSTANDING FEATURED ACTRESS IN A PLAY

Eileen Atkins, *The Night of the Tribades*

The Cast of *The Mighty Gents*

OUTSTANDING FEATURED ACTOR IN A PLAY

Morgan Freeman, *The Mighty Gents*

OUTSTANDING PRODUCTION OF A MUSICAL

Ain't Misbehavin'

OUTSTANDING FEMALE PERFORMANCE IN A MUSICAL

Nell Carter, *Ain't Misbehavin'*

OUTSTANDING MALE PERFORMANCE IN A MUSICAL

Ken Page, *Ain't Misbehavin'*

OUTSTANDING FEATURED FEMALE PERFORMANCE IN A MUSICAL

Bobo Lewis, *Working*
Swoosie Kurtz, *A History of the American Film*

OUTSTANDING FEATURED MALE PERFORMANCE IN A MUSICAL

Kevin Kline, *On the Twentieth Century*

OUTSTANDING SCENIC DESIGN

Robin Wagner, *On the Twentieth Century*

OUTSTANDING COSTUMES

Florence Klotz, *On the Twentieth Century*

OUTSTANDING LIGHTING DESIGN

Jules Fisher, *Dancin'*

Estelle Parsons

UNIQUE THEATRICAL EXPERIENCE

Estelle Parsons, *Miss Margarida's Way*

SPECIAL AWARD FOR OUTSTANDING CONTRIBUTION TO THE PROFESSIONAL THEATRE

The off-Off Broadway Movement

Outer Critics Circle Awards

OUTSTANDING MUSICAL

Ain't Misbehavin'

OUTSTANDING PLAY

"Da," by Hugh Leonard

OUTSTANDING DRAMATIC PERFORMANCE

Barnard Hughes, *"Da"*

OUTSTANDING STAGE DIRECTION

Melvin Bernhardt, *"Da"*

Martin Balsam

OUTSTANDING PERFORMANCE

Martin Balsam, *Cold Storage*

OUTSTANDING PERFORMANCE

Vicki Frederick, *Dancin'*

OUTSTANDING LIGHTING DESIGN

Jules Fisher, *Dancin'*

OUTSTANDING DRAMATIC PERFORMANCE

John Wood, *Deathtrap*

John Wood

OUTSTANDING SCENIC DESIGN

Robin Wagner, *On the Twentieth Century*

OUTSTANDING PERFORMANCE

Nancy Snyder, *The 5th of July*

JOHN GASSNER PLAYWRITING AWARD

David Mamet

KANSAS CITY STAR-JOSEPH KAYE MEMORIAL AWARD

The Circle Repertory Company

Obie Awards

(presented by *The Village Voice*)

LIFETIME ACHIEVEMENT

Peter Schumann's Bread & Puppet Theatre

BEST PLAY

Lee Breuer, *Shaggy Dog Animation*

PERFORMANCES

Richard Bauer, *Landscape of the Body* and *The Dybbuk*
Nell Carter, *Ain't Misbehavin'*
Alma Cuervo, *Uncommon Women*
Swoosie Kurtz, *Uncommon Women*
Kaiulani Lee, *Safe House*
Bruce Myers, *The Dybbuk*
Lee S. Wilkof, *The Present Tense*

Swoosie Kurtz

Laurence Luckinbill and George Dzundza

DIRECTORS

Robert Allan Ackerman, *A Prayer for My Daughter*
Thomas Bullard, *Statements After an Arrest Under the Immorality Act*
Elizabeth Swados, *Runaways*

Gibson Glass and members of the Company

DESIGN

Garland Wright and John Arnone, *K*
Robert Yodice, *Museum*

Nancy Nelson

Robyn Goodman and Larry Bryggman

164

SPECIAL CITATIONS

Ain't Misbehavin'
Eric Bentley
Joseph Dunn and Irja Koljonen, *Preface*
James Lapine, *Photograph*
Jerry Mayer, *Taud Show*
Stuart Sherman
Squat
Winston Tong

The Rosamond Gilder Award

of the New Drama Forum Association
(for outstanding creative achievement in the theatre)

Michael Lessac, Colonnades Theatre Lab

Peter Kingsley (above), Marcia Hyde
and Tom V. V. Tammi

Peter Simon and Vasili Bogazianos

Christopher Goutman and Marilyn McIntyre

Clarence Derwent Awards

Margaret Hilton, *Molly*
Morgan Freeman, *The Mighty Gents*

William Hurt, Circle Repertory Theatre productions
Judy Kaye, *On the Twentieth Century*
Florence Lacey, *Hello, Dolly!*
Armelia McQueen, *Ain't Misbehavin'*
Gordana Rashovich, *Fefu and Her Friends*
Bo Rucker, *Native Son*
Richard Seer, *"Da"*
Colin Stinton, *The Water Engine*

Theatre World Awards

Vasili Bogazianos, *P.S. Your Cat is Dead*
Nell Carter, *Ain't Misbehavin'*
Carlin Glynn, *The Best Little Whorehouse in Texas*
Christopher Goutman, *The Promise*

1978 SPECIAL THEATRE
WORLD AWARD

Joseph Papp and the New York Shakespeare Festival

Photo Credits

Act, The — Martha Swope
Agamemnon — Jos. Abeles Studio
Angel — Gerry Goodstein
Annie — Martha Swope
Ashes — Ken Howard
Biko Incident, The — Elaine Kirsch
Bistro Car on the CNR, A — Laura Pettibone
Brontosaurus — Michael Goldstein
Bully — Ken Howard
Cabin 12 — Michael Goldstein
Catsplay — Gerry Goodstein
Cherry Orchard, The — Sy Friedman
Chez Nous — Gerry Goodstein
Chorus Line, A — Martha Swope
Club, The — Martha Swope
Creditors — Sy Friedman
Curse of the Starving Class, The — Frederic Ohringer
Dancin' — Martha Swope
Devil's Disciple, The — Frederic Ohringer
Dressed Like an Egg — Richard Landry
Dybbuk, The — Inge Morath
Elusive Angel, The — Roger Greenawalt
Esther — Bette Marshall
Eulogy for a Small Time Thief — Gerry Goodstein
Exiles — Ken Howard
Feedlot — Ken Howard
Fifth of July, The — Ken Howard
For Colored Girls . . . — Sy Friedman
Gemini — Joan James
Green Pond — Martha Swope
Hair — Curt Kaufman
Happy End — Martha Swope
History of the American Film, A — Martha Swope
Ice Show — Martha Swope
Julius Caesar — Jack Mitchell
K — Laura Pettibone
Landscape of the Body — Martha Swope
Life in the Theatre, A — Martha Swope

Lulu — Ken Howard
Man and His Women, A — Frederic Ohringer
Mandrake, The — Sy Friedman
Merchant, The — Zoe Dominic
Mighty Gents, The — Martha Swope
Miss Margarida's Way — Sy Friedman
Museum — Jos. Abeles Studio
Naked — Geoffrey Fried
Night of the Tribades — Cliff Moore
On-the Lock-In — Martha Swope
One Crack Out — Roger Greenawalt
Othello — Geoffrey Fried
Patio/Porch — Jack Mitchell
Paul Robeson — Bert Andrews
Photograph, A — Frederic Ohringer
Play and Other Plays — Gerry Goodstein
Play's the Thing, The — Fred Ohringer
Prayer for My Daughter, A — Gerry Goodstein
Promise, The — Geoffrey Fried
Red Fox/Second Coming — Gerry Goodstein
Rum an Coca Cola — Martha Swope
Runaways — Martha Swope
Saint Joan — Martha Swope
Show-Off, The — Ken Howard
Side by Side by Sondheim — Zoe Dominic
Statements After an Arrest . . . — Gerry Goodstein
Tartuffe — Martha Swope
13 Rue de l'Amour — Martha Swope
Twilight Dinner, The — Bert Andrews
Ulysses in Traction — Ken Howard
Uncommon Women and Others — Roger Greenawalt
Unsung Cole — Ken Howard
Waiting for Godot — Thomas Victor
Wayside Motor Inn, The — Gerry Goodstein
Where the Mississippi Meets the Amazon — Martha Swope
You Never Can Tell — Ken Howard

Index of Plays

Index of Plays

Index of Individuals
and Organizations

Index of Individuals and Organizations